LISTENING TO THE NEIGHBOR

American Society of Missiology Monograph Series

Series Editor, James R. Krabill

The ASM Monograph Series provides a forum for publishing quality dissertations and studies in the field of missiology. Collaborating with Pickwick Publications—a division of Wipf and Stock Publishers of Eugene, Oregon—the American Society of Missiology selects high quality dissertations and other monographic studies that offer research materials in mission studies for scholars, mission and church leaders, and the academic community at large. The ASM seeks scholarly work for publication in the series that throws light on issues confronting Christian world mission in its cultural, social, historical, biblical, and theological dimensions.

Missiology is an academic field that brings together scholars whose professional training ranges from doctoral-level preparation in areas such as Scripture, history and sociology of religions, anthropology, theology, international relations, interreligious interchange, mission history, inculturation, and church law. The American Society of Missiology, which sponsors this series, is an ecumenical body drawing members from Independent and Ecumenical Protestant, Catholic, Orthodox, and other traditions. Members of the ASM are united by their commitment to reflect on and do scholarly work relating to both mission history and the present-day mission of the church. The ASM Monograph Series aims to publish works of exceptional merit on specialized topics, with particular attention given to work by younger scholars, the dissemination and publication of which is difficult under the economic pressures of standard publishing models.

Persons seeking information about the ASM or the guidelines for having their dissertations considered for publication in the ASM Monograph Series should consult the Society's website—www.asmweb.org.

Members of the ASM Monograph Committe who approved this book are:

Craig Ott, Trinity Evangelical Divinity School
Roger Schroeder, Catholic Theological Union
Gary Simpson, Luther Seminary

RECENTLY PUBLISHED IN THE ASM MONOGRAPH SERIES

Kim Marie Lamberty, *Eyes from the Outside: Christian Mission in Zones of Violent Conflict*

Runchana P. Suksod-Barger, *Religious Influences in Thai Female Education (1889–1931)*

Darren Todd Duerksen, *Ecclesial Identities in a Multi-Faith Context: Jesus Truth-Gatherings (Yeshu Satsangs) among Hindus and Sikhs in Northwest India*

Listening to the Neighbor
From a Missional Perspective of the Other

BYUNGOHK LEE

Foreword by Craig Van Gelder

American Society of Missiology Monograph
Series vol. 24

☙PICKWICK *Publications* · Eugene, Oregon

LISTENING TO THE NEIGHBOR
From a Missional Perspective of the Other

American Society of Missiology Monograph Series 24

Copyright © 2015 Byungohk Lee. All rights reserved. Except for brief quotations in critical publications or reviews, no part of this book may be reproduced in any manner without prior written permission from the publisher. Write: Permissions, Wipf and Stock Publishers, 199 W. 8th Ave., Suite 3, Eugene, OR 97401.

Pickwick Publications
An Imprint of Wipf and Stock Publishers
199 W. 8th Ave., Suite 3
Eugene, OR 97401

www.wipfandstock.com

ISBN 13: 978-1-4982-1944-0

Cataloging-in-Publication data:

Lee, Byungohk

    Listening to the neighbor : from a missional perspective of the other / Byungohk Lee.

    xiv + 218 p. ; 23 cm. —Includes bibliographical references and index(es).

    American Society of Missiology Monograph Series 24

    ISBN 13: 978-1-4982-1944-0

    1. Missions—Korea. 2. Missions, Korean. 3. Christianity and culture—Korea. I. Title. II. Series.

BV3460 L35 2015

Manufactured in the U.S.A.   05/06/2015

Contents

List of Illustrations | vii
Foreword by Craig Van Gelder | ix
Acknowledgments | xiii

1 Introduction | 1
2 The Understandings of Mission and the Church: The PCK and Calvin | 16
3 Methodology | 48
4 Research Findings and Analysis | 71
5 Theoretical Reflections on the Research Findings | 114
6 Biblical and Theological Reflections on the Research Findings | 140
7 Conclusion | 181

Appendix A: Personal Interview Questions | 199
Appendix B: Focus Group Interview Questions | 201
Appendix C: Informed Consent Form (Personal Interview) | 203
Appendix D: Informed Consent Form (Focus Group) | 205
Appendix E: Consent Form (Translator/Auditor) | 207

Bibliography | 209
Index | 215

Illustrations

TABLES

Table 1: The Primary Conceptual Categories | 84
Table 2: Overview of Personal Interview Participants | 84
Table 3: Overview of Focus Groups | 85

FIGURES

Figure 1: The Process of Listening to the Neighbor | 113, 182

Foreword

ONE OF THE MOST challenging issues facing the work of mission and the discipline of missiology in the world today concerns the relationship of the church to persons who do not profess the Christian faith. This is usually framed in terms of the relationship of the church and the *other*. Embedded in this issue are a whole series of important missiological questions which must be addressed, such as: What is the gospel and how is the church to bear witness to it? What is the appropriate posture of the church as it seeks to participate in God's mission in the world? And even more substantively, How are we to understand the personhood of God as well as God's works of creating and redeeming?

Numerous books have appeared over the past decade which attempt to take up this issue of the relationship of the church to the other. But the majority of them are still being written by persons from the Western world. These persons, some by intent but most by default, share in the legacy of the modern missions movement with its complicity to the realities of colonialism which problematized the matter of the other due to unequal power dynamics. Many of these authors, helpfully, are working to reframe the mission enterprise in new terms regarding the relationship of the church and the other by focusing on the reciprocity inherent in the gospel. But the hermeneutic of suspicion lingers as to whether persons working from the position of the power dynamics and resources of the Western world can adequately make the move to understanding the nature and power of the gospel from the viewpoint of the other—from the *outside in*.

This book by Dr. Byungohk Lee provides an alternative way for opening up and examining this issue. As a Korean Christian, he has lived the majority of his life within a context where Christianity is a minority faith. This requires the Korean church to have to think and act differently as it seeks to bear witness to the gospel and thus provides a different way for the church to be in relationship with the other.

Dr. Lee chose to pursue his dissertation research in completing his PhD studies by engaging the issue of the relationship of the church and the other in this context—his native country of Korea. He did so by employing a social science research methodology known as "grounded theory." This inductive approach examines a particular phenomenon by seeking to discover the dynamics of what is being experienced by those embedded within a particular context, and then from these experiences attempt to discover and describe what is actually taking place—to develop an hypothesis of explanation.

This research methodology is typically used when there are a lack of existing theories and previous research to guide and inform the gathering and interpretation of data. One does not yet know what is actually happening or how to explain it, even though what are known as "sensitizing concepts" are employed to offer some perspective for orienting the direction of the research. Especially important sensitizing concepts of value in this research were: the use of missional theology to consider the work of God in the world and the perspectives of Gadamer and Levinas regarding their differing views of a hermeneutic of the other. Dr. Lee employed the methodology of grounded theory to study three Presbyterian Church of Korea (PCK) congregations which had a reported reputation of actively seeking to relate to their neighbors. He focused on studying how these congregations actually engaged, related with, and listened to their neighbors who did not profess the Christian faith.

The findings of this study, framed within the *grounded theory* that emerged, are of great value to those seeking to understand more substantively what the posture of the church might look like when one takes seriously the practicing of a genuine reciprocity in relating to the other in contexts where the Christian church is the minority faith. Of particular interest is his discussion of minjung theology in relation to this emerging theory. While one cannot generalize from a grounded theory study to a broader population, this particular study does offer some helpful clues to consider for churches which are struggling to connect with their neighbors. It also offers some provocative hypothesis for future research around the issue of the relationship of the church and the other. As such, this type of research conducted by a majority-world person in a global-south context represents what, I believe, must increasingly become the norm if we are to better understand the churches participation in God's mission in the world today.

Craig Van Gelder, Ph.D.
Emeritus Professor of Congregational Mission, Luther Seminary

Acknowledgments

I PRAISE YOU, GOD, who have completed what you began in me. Your Trinitarian guidance has enriched my life and vision. Through the journey of my PhD program and thesis, you have led me to realize who I am and that I am unable to live a faithful life without help and assistance from others by your merciful grace.

My deep gratitude first goes to my thesis committee members, Drs. Paul Chung, Dwight Zscheile, and Craig Van Gelder. Dr. Chung has helped me become aware of the audacity of theology and the importance of both solid theological bases and creative hermeneutical praxis. His insights have sharpened my theological thoughts. I am indebted to Dr. Zscheile who has offered new impetus to my understandings of missional theology and leadership through his thoughtful comments and fresh works. I am grateful to him for helping me take seriously missional leadership. I wish to express my deepest gratitude to Dr. Van Gelder for my entire academic journey in America, including my thesis process. He has encouraged me to move forward when I was lost and pushed me to keep focused when I was lazy. I could not have completed this thesis without his critical reading of its earlier drafts. He has shown me a good model of an excellent researcher, scholar, leader, and adviser.

I would like to give my special thanks to all the research participants in Heavenly Creek, New Community, and Holy Hill (pseudonyms) who contributed to sharing their vivid meaningful experiences with me. Their long-term involvement in serving their neighborhoods made my thesis possible. Their active participation in my research and humble assistance during my visits made my study more fruitful.

I am greatly indebted to many people's assistance for my thesis. I thank Peter Susag for proofreading and encouragement. He has been also a good counselor and friend. I wish to express my appreciation to

Eunkyung Jo, Tony Chung, Tae Woong Lee, and Tae-Hyung Ha who helped with the process of translation or auditing. Karen Alexander, Jennifer Bartholomew, and Bruce Eldevik have kindly provided me with what I needed for my research at the library.

Many thanks also go to Luther Seminary and its community. Luther Seminary has been a good institution and sweet home for me and my family. For helpful comments and insightful teachings, I am grateful to Drs. Gary Simpson, Alvin Luedke, Patrick Keifert, Alan Padgett, Charles Amjad-Ali, and many professors. My colleagues at Luther Seminary (Hrang Hlei, Marty Tollefson, Harvey Kwiyani, John Ogren, Mark Love, Dinku Bato, David Hahn, William Obaga, Margaret Obaga, Imliwabang Jamir, Michael Jinteh, and others) have guided and stimulated my thoughts about missional theology. For academic affairs, I wish to give my appreciation to Dr. Paul Lokken, Katie Dahl, and Sarah Grow at the Graduate Theological Education Office. In particular, Dr. Lokken has always tried to understand my situation and do his best whenever I needed his help. I thank Marie Hayes, Chenar Howard, and Elizabeth Flomo for helping me feel at home at Luther Seminary.

I owe special thanks to my family, friends, and churches in Korea for prayers, support, and encouragement. My beloved parents and sisters (Mikyung, Mihwa, Hyunyoung, and Joungyun) have loved and trusted me, and have spiritually and financially supported for my study and my family in the U.S. I am indebted to the elder Lees (Woonhyung and Jungsun) for their valuable grants and priceless trust. I certainly owe a debt of gratitude to Daesin Presbyterian Church for incubating my faith and providing me with financial support and Bokwang Presbyterian Church for sending me as the chief leader of mission teams to many countries and allowing me, as its pastor, to study at Luther Seminary.

Finally, my deepest thanks go to my sons, Heejae and Eunjae, and my wife, Yunjoung, for their love, encouragement, patience, and sacrifices. Heejae has brought joy to my family and his pure prayers have boosted my faith. Eunjae has made me smile even when I have been frustrated with my study. I am certainly sure that my completion of this study would be impossible without Yunjoung's wholehearted love and countless support. She has been dedicated to taking care of two active sons and all the chores so as to help me focus on my study. Yunjoung, I cannot express my gratitude enough for you. You have always made me feel special in any circumstances. I believe that we will walk together to the end of our life's journey to the kingdom of God, as we have done so far.

1

Introduction

Son [the Stated Clerk of the General Assembly of the Presbyterian Church of Korea (PCK)] emphasized that the Korean church would not restore trust from the Korean society until it would become a friend of the least—the poor, disabled, interracial marriage families, North Koreans, the next generation, and so on. By asking himself "what should we do to become a hope again?" Son answered, "the church and Christians will be able to become a hope for the world again when we do not enjoy the power by standing by the big men, but return to the least and become their friends."[1]

THE THEME OF THE PCK's General Assembly for fall 2012–summer 2013 is "A Christian, A Friend of the Least: We Will Be a Hope Again."[2] It is obviously a result of the PCK's reflection on the present-day crises of churches in Korea. Those who prepared for this one-year theme shared an agreement that most Koreans outside the church had critical and negative assessments on the Korean church.[3] In a word, many Koreans outside the church do not regard the Korean church as their friend.

A study which was conducted in 2010 by the Christian Ethics Movement of Korea, a Christian association aiming at Christian ethical practices in Korea, said that Koreans ranked Protestantism third behind

---

1. Choi, "The Church Has to Be a Friend of the Least." The author's translation.
2. The PCK's website. The author's translation.
3. The Korean church in this study means the Korean Protestant church unless otherwise stated.

Roman Catholicism and Buddhism in terms of social credibility.[4] The same report also pointed out that approximately 55 percent of non-Protestants did not trust in the Protestant church, while 8 percent of them did.[5] Some scholars and leaders argue that the current crises are rooted in the church's lack of communication with people outside the church, although there are other perspectives concerning the same issues.[6] The Protestant churches in Korea have been accustomed to speaking the gospel to the world without listening to the world.

Koyama's *Water Buffalo Theology* is concerned with contextualization of theology and mission, emphasizing the locus and people of the Asian context, including Korea.[7] This concern is based on Koyama's reflection that Christianity has been perceived as being western or foreign to Asians and that Christian mission has had no dialogue with local cultures and people. Koyama suggests that mission should be "neighborology" which is not monologue for treating living neighbors simply as objects, but dialogue with them.[8] His neighbors today live in local cultural situations characterized by the interaction between traditional, cultural, and religious heritage and our technological civilization.[9] David Bosch similarly reflects that mission has tended to be one-way, *monological* approach to the non-Christian world. Bosch maintains that in a newly-emerging postmodern world, mission should be a dialogue with other peoples and faiths in creative tension.[10]

---

4. The Christian Ethics Movement of Korea, http://cemk.org/ (accessed December 21, 2012). This organization conducted research regarding the social credibility of the church in Korea. The author's translation.

5. Ibid.

6. Theologians were concerned with the publicity of the church and the church's communications with the world in order to overcome the current crises in a theological forum in Presbyterian College and Seminary in Seoul, April 2012. See http://www.igoodnews.net/news/articleView.html?idxno=34540 (accessed January 20, 2013); Rev. Dongho Kim, the director of the Good Church Academy and a leading figure regarding reforming the Korean church, argued that these crises of the Korean church were essentially rooted in its lack of communications. See http://news.c3tv.com/news_vods_view.asp?idx=437&category=NEWS&curpage=1&curpage2=1 (accessed January 12, 2013). All contents addressed above are based on the author's translation.

7. Koyama, *Water Buffalo Theology*, vii–xiv.

8. Ibid., 64–67.

9. Ibid., 45.

10. Bosch, *Transforming Mission*, 483–89.

Stephen Bevans and Roger Schroeder, in *Prophetic Dialogue: Reflections on Christian Mission Today*, emphasize mission for the twenty-first century as prophetic dialogue.[11] This book results from Bevans and Schroeder's reflection on their Society of the Divine Word's mission. They critically accept arguments of mission as both justice for the poor/oppressed in Latin America and as dialogue with other faiths in Asia in articulating mission as prophetic dialogue.[12] Bevans and Schroeder argue that both prophecy and dialogue have worked together as two primary aspects of mission practice throughout the history of the church, with emphasis being placed on one or the other according to different contexts.[13] Since they understand prophecy in relation to proclamation, both prophecy and dialogue are inseparable, albeit distinguishable. They hold that this understanding is essentially rooted in the Trinity. They understand the Trinity as *dialogue* in light of God's Word and mission.[14] Bevans and Schroeder contend that mission must be founded in God and be practiced in a dialogical manner, as long as the triune God is the subject of mission. In this light, Bevans states,

> God's mission-in-dialogue, always present through the Spirit and incarnate and concrete in Jesus, has now been entrusted to the church. Through Baptism, Christians share the very life and of [sic] the Trinity, and so they are enjoined to carry out God's mission in the same dialogical way.[15]

Thus, the Trinity is a social community *speaking and listening to one another in love*.

The missional church conversation, likewise, embraces the dimension of dialogue in terms of the relationship between the church and its local context or neighborhood. It has sought to understand the church's identity related to mission within the rapidly-changing post-Christendom and postmodern world of the United States in terms of *missio Dei*, as we will see in more detail. Missional ecclesiology has rediscovered the church as a Spirit-led community and its local context as a mission location. The triune God, rather than the church, is at the center of mission.

---

11. Bevans and Schroeder, *Prophetic Dialogue*.

12. In this respect, Bosch keeps highlighting *tension* in the process of mission, while focusing on the dialogical aspect of mission.

13. Ibid., 5.

14. Ibid., 41.

15. Bevans, "Mission as Prophetic Dialogue."

Regarding the gospel, it is God who speaks the Word—Jesus Christ—by the power of the Spirit to the church as well as the world. The Spirit is actively working within both the church and its local neighborhood. The church needs to listen to its larger neighboring community in order to speak, from the missional, dialogical perspective of mission. In other words, God's mission is located in dialogue between the church and its neighborhood.

STATEMENT OF PROBLEM

The PCK, along with other denominations, has enjoyed the unique success of explosive church growth since the introduction of Protestantism to Korea in 1884.[16] The Korean Protestant church took it for granted that church growth was *the primary indicator* of *the success for church mission*, focusing on growing in numbers. The Korean church, separated from the world, tried to continue to expand primarily for its own survival, as we will see later. Regarding this, Craig Van Gelder points out precisely that "Survival, in itself, is not a sufficient reason for existence."[17]

However, the Protestant population in Korea, including the PCK's membership, has been declining since the middle 1990s. What is worse, other religions, including Roman Catholicism, have continually grown in numbers during the same period.[18] Korean Protestant scholars have explored the reasons for this continuing decline in recent years, trying to find various ways to reform and revive the church. Most of them have a common agreement, despite various factors and/or causes, that the Korean Protestant church has been a self-centered and growth-driven church. The Protestant church pays little attention to *others'* suffering in the society due essentially to its narrow understanding of the church and mission.[19]

---

16. In this paper, all references to "Korea" after the division of Korea in 1945 apply to *South* Korea unless otherwise stated.

17. Van Gelder, *The Ministry*, 137.

18. KOSIS., http://kosis.kr (accessed April 2, 2012). According to a 1995 survey by the South Korean Statistics Office, Protestants were counted as numbering about 8,760,000 (20 percent of the entire South Korean population). However, according to a 2005 survey by the same office, Protestants constituted about 19 percent of the Korean population, numbering around 8,620,000, which was a decrease of 142,000 persons compared with the previous survey.

19. See Kim, "Modernization and the Explosive Growth and Decline of Korean Protestant Religiosity," and Lee, "Beleaguered Success," in Buswell and Lee, *Christianity in Korea*.

The PCK's mission has tended to be more monological than dialogical, although the PCK has emphasized mission since its beginning. The PCK regards itself as a missionary or missional church in terms of missionary zeal and work. It is proud of its explosive growth compared to the relatively short history of mission in Korea. It also enjoys playing a role as one of the dominant emerging forces of the world missionary movement. The PCK, however, has a tendency to relate mission to the concepts of numbers, territory, and activity. This shows that the PCK treats mission as being dependent on its own work, while a missional ecclesiology emphasizes God as the acting subject of mission. The PCK's notion of mission sheds light on the view that mission is reduced to the church's activities in the world alone and that God works through this process only. Thus, the world is regarded simply as the object of the PCK's mission.

The PCK regards mission primarily as *evangelization* and *church growth* and as *the extension of God's kingdom*, while the *Constitution*, as its official, theological basis on mission, pays relatively little attention to mission. Strictly speaking, the PCK's primary notion of mission is a church-centered mission based on the Great Commission, aiming at church growth, although the *Constitution* ambiguously uses both the terms God's *mission* and *church-centered mission*. The PCK further divides mission into both *domestic mission* and *overseas mission*, focusing on the Great Commission. The PCK generally relates the former to the category of evangelization and the latter to the category of mission. It also provides few pneumatological accounts in terms of mission outside the church, while it deals with the work of the Spirit in relation to internal aspects of the church.

The PCK has identified local mission with evangelization in terms of its historical and practical understandings of mission. Overseas mission is also primarily concerned with evangelization, while the term "mission" has generally meant "overseas mission." The PCK's primary focus on evangelization results from the strong influence of the early missionaries in Korea. These early missionaries, based on the belief that the world would gradually deteriorate until the return of Christ, devoted themselves to an exclusively *literal evangelism* for the expansion of God's kingdom, although they used educational and medical services as secondary, complementary tools in the process. They did not want Korean Christians to get involved in socio-political issues in terms of *socio-political engagement*. They, however, did try to make extensive use of political relations between the U.S. and Korea before the colonial period of Korea and between the U.S. and Japan during that period.[20] The PCK, in this light, has narrowly interpreted Calvin's ecclesiology, regarding the church as the kingdom of God or a *lifeboat* to *save people from the world* which is evil and tragic. All people in the world have to do is listen to the church in order to be saved from the world, but not *vice versa*. This is a very monological approach to mission in terms of the church and people in the world.

Most congregations within the PCK, based on such a traditional, monological notion of mission, have tried to grow once again by renewing the previous successful approaches or launching new programs in the face of the decline since the mid-1990s. In contrast, some congregations have focused on being closely engaged with their neighborhoods in terms of local mission and have kept growing. Almost all academic writings in Korean since the mid-1990s have addressed "local mission" with regard to a congregation's relationship with its own neighborhood.[21] I wonder how these congregations are connected with their neighborhoods in light of mission, given that most congregations are somewhat self-centered in Korea. In particular, I am curious about *how they listen to their neighborhood*, considering the PCK's *general, monological* relationship with the world.

PURPOSE OF THE STUDY

There are three core beliefs undergirding this study. First, God's mission involves mission-in-dialogue, as discussed earlier, since dialogue is one

---

20. For example, the early missionaries did not want Korean Christians to get involved in defense against Japan even before Japan eventually colonized Korea in 1910. In contrast, the Korean-American treaty, which was signed in 1882 and Korea's first treaty with a western power, guaranteed American missionaries their status securely in Korea and gave them a good opportunity to start missionary work. Horace N. Allen, as the first Presbyterian missionary to Korea, first worked for both the Presbyterian mission and the U.S. Legation in Korea and later only for the latter. Later, most missionaries supported for Japanese colonial rule over Korea for the purpose of their mission in Korea. This is because, after Japan's victory in the Russo-Japanese war of 1904–5, the U.S. strongly supported Japanese regency over Korea by recognizing the so-called Taft-Katsura Agreement of 1905 relevant to American rule over the Philippines and Japanese rule over Korea. See Paik, *The History*, 53–114; Wells, *New God*, 1–42; Nagata, "American Missionaries in Korea and U.S.–Japan Relations 1910–1920," 159–79.

21. Digital Library of Korean Assembly Library, http://dl.nanet.go.kr/SearchList.do (accessed April 15, 2012).

reality within the life of the Trinity.[22] Second, the Spirit leads the church into God's mission by speaking through people/contexts outside the church, as the Spirit is working in the world as well as in the church. We can find this aspect in missional theology, minjung theology, or liberation theology.[23] Third, now is a time for "the return of the congregation to the study of theology," as congregations are no longer just places where theologies and theories are applied.[24] Conversely, we need to address congregations as incubators of theology, as they were in the era of the early church.

With this in mind, I focused primarily on PCK congregations which have been actively involved in their neighborhoods in light of mission. This study attempts to explore the dynamics of their listening to their neighbors. Its specific aims are: (1) to explore the ways and phenomena of congregational listening to the neighborhood in terms of local mission, (2) to describe the congregations' understandings of their listening to their neighbors, and (3) to construct a grounded theory of their listening experiences in relation to their neighborhoods. However, this study does not aim to explore congregational strategies relating to local mission, types and ranges of congregational connections with the neighborhood, or the relationship between church growth and listening to the neighborhood.

I am concerned with the following primary question:

> For the PCK congregations which have been actively involved in their neighborhoods in light of mission, what are the understandings and practices of their listening to their neighbors?

Related sub-questions are as follows: (1) Why do they listen to their neighbors? (2) What helps them to listen better to their neighbors? (3) What do they learn from this listening process? (4) What commonalities, if any, exist between such congregations within the PCK?

---

22. For example, Luther understands the Trinity as "conversation." See Luther, *St. John Chapters*, 5–14; Based on Luther's commentaries on the Word, Bayer highlights that "the Trinity is to be comprehended as dialogue." See Bayer, *Martin Luther's Theology*, 340–41; In a broad sense, in commenting on John 14:17–28, 16:7–15, 17:1–25, and so on, Calvin construes the three persons of the Trinity as being in dialogue, although mostly regarding the Spirit as one who hears. See Calvin, *According to John*.

23. See Van Gelder, *The Ministry*, 47–68; Chung, *Public Theology*, 200–239; Mayama, *Emmanuel Levinas' Conceptual Affinities with Liberation Theology*, 45–93.

24. Keifert, *Testing the Spirits*, 17.

SIGNIFICANCE OF THE STUDY

This research helps me illustrate that the church should take seriously its listening to the neighbor as well as to God, as long as mission is at the heart of the church. I, previously, tried my best to evangelize my acquaintances who believed in other religions such as Confucianism and Buddhism in a very aggressive way. Many of them complained that I left no room for dialogue with them in the process. This experience led me to reflect on what I had done in terms of evangelism. The experience of poverty in my childhood also gave me a sense that many congregations helped their neighbors only from the congregations' point of view. Put in more detail, they tended to not ask what their neighbor really wanted, although they conducted social aid activities for their poor neighbors. These activities also generally were used as a means for promoting church growth and tended to be very similar regardless of their different local contexts.

Short-term mission trips to India, Tanzania, Mongolia, and China also provided me with a new viewpoint to see the church and mission in light of what God is up to in the world. As a mission team leader, I needed to carefully listen to missionaries, team members, and indigenous church members in each mission field. I had to pay careful attention to both voices of people outside the church and continually changed contexts in particular. Missionary activities of my team had to vary, even in a local context. My team sometimes felt that God worked in the process, although they did nothing or failed in their plans in some mission fields. The above experiences led me to envision that this study would help me see how congregations that have been actively involved in their neighborhoods have listened to their neighbors.

This study also helps the PCK see that mission is *mission-in-dialogue* with its neighbors. The PCK has tended to separate itself from people in the world. It has treated its neighbors as only *heathens* or *objects* to be converted for the sake of God's kingdom. The PCK's *aggressive* and *one-sided* attitude toward non-Christians tends to prevent it from listening to voices outside the church. The PCK does not have listening ears for the groaning of the people who suffer under desperate situations, as long as it still regards church growth as its ultimate purpose in terms of mission. In this regard, we need to take seriously minjung theology as a Korean contextual theology focusing on the *minjung*—the poor and the oppressed in socio-political terms. On the one hand, minjung theology has helped the PCK to pay attention to people's suffering in the world since the 1970s to some extent in light of God's preference for the oppressed. On the other hand, minjung theology has paid more attention to the relationship between God and the *minjung*, rather than the relationship between God and the church. It has tended to emphasize God's mission as God's responsibility toward and solidarity with the *minjung*, often separately from the church in the process. The Korean church has confronted the new issues of the increased presence of *the other*, such as foreign workers and internationally married women from poor countries, along with existing *religious* others in the face of globalization since the 1990s. Given the above, this study helps many other congregations, to say nothing of the PCK, to better listen to their neighbors.

Furthermore, this study provides the larger church with concrete examples and practices of mission-in-dialogue from local congregations. Bevans and Schroeder bring few practical examples of how local congregations conduct this kind of mission, while they emphasize a dialogical approach to mission.[25] The existing literature regarding the missional church, moreover, does not seem to fully develop the so-called hermeneutics of "the other." On the one hand, missional ecclesiology is primarily concerned with the church's participation in God's mission in the world. On the other hand, the God and church relationship tends to be more dominant than the God and world relationship in the missional church conversation.

The initial stage of the missional conversation focused on the triune God's sending of the church, which tended to miss the social, interrelated aspect of the Trinity and otherness in the unity of the three divine persons. Later, some missional theologians brought relational aspects of the Trinity into the missional conversation, based on the eastern notion of the social Trinity.[26] The Eastern Church's emphasis on *perichoresis* (interrelatedness) of the Godhead has helped missional theology to view God's mission and the nature of the church in relational terms.[27] John Zizioulas's understandings of being as communion and the person as including otherness in terms of the Trinity have enabled missional theologians who follow the relational, social notion of the Trinity to pay more attention to the church as communion-in-mission and the otherness within and out-

25. See Bevans and Schroeder, *Prophetic Dialogue*.
26. Van Gelder, *The Ministry*, 87–88.
27. Ibid.

side the church.[28] Drawing from Jürgen Moltmann's notion of the social Trinity, missional theologians who follow such a notion of the Trinity posit that our fellowships with God precede our participation in God's mission and that God's existence as a social community renews the social nature of the church and God's mission.[29]

This approach has brought the concern for the other to the fore and has developed plausible arguments that the church has to listen to its neighbors, whereas it has offered us few examples of how missional congregations have listened to their neighbors in practical terms.[30] We can find the emphasis on the church's *hospitality to the stranger* within the literature of the missional church conversation.[31] If the *stranger* is a reference to *the other*, the gap between people within and outside the church still seems to remain wide and deep. The metaphor of *hospitality to the stranger* generally reminds us of the *asymmetrical* relationship between *the host* and *the guest* or between *the benefactor* and *the beneficiary*.[32] In contrast, missional literature which addresses hospitality to the stranger tends to take seriously the role of the stranger or the other in relation to spirituality or mission.[33] Missional theologians, such as Alan Roxburgh, Patrick Keifert, and Dwight Zscheile, have developed arguments for the church's need for listening to the stories of the people in its neighborhood,

---

28. See ibid; Van Gelder, *The Missional Church in Context*, 29, 46–50; Van Gelder, ed., *The Missional Church and Denominations*, 146, 167–69.

29. See Moltmann, *God in Creation*, 216–43. Since *imago Dei* mirrors the Trinitarian life of the three Persons, Moltmann interprets *imago Dei* as "*imago[T]rinitatis*." *Imago Dei* essentially refers to human relationships with God as God's gift of fellowship, which indicates God's initiation of his relationship with us. Second, *imago Dei* corresponds to Trinitarian relationship. In this regard, *imago Dei* is a social and interpersonal reality. Thus, Moltmann holds that "person and community are two sides of one and same life process"; See Van Gelder and Zscheile, *The Missional Church in Perspective*, 101–23.

30. See Roxburgh and Romanuk, *The Missional Leader*; Roxburgh and Boren, *Introducing the Missional Church*; Barrett et al., *Treasure*.

31. See Guder, *Missional Church*, 175–80; Barrett, *Treasure*, 84–99, 167–70.

32. For example, Bosch points out that the relationship between Western missionaries and natives or churches of the West and those of the East/South has been a one-way-street relationship between the benefactor and the beneficiary. See Bosch, *Transforming Mission*, 290, 456.

33. See Dietterich, "Missional Community: Cultivating Communities of the Holy Spirit," 142–82; Van Gelder and Zscheile, *The Missional Church in Perspective*, 132–33, 148–55.

and have provided several practical steps for doing so.[34] Roxburgh, Keifert and others have called for a posture of learning from neighbors but there has been little published research of congregations actually doing so. Therefore, I expect, in light of this study of congregations' listening to their neighbors, that congregations will be able to cultivate their own ways of listening to their neighbors, who are located in the contexts in which God is working. Congregations may understand that listening to their neighbor is a starting point of their participation in God's mission, because God's mission is mission-in-dialogue.

CONSTRUCTIVIST GROUNDED THEORY

A constructivist grounded theory method was used for this study. There were two essential reasons regarding the reason why I chose grounded theory. First, few studies undertaken subscribed to listening to the neighbor in terms of congregational relationships with the neighborhood. A grounded theory approach seemed to be suitable to engaging these. This is because grounded theory is generally regarded as being helpful in cases where there are no overarching theories/hypotheses from previous research that inform the present research. It is invaluable as an explanatory tool that explicates all constituent elements of the research phenomenon and their interrelationships.[35] Second, grounded theory enables us to discover the primary concerns of research participants and the basic social/phenomenological process that facilitates those concerns.[36] Grounded theory helped me find out what was happening in relation to participants' listening to their neighbors and to identify the process of it.

Grounded theory was developed as an attempt to shorten the distance between theory and empirical research in the social sciences. Barney G. Glaser and Anselm L. Strauss first developed grounded theory through the publication of *The Discovery of Grounded Theory* in 1967.[37] They held that grounded theory approach aimed to offer empirical grounding for theories based not in hypothesis but in data, suggesting a specificity and logic to those theories and legitimizing qualitative research. The four central criteria for judging the applicability of grounded

---

34. See Roxburgh, *Moving Back* and *Missional*; Keifert, *We Are Here Now*, 29, 35, 44, 98; Zscheile, *People of the Way*, 74–86.

35. Charmaz, *Constructing Grounded Theory*, 5–10, 14–18, 125–32.

36. Ibid., 21–25.

37. Glaser and Strauss, *The Discovery of Grounded Theory*.

theory are *fit, understanding, generality,* and *control*.³⁸ Creswell explains grounded theory as follows:

> Grounded theory is a strategy of inquiry in which the researcher derives a general, abstract theory of process, action, or interaction grounded in the views of participants. This process involves using multiple stages of data collection and the refinement and interrelationship of categories of information (Charmaz, 2006; Strauss and Corbin, 1990, 1998). Two primary characteristics of this design are the constant comparison of data with emerging categories and theoretical sampling of different groups to maximize the similarities and the differences of information.³⁹

I employed Kathy Charmaz's approach to grounded theory for this study, considering that her grounded theory approach developed in ways different from the initial approach of Glaser and Strauss. Glaser developed his approach by emphasizing its positivist, objectivist leanings and dimension of induction, while Strauss strengthened his approach by developing a more technical and systematic process of data analysis.⁴⁰ Charmaz points out that classic grounded theory overlooks that the researcher could not be separated from discovered data or theories.⁴¹ Charmaz, in this regard, contends that any discovered theories offer "an *interpretive* portrayal of the studied world, not an exact picture of it."⁴² Charmaz argues in opposition to the classic grounded theory texts of Glaser and/or Strauss that grounded theory methodology can complement other qualitative approaches, and vice versa.⁴³ Grounded theory is an inductive, comparative, and interactive approach to inquiry that offers several open-ended strategies for conducting emergent inquiry.

I was primarily interested in Charmaz's argument for the interpretive aspects of the research process and results. I basically made use of missional theology as the primary interpretive tool in the entire process of this study. The interpretive aspects of this study stems from missional theology as follows. The Holy Trinity is the subject of the church and mission. Mission and the church have to be understood as being Trinitarian.

38. Strauss and Corbiton, *Basics of Qualitative Research*, 25.
39. Creswell, *Research Design*, 13.
40. Charmaz, *Constructing Grounded Theory*, 129–35, 177–85.
41. Ibid., 10.
42. Ibid. Emphasis in original.
43. Glaser and Strauss, *The Discovery of Grounded Theory*; Glaser, *Theoretical Sensitivity*.

The *missio Dei* means God's own self-sending in Christ by the Spirit to redeem and transform creation. The church is not the subject of mission, but a community of witness that is called into being and equipped by God, and sent into the world to testify to and participate in Christ's work. Therefore, mission and the church must be understood in light of the Trinity. In addition, I gave "priority to the studied *phenomenon* or *process*—rather than to a description of setting," as Charmaz suggests.[44]

DEFINITION OF LISTENING

When it comes to the definition of listening, a majority of listening research has focused on behavioral and cognitive, rational aspects of daily and professional communication.[45] Listening always recognizes "the other."[46] We cannot speak, communicate, or live without listening in a true sense. Many fields, including practical theology, conduct listening-enhancing training in order to achieve better communication. Listening in human communication has become more significant from theoretical, spiritual, and practical points of view. "The definition of listening as a concept is extremely broad" to the extent that listening is defined from various academic fields.[47] As a result, listening is widely and interchangeably used with hearing, attending, meditating, contemplating, and focusing.[48]

Given the above, I use *listening*, relating to dialogue, as an open-ended term in a more missional and hermeneutic sense. The term "dialogue" has gained prominence in missiology since the 1960s. Lamin O. Sanneh makes explicit translation the primary path of Christian mission, drawing on the social nature of language and highlighting the recipient culture as the true and final locus of the gospel.[49] Sanneh also contends that Christianity has grown as a result of its encounter with the *other*.[50] Thus, mission is God's invitation to dialogue with diverse cultures and religious traditions.

---

44. Charmaz, *Constructing Grounded Theory*, 22. Emphasis in original.

45. Purdy, "Listening, Culture, and Structures of Consciousness," 50.

46. Shotter, "Listening in a *Way* that Recognizes/Realizes the World of 'the Other,'" 21.

47. Schnapp, "Listening in Context," 134.

48. Ibid.

49. Sanneh, *Translating the Message*, 229–51.

50. Ibid., 3.

Dialogue, however, is not new in missionary discourse. The theological foundation for dialogue in mission is the triune God, as noted earlier. God has revealed that dialogue is an essential element of God's missional praxis. Therefore, Spirit-led congregations have a dialogical relationship with their neighborhoods as long as the triune God is the agent of mission. In this regard, *listening* to the neighborhood also includes the aspect of *attending* in a broader sense, although it is mainly used to emphasize the dialogical relationship between a congregation and its neighborhood.

CONCLUSION

I employ Charmaz's constructivist grounded theory to explore the following question: For the PCK congregations which have been actively involved in their neighborhoods, what are the understandings and practices of their listening to their neighbors? Related sub-questions, as noted earlier, are as follows: (1) Why do they listen to their neighbors? (2) What helps them to listen better to their neighbors? (3) What do they learn from this listening process? (4) What commonalities, if any, exist between such congregations within the PCK?

This thesis is presented in seven interrelated chapters. The first three chapters lay the foundation of the research. Chapter 1 provides a synopsis of the development of the study. It reveals the rationale for undertaking the study and a brief background on its theological and theoretical underpinnings. Accordingly, it briefly addresses the statement of the problem, purpose of the study, significance of the study, Charmaz's constructivist grounded theory, and a working definition of listening.

Chapter 2 focuses on the PCK's notions of mission and ecclesiology, briefly addressing the history of the PCK in the process. It then revisits Calvin's notions of mission and the church by comparing them with those of the PCK in light of missional theology.

Chapter 3 deals with methodology. It addresses the following topics: the key research question and method, sensitizing concepts, the research process, the role of the researcher, and ethical concerns.

Chapter 4 focuses primarily on research findings and their analysis, including profiles of research participant congregations. Based on these, it provides an emerging grounded theory of listening to the neighbor.

Chapter 5 undertakes a dialogue between the research findings or the emerging theory and theoretical sensitizing concepts. These sensitizing concepts consist of hermeneutics of the other and Open Systems

Theory (hereafter, OST). It also draws other related literature into the dialogue in the process.

Chapter 6 provides a dialogue between the research findings or the emerging theory and biblical/theological sensitizing concepts. These sensitizing concepts include biblical notions of neighbor and listening to the neighbor, the kingdom of God, the church as a Spirit-led community, Calvin's ecclesiology, and missional ecclesiology. It also addresses holistic mission, minjung theology, and missional theologians' notions of listening to the neighbor in relation to the research findings or the emerging theory.

Chapter 7 briefly addresses achievements and limitations of the study. It provides an overview of the research findings and the emergent theory of the church's listening to the neighbor. The implications of the research findings and the emergent theory are highlighted. I close the thesis with recommendations of future research and a short reflection of the research journey.

2

The Understandings of Mission and the Church
The PCK and Calvin

THIS CHAPTER DESCRIBES THE understandings of the PCK and Calvin regarding mission and the church before turning to the research methodology. We need to compare Calvin's understanding of mission and the church with that of the PCK because the PCK's understanding of the church and mission is deeply rooted in Calvin's work. When it comes to the PCK's understanding of mission and the church, this chapter focuses on its historical and practical understanding of mission and the church, along with its official understanding in its *Constitution*.[1] It also rests chiefly upon the 1559 edition of Calvin's *Institutes of the Christian Religion* (hereafter, *Institutes*) to the objective of this study, including complementarily his other works, although it would be fruitful to consult Calvin's entire work and life.

THE PCK'S UNDERSTANDING OF MISSION

The PCK's doctrine is essentially based on the Calvinist tradition, seeking to acknowledge God's sovereignty and to glorify Him as God alone through all it can do. The PCK has been theologically and historically concerned with mission as the Great Commission given to all Christians. It generally understands mission as involving evangelization and church growth, which are closely interrelated. Given this, the PCK has regarded

---

1. The Presbyterian Church of Korea, *Constitution*, http://www.pck.or.kr/PckInfo/Law01.asp# (accessed January 3, 2013). This English translation of the *Constitution* is the author's.

itself as responsible for building and expanding the kingdom of God. Therefore, the PCK has tended to place the church as primary agent, rather than God, at the center of mission.

The PCK only mentions the concept of *missio Dei* within the "Twenty-First Century Confession of Faith (TFCCF)" within its *Constitution*, while it does not fully develop this concept.[2] The PCK included the TFCCF in the *Constitution* in 2001 by theologically and historically reflecting on its growth and mission. The TFCCF is the product of the PCK alone within its "Volume 1 Doctrine" of the *Constitution*, except for "The PCK's Confession of Faith (PCKCF)" which was included in the *Constitution* in 1986.[3] The TFCCF emphasizes, in light of God's mission, that the PCK needs to be confessional and ecumenical by renewing its identity within rapid cultural change. It calls the PCK's attention to mission of reconciliation and *koinonia* between South and North Korea and among diverse groups or regions in South Korea, emphasizing the church's social mission in relation to God's kingdom. The TFCCF, on the one hand, ostensively addresses the work of the Spirit within and outside the church in relation to mission. On the other hand, the TFCCF still places the PCK's priority of mission on saving souls over other aspects of the PCK's mission. It does parallel evangelism to God's mission. The TFCCF continues to be primarily concerned with church growth, while pointing out its negative effects. It also notes that the PCK should build and expand the kingdom of God through its evangelism and social services. Therefore, the TFCCF still tends to consider the church rather than God to be the primary agent of mission from a missional perspective of God's mission.

Mission as Evangelization

The PCK understands mission as evangelization. The PCK, on the one hand, divides mission into domestic and overseas missions according to

2. See *Constitution*, 1:6. This Confession was included in the *Constitution* in 2001.

3. Volume 1 of the *Constitution* consists of "the Apostles' Creed," "the 12 Creeds," "the Westminster Shorter Catechism," "the Westminster Confession of Faith," "the PCKCF," and "the TFCCF," which includes "The Nicene-Constantinopolitan Creed." In 1907, the "12 Creeds" as a revision of "The Confession of Faith" of the independent, national Presbyterian Church of India in 1903 was adopted by the early missionaries. Moreover, the Westminster Confession of Faith is the 1903 version in which the Presbyterian Church of the United Church of America added two chapters, "Of the Holy Spirit" and "Of the Gospel of the Love of God and Missions" to the original version of the Confession (1646).

geographical locations of its mission field, and ordinary and extraordinary missions according to the degree and kind of mission activity. On the other hand, the PCK emphasizes that all mission activities focus on evangelization based on the Great Commission. There is no mission apart from evangelization.

The PCK has placed its primary interest in evangelism for saving souls since its beginning. The PCK's notion of evangelization consists of proclaiming the gospel to save individual souls and bringing them into the church. This has encouraged Korean Christians to view carrying the gospel to their neighbors as the biggest and most important mission. The PCK understands the gospel as God's love and mercy, which seems to be reduced to saving souls from the world. The PCK, in this vein, undertook the Movement of Saving One Million Souls in 1909 for the sake of saving souls, and promoted the Three-Million-Member Movement as its denominational mission policy in the late 1990s–2000s.

The PCK's primary focus on evangelization results from the strong influence of the early missionaries in Korea.[4] The early missionaries made great contributions on the growth of the early church. They devoted themselves to mission in Korea. Their mission consisted of evangelical, educational, and medical activities, though the last two activities were complementary to the first activities. They believed church-founding to be the most essential task for evangelization. Their educational and medical services also provided Koreans with the initial basis of modern infrastructure for education and medicine.

---

4. The early leaders of the PCK, such as Horace G. Underwood, Samuel H. Moffett, William N. Blair, and Sun Chu Kil (a native leader), were regarded as fundamentalist. The initial stage of the PCK was strongly influenced by Presbyterian missionaries, who came mostly from the United States. American Presbyterian missionaries were sent out by both the northern and southern Presbyterian Churches (or *The Presbyterian Church in the U.S.A.* and *The Presbyterian Church in the U.S.*). Most of them graduated from McCormick, Princeton, and New Brunswick seminaries. They, regardless of their denominations, followed the theological position of the Old School of Princeton Seminary, which held a high view of the Scriptures against the higher biblical criticism and a strict adherence to the seventeenth-century Westminster Confession of Faith and Catechisms. They were also motivated by Dwight L. Moody's revival meetings and the Student Volunteer Movement, which was founded to recruit college and university students for foreign missions in 1886. The Great Commission and premillennialism were at the heart of their primary concern. See Paik, *The History*, 83–102, 149–50, 171–73, 177–79; Wells, *New God*, 32–46, 76; Adams, *Christ and Culture*, 86–87; Park, *Protestantism and Politics*, 53–60; Pak, *Millennialism*, 139, 231; regarding the theology of the Old Princeton School, see McConnel, "The Old Princeton Apologetics: Common Sense or Reformed?" 647–72.

Most of the early missionaries came from America and were influenced by fundamentalism, which tended to regard the gospel as only related to individuals' personal salvation and native cultures as negative or evil against evangelism.[5] They dealt with the following themes as key concepts and catch phrases: "conversion," "call," "gospel," "heathen," "the sense of urgency," "the heathen are lost," "salvation through Christ," "before he comes," and so on.[6] Spencer J. Palmer compares their characteristics of mission to "Puritanic zeal and Wesleyan fervor" based on fundamentalism.[7] On the one hand, this tendency helped missionaries, with the pre-millenarian view of the second coming of Christ, passionately focus on evangelism and church-founding. On the other hand, the early missionaries' fundamentalist understanding of mission unavoidably led Korean Christians to separate evangelism from socio-political involvement and to understand the church as separated from the tragic or evil world. Their teachings of the Spirit focusing primarily on personal conversion also resulted in both individual morality-centered and other-worldly spiritualism.

The missionaries' fundamentalist understanding of the gospel somewhat seemed to be compatible with Neo-Confucianism, which had played a primary role as a national religion and ethic in Korea, in regard to legalism, orthodox thought, authority, etc. Some Koreans consented to the missionaries' exclusive understanding of Korean religious traditions because their traditions could not answer Koreans' mental suffering properly with regard to their spiritual thirst. Koreans, who had experienced colonization by Japan, the Korean War, dictatorships, etc., viewed the *urgent return of Christ* as real *good news*. Since the present world was utterly lost, the eyes of the Korean Christians were fixed on the next world. The faster they would evangelize the world, the sooner Christ would come. Korean Christians, in light of puritanism, felt a kind of a holy sense of mission and sense of pride as a *chosen people* in the end. For this reason, the PCK maintains that national evangelization has meant a kind of a national hope.

The early missionaries' emphasis on the Bible in general and the gospel in particular caused promotion of the *Hangul*—Korean vernacular—translation of the Bible. They thought that Koreans would need it

---

5. See previous footnote.
6. Hunt, *Protestant Pioneers in Korea*, 84–92.
7. Palmer, *Korea and Christianity*, 26.

in order to understand the gospel correctly. This vernacular translation greatly influenced the development of the Korean culture as well as the church growth of the early Korean church, although missionaries generally avoided relating the gospel to the Korean culture. Considering that a language is a container of any particular culture, we can understand that the Korean vernacular translation already embraced the Korean culture regardless of the intention of missionaries.

It is surprising that, before the coming of many official missionaries to Korea, there existed Korean vernacular translations of the New Testament by the Rev. John Ross, a missionary of the Scottish Presbyterian Church to China, with the assistance of a Korean teacher Sang-yun Suh.[8] This can be regarded as a case of the Spirit being ahead of the church in missional terms. Ross completed Korean translation of the whole New Testament in 1887. Suh spontaneously established the first Protestant church—*Sorae* church—in 1883, before the first official missionary ever came to Korea.[9] This is likely to be regarded as an example of how the Korean vernacular translation of the Bible influenced Korean Christians. Missionaries to Korea finished translating the whole Old Testament into Korean in 1911, along with a new Korean version of the New Testament in 1900.

The choice to use *Hangul* had a significant meaning beyond the choice of language. The use of the Korean vernacular translation of the Bible focused primarily on evangelizing the Korean populace because an overwhelming majority in the Korean population of that time used Korean vernacular, mainly in its spoken form. At the same time, Chinese was used as an official language by the educated aristocracy. Missionaries indirectly popularized *Hangul* through the dissemination of the Korean translation of Christian literature, including the Bible, and through teachings of *Hangul* in Christian schools and local churches. What is more, Protestant churches also "made literacy in *Hangul* a prerequisite for admission to Holy Communion."[10] Missionaries' strategy of

---

8. Paik, *The History*, 46. Because of Suh's profound knowledge of Chinese, three thousand copies of the Gospel of St. Luke in Korean were published on March 24, 1882, and an additional three thousand copies of the Gospel of St. John were published on May 12 in the same year.

9. Clark, *Christianity in Modern Korea*, 6. It is also regarded as the first church of the PCK.

10. New World Encyclopedia, "Christianity in Korea," New World Encyclopedia, http://www.newworldencyclopedia.org/entry/Christianity_in_Korea (accessed April 27, 2013).

teaching *Hangul* led to replacing the existing feudal social structure by granting more opportunities for women and underprivileged people. The renaissance of *Hangul* directly provided the basis for a new vernacular literature closely associated with reformist-nationalist movements, and the use of *Hangul* also acquired a patriotic anti-Japanese meaning in the colonial era (1910–1945). Sanneh, in the similar vein, argues that "missionary translation was instrumental in the emergence of indigenous resistance to colonialism" in Africa.[11] Therefore, the productive result of the Korean translation of the Bible resonates with that of Martin Luther's translating work of the Latin Bible into the German language.[12]

Vernacular translations of the Bible, from a missional perspective, do not mean only translations into local languages, but also into local cultural settings. This is true because a language is always specific and particular and is "the primary vehicle of a culture."[13] Andrew F. Walls highlights that missionaries' vernacular translations of the Bible are available due not to their ability of translation or the reformers' emphasis on vernacular translations but to the translatability of the Bible itself.[14] Walls also emphasizes that the translation of the Bible rests on "the first divine act of translation into humanity," that is, incarnation.[15] In other words, "Incarnation is translation."[16] Sanneh, in the similar vein, maintains that God's mission is "the hidden force" for vernacular translations, regarding mission as translation.[17] Sanneh understands that the Holy Spirit has worked through the vernacular translations, enabling all peoples to understand God's message in their own languages.[18] Sanneh argues in light of the translatability of the gospel that the receptor culture is the true and final locus of the gospel. The PCK, in this regard, seems to miss the translatability of the gospel and the Bible translation as the work of the Holy Spirit. The PCK has to pay attention to the contexts and cultures of

---

11. Sanneh, *Translating the Message*, 161.

12. Luther's German translation of the Bible awakened the national identity of the German populace and had a strong impact on cultural German developments, for instance, the creation of the modern German language and educational reform throughout Germany.

13. Newbigin, *The Gospel*, 188.

14. Walls, *The Missionary Movement*, 26–42.

15. Ibid., 27.

16. Ibid.

17. Sanneh, *Translating the Message*, 37.

18. Ibid., 113, 117.

its neighborhood to evangelize them because, as Van Gelder states, the Spirit-led church takes its context seriously for its mission as long as the gospel is inherently translatable.[19]

Mission as Church Growth

The PCK has understood church growth to be its primary mission. This is because the PCK treats church growth as the extension of the kingdom of God. The PCK is still concerned with church growth as a central theme in regard to mission although taking seriously the shadow of its explosive church growth within both the PCKCF and the TFCCF. Even the TFCCF, which is concerned with God's mission, deals with the church as the subject of building and expanding the kingdom of God. It is natural for the PCK to link church growth with the extension of the kingdom of God.

This notion of the kingdom of God is concerned only with God's kingdom's dimension of *being already on earth* with little consideration of its dimension of *not yet being fulfilled*, considering that God's kingdom is *already* come, but *not yet* accomplished. This notion tends to identify the church with the kingdom as long as the church growth means the extension of God's kingdom. However, Van Gelder points out that the church cannot "build, extend, promote, [or] establish," but must "receive, enter, seek, [or] inherit" the kingdom of God.[20] The church, instead, is an eschatological community in relation to the coming kingdom of God.

The PCK has regarded increasing the number of believers as the extension of God's church, which has meant the progress of God's kingdom. The PCK has concentrated on planting churches as well as personal evangelism to save souls. Such a tendency has been influenced by Underwood, the father of the Protestant mission and the first Presbyterian pastor in Korea. Underwood regarded the phenomenal growth of the Korean church as the progress of God's kingdom.[21]

Underwood employed the Nevius Method (named after John Nevius, who was American Presbyterian missionary in Shantung China) of self-support, self-propagation and self-government for the sake of more effective mission in Korea.[22] Underwood stated succinctly as to the Nevius Method,

19. Van Gelder, *The Ministry*, 61–63.
20. Van Gelder, *The Essence*, 87–88.
21. Underwood, *The Call of Korea*, 5.
22. See Nevius, *The Planting*; Underwood, "Principles of Self-Support in Korea,"

First, to let each man "Abide in the calling wherein he was found," teaching that each was to an individual worker for Christ, and to live Christ in his own neighborhood, supporting himself by his trade.

Secondly, to develop Church methods and machinery only so far as the native Church was able to take care of and manage the same.

Third, as far as the Church itself was able to provide the men and the means, to set aside those who seemed the better qualified, to do evangelistic work among their neighbors.

Fourth, to let the natives provide their own church buildings, which were to be native in architecture, and of such style as the local church could afford to put up.[23]

This Nevius Method has paved the way for explosive church growth of the PCK and is still operative within the PCK in practical terms. The PCK has tended to emphasize church growth as its primary mission, because Korea has been a mission field. Such an understanding is inseparably related to the PCK's church-growth-centered ecclesiology, as will be discussed later. Therefore, the PCK's understanding of mission as church growth is grounded in the notion of the church rather than God as the primary agent in terms of mission.

THE PCK'S UNDERSTANDING OF THE CHURCH

It is important to note that the PCK's understanding of the church is rooted in Calvin's ecclesiology in theological terms. The PCK uses the same or similar terms from Calvin's ecclesiological concepts or images, as will be seen later, such as "the body of Christ," "the kingdom of Christ," "the visible/invisible church," "the people of God," "the temple of the Spirit," and so on within its *Constitution*.

The PCK has developed relatively functional ecclesiologies at the practical level, as compared with its doctrinal understanding of the church. The PCK's condition as a mission field, *inter alia*, has prompted the PCK to concentrate on practical issues relating to its local context, rather than its theological heritage. It is surprising that most of the early missionaries to Korea already spoke about the success of the Protestant mission after only sixteen years of missionary work in Korea. For instance, the factors for its success were described with expressions such as

---

91–94.

23. Underwood, *The Call of Korea*, 109–10.

"miracles" and "the work of the Holy Spirit" at the New York Ecumenical Missionary Conference in 1900.[24] The early Korean church has functioned as an archetype of the PCK, with key characteristics such as the self-support of the church, dynamic evangelism, spiritual renewal, dawn prayer meetings, and the like. Functional ecclesiologies within the early Korean church have been regarded as archetypal for the PCK. With this in mind, we address the themes of the church as (1) an institution, (2) a self-supporting church, (3) a spiritual-renewal-driven church, (4) a lifeboat, and (5) a growth-driven church—functional ecclesiologies within the PCK. These functional ecclesiologies are embedded in each other.

The Church as an Institution

The PCK has had a tendency to regard itself as an institution for saving souls since its beginning. The early missionaries took seriously the establishment of the church as an institution and *the training of a native pastorate*, which were their primary concerns because they believed that the evangelization to the end of the world was the most important task. The Presbyterian missionaries, including Underwood, based the Korean church on the Presbyterian system and strictly applied the *Westminster Shorter Catechism* from the very beginning although they dreamed of an organized church in Korea beyond denominational barriers. They, as children of their time, could not help but be concerned with the institutional church and ecclesiastical ecclesiology. The most crucial motive for setting up the Presbytery of Korea in 1907 was that Presbyterian missionaries wanted to ordain the first native pastors, including Sun Chu Kil, and needed a Presbytery to do so according to the Presbyterian Form of Government.

Underwood considered seriously whether the church could pay for the pastor, as we shall see, when he emphasized a self-supporting church. Underwood understood that the church could not be the church without the role of the pastor, because the church could be a true church only when the Word was preached and the sacraments were administered. Missionaries, in this regard, did not officially recognize Sorae Church, which was established by Sang-yun Suh in 1883 before missionaries officially came to Korea, as a *true* church because of the absence of an ordained pastor, as the Roman Catholic Church did not acknowledge the first Korean Catholic church established by Korean lay members until

24. Chung, *Syncretism*, 13–20.

it had a priest, approximately one century later. For this reason, Bosch points out that "mission [of Underwood's time] was the road from the institutional church to the church that still had to be instituted."[25]

The Church as a Self-Supporting Church

The early missionaries' implementation of the Nevius Method is still operative as a primary ecclesiology and theory of congregations because it has contributed greatly to the growth of the PCK. The Nevius Method emphasized a self-supporting, self-propagating and self-governing indigenous national church. Korean Christians viewed missionaries' emphasis on the *self* as positive since the Koreans' desire for independence from Japan's influence became closely linked with the self-supporting church during that time.[26] This method stressed the church's self-determination and the need for natives to carry on evangelical work.[27] For the sake of quick and efficient evangelization of Koreans, such missionaries' question was not what kind of church it should be in biblical terms, but how the church should be built and extended. Missionaries put the strongest stress on financial self-support among the Korean churches in the process.[28]

Strictly enforcing this principle throughout all of Korea sometimes hindered balanced development of churches, especially in the poor farming areas, although the adoption and adherence of the Nevius Method was inevitable and the best policy for the *survival* of the church under the fragile political condition and disastrous economic dislocation in Korea. The economic ability of the church gradually became the decisive standard for judging whether or not the church could be regarded as independent. For example, when a church could pay for its minsters and buildings, this church would be admitted as a real church. Thus, such

---

25. Bosch, *Transforming Mission*, 332.
26. Nevius, *The Planting*.
27. See Clark, *The Korean Church*; Rhodes and Campbell, *History*, 86–90.

28. Historically, though Korean self-supporting churches became independent with regards to finance, they, as an infant church, were still under the oversight of missionaries and the parent church in terms of self-government. For the PCK, self-government was not given until missionaries left Korea around the turn of the 1940s. During that time, the worsening international situation due to World War 2 and the Japanese colonial government's mandate to participate in Shinto shrines inevitably led missionaries to withdraw from Korea.

an ecclesiological notion of a self-supporting church within the PCK has been almost completely related to the financial dimension of the church.

The Church as a Spiritual-Renewal-Centered Church

The PCK has sought to be a spiritual-renewal-centered church in the legacy of the Great Revival of 1907. The Great Revival has very often been called "the Great Awakening in Korea." The Great Revival led to the spiritual rebirth of the Korean church and had the most profound effect on its character and nature, leading to fervent prayer and dynamic personal evangelization through strong indigenous leadership and unique spiritual activities such as dawn prayer meetings.[29] Sun Chu Kil, as one of the first indigenous Presbyterian ministers, took the lead in the Great Revival and initiated dawn prayer meetings. In the face of the collapse of Joseon—the final dynasty in Korea and Japanese colonialism, Kil, like other educated people, sought to transform the Korean nation. Missionaries' emphasis on the self and the individual soul helped Kil become aware of the value of individuals. Kil posed that individual spiritual weaknesses had caused the national problems of his time.[30] Kil held that individuals' change would result in national change. The country could never achieve true national liberation without individuals' inner, spiritual transformation. The spiritual revival of individuals, thus, would cause the revival of the church and the nation.

Kil, however, tended to understand the Spirit as the One who works for personal blessings through a nuanced understanding of the work of the Holy Spirit. He treated spirituality in terms of private rather than public ethics. Kil, doubtless, saw that the spiritual regeneration of the church was accomplished by spiritually reborn individuals, with the help of the Holy Spirit. After the failure of the March First Movement of 1919—an independence movement against Japanese colonialism in which many Korean Christians got involved—Kil paid more attention

---

29. In 1907, the Great Revival as a mass revival movement began in Pyongyang, the capital and largest city of North Korea as of 2013, during an annual Bible conference. This revival originated from a series of prayer and Bible study meetings that had already been held for spiritual revival by missionaries and Korean church leaders from the early 1900s. Expecting an outpouring of the Holy Spirit, all attendees were eventually moved by the Spirit, repented of their sins, and made public confession of them. This revival was continued as a movement of mass prayer and confession in the early Korean church.

30. Wells, *New God*, 40.

to other-worldly spiritualism. On the one hand, the PCK's emphasis on personal spiritual renewal mainly through dawn prayer meetings and revival meetings has helped Christians satisfy their spiritual-psychological quests for redemption in Korea's continued tragic situations in light of Kil's legacy. On the other hand, such a notion also seems to have been closely related to other-worldly spiritualism, which encouraged Christians not to relate to burning politico-economic issues within Korea.

The Church as a Lifeboat

The PCK understands the church to be a lifeboat. One of the primary factors in regard to the early Korean church's explosive growth was Korea's tragic situation of that time, as noted above. Many Korean Christians saw the total crisis throughout the entire country as a sign prior to the Second Coming of Christ under the strong influence of missionaries' pre-millennialism.[31] For example, it was near Pyongyang, in which the Great Revival began in 1907, that the Sino-Japanese war (1894–95) and the Russo-Japanese war (1904–05) took place in order to occupy Korea. The Korean palace was busy begging for her survival, although these two wars brought massive suffering to the Korean populace in both psychological and material terms. It seemed very natural for Korean Christians that the church naturally represented a rescue ship saving the people who suffered in this world under such circumstances. Simply put, the church was a lifeboat for saving people *from* the world. Such a church was a called-out community from the world, a literal *ekklesia*, and as such, a church-centered church separated from the world. Missionaries' policy of separation of church and state also tended to make the PCK separated from the world. Daniel J. Adams, in this regard, compares such a notion of the early Korean church to "Noah's Ark," saving people from Satan's tragic world.[32] The continued unsafe circumstances due to the Korean War, military dictatorships, radical industrialization, rapid urbanization, and the like have made it possible for Christians to understand the church as a lifeboat no matter how much this ecclesiology has worked.

---

31. For example, in *Haetaron*, Kil already described metaphorically that Satan ruled over this world and God would accomplish God's kingdom at the end of human beings' history. He viewed the worsening circumstances of that time as increasing Satan's power in the world and a sign before the return of Christ. Kil, *Haetaron* [*Treatise on Laziness*].

32. Adams, "Church Growth in Korea," 21–23.

The Church as a Growth-Driven Church

A growth-driven church can be regarded as a functional ecclesiology in the PCK. Given that church growth means the expansion of God's kingdom, the PCK has treated church growth as positive, rather than negative. Both the PCKCF (1986) and the TFCCF (2001) overall take seriously church growth, despite the time gap of twenty-five years between them, while partly criticizing the shadow of church growth. This is a good example of regarding a growth-driven church as operative in terms of functional ecclesiology.

The explosive growth of the early Korean church has continued to motivate the PCK to concentrate on church growth. The term "growth" was treated as a popular motto for all, including the PCK, given that the ruin and poverty due to the Korean War led people to hope for economic growth through modernization and industrialization. In the midst of such a culture, it was natural for the PCK to be primarily concerned with its growth. Explosive economic growth and rapid industrialization/urbanization during the 1960s–80s contributed to church growth. On the one hand, many urban congregations were able to cater to the needs and demands of the new society in that juncture—a time of economic growth in which many farmers were moving to the cities. The church provided people amidst rapid social disorganization with meaning for life, a place of rest, and a new community for a sense of belonging.[33] On the other hand, during that time, the government could hardly address people's needs due to rapid urbanization and other religions had few gathering places in cities. Over time, economic success came to mean success of religious life and emphasis came to be placed on the size of the congregation. The message of immediate material success encouraged people within the church who were afraid of failure. Pastors' preaching as a firsthand method to attract people into the church has been at the heart of evaluating the church in the process of competitions among local churches for the sake of growth. Naturally, pastors' ability and leadership have played a central role in church growth. Sacraments have been relatively rarely held within the PCK, as compared with preaching, while Calvin emphasized both the pure preaching of the Word and the due celebration of sacraments.

---

33. Kim, *Protestant Church Growth in Korea*, 122.

CALVIN'S UNDERSTANDING OF MISSION

Over the centuries, it has been widely accepted that Calvin, along with other reformers of the sixteenth century, was not involved in foreign missions because he believed that the Great Commission was fulfilled by the apostles.[34] This is based on the notion that mission has typically been understood in relation to foreign missions. There has also been criticism of Calvin, in that he did not develop a systematic theology of mission.[35] Calvin's doctrines of election and predestination have been to some extent considered as preventing believers from getting involved in evangelistic and missionary activities. In brief, this argument holds that Calvin had no concern for mission to non-Christians.

However, recent studies of Calvin have drawn a sharp contrast to such criticisms of Calvin's teachings and activities regarding mission.[36] Calvin was involved in the work of sending missionaries to Brazil, although this eventually failed. Calvin also sent trained ministers back to not only his native land, France, but also the rest of Europe for the reformation of the church, such as Scotland, England, Hungary, etc. Calvin's biblical and theological teachings, including those regarding God's election and predestination, seem to support evangelism and mission work. Calvin posits that the kingdom of Christ is not yet fulfilled in commenting on Micah 2:1–4.[37] Calvin maintains that although the extension of Christ's kingdom is all God's work completely, God uses humans as his instruments in the process.[38] Calvin does not treat the doctrines of election and predestination as fatalistic. When examining his views, these doctrines, rather, highlight that humans achieve salvation only through God's sovereignty and grace, and that Christians must make the effort to evangelize everyone, admitting that only God knows who will be saved. Calvin, in this regard, does not limit preaching of the gospel to the elect. For example, Calvin writes in his commentaries on 1 Tim 2:4–5:

---

34. Bosch, *Transforming Mission*, 243–48.

35. Ibid.

36. See Hughes, "John Calvin: Director of Missions," 40–54; Beaver, "The Genevan Mission to Brazil," 55–73; Calhoun, "John Calvin: Missionary Hero or Missionary Failure?" 16–33; Schirrmacher, *Calvin and World Mission*; Barro, "Election, Predestination and the Mission of God," 181–98; Chung, *Hermeneutical Theology*, 22–23.

37. Calvin, "Commentaries on Micah," 184–92.

38. Calvin, "Commentary on a Harmony of the Evangelists," 380–91.

> [T]here is no people and no rank in the world that is excluded from salvation; because God wishes that the gospel should be proclaimed to all without exception. Now the preaching of the gospel gives life; and he justly concludes that God invites all equally to partake salvation . . . this Mediator was not only given to one nation, or to a small number of persons of some particular rank, but to all; because the fruit of sacrifice, by which he made atonement for sins, extend to all.[39]

From this example, we perceive that Calvin was primarily concerned with Christians' responsibility for preaching the gospel to all, rather than the elect.

We can find that there exist rich missional insights in his writings and teachings, although Calvin does not use missionary language explicitly, as we shall see later. Calvin was concerned with the renewal of his contemporary churches from the spirit of the gospel as his primary missional task. Calvin's teachings also have implications and inherent connections in relation to the theology of God's mission. Calvin's emphasis on God's election and predestination in light of God's sovereignty is well in accord with Karl Barth's view of election. It is needless to say that Barth paved the way for a paradigm shift from the *missio ecclesiae* to the *missio Dei*.[40] Such a notion of mission, which has strongly influenced

---

39. Calvin, "Commentaries on the First Epistle to Timothy," 54–56.

40. See Bosch, *Transforming Mission*, 389–90. According to Bosch, although Barth did not use the exact term *missio Dei*, he was the first theologian to denote mission as God's activity rather than human activity of the church, as evidenced in a paper at the Brandenburg Missionary Conference in 1932; However, there is some disagreement regarding the general genealogy of *missio Dei* in which Karl Hartenstein mediated Barth to Willingen and developed a Trinitarian grounding for mission. See, for example, Flett, *The Witness of God*. Flett rejects the accepted genealogy of *missio Dei*. According to Flett, Barth and Hartenstein did not develop God's mission in Trinitarian terms until the 1950s. Barth did not develop a Trinitarian basis for mission until 1965. Hartenstein almost fully accepted Barth's dialectical theology, emphasis on God as acting subject, and centrality of God's word. He agreed with Barth's intention that Barth harshly rejected human mediation in mission in order for the German church to have room to support the Nazis' National Socialism. However, he viewed that this rejection did not provide the church with a positive theological basis for its missionary work. In this regard, Hartenstein followed Oscar Cullman's eschatology regarding Jesus Christ as the midpoint of sacred history and sacred history as objectively real in general history. For Hartenstein, "mission is not based on the Trinity; mission is grounded in the sending of the Son and in expectation of his return" (ibid., 130–31). Further, he developed *missio Dei* as "an apologia for the missionary existence of the Christian community" (ibid., 132). In brief, Barth and Hartenstein had not grounded mission in the Trinity, even by the time of the Willingen Conference, in 1952. In contrast to

the development of the missional church conversation in England and North America, is closely related to God's election. Barth regards God's election as "the sum of the gospel."[41] Barth understands, in light of God's election, that God already decided God's reconciliation to the world in Jesus Christ by the power of the Holy Spirit.

Barth developed his notion of God's election based on Calvin's overall notion of election in a supralapsarian manner. It, in this regard, is worth briefly mentioning the primary issue surrounding this controversy, while I do not wish to enter into the full complex debate of whether Barth did justice to Calvin's notion of election. Barth rejects Calvin's idea that God chose either some to be saved or others to be damned. This is because this notion does not support universal reconciliation in Christ. For this reason, Barth asserts that Jesus is the only object of God's election and damnation. Jesus Christ is "both the electing God and elected man," thus God's election and damnation took place only in Jesus Christ before the foundation of the world.[42] This is Barth's notion of dialectical predestination in contrast to the Calvin's double predestination. However, Barth tends to pay little attention to Calvin's emphasis on the Spirit in relation to election and predestination, as Paul Chung points out.[43]

Calvin develops his soteriology and ecclesiology relating to God's election in a Trinitarian fashion. God's election and predestination as the consequence of such election are the essential proof that everything regarding salvation is grounded in God's sovereignty and grace. For Calvin, these are not the products of theological or metaphysical speculation, but are grounded in biblical revelation. Their basis is biblically hidden

---

the received genealogy of *missio Dei*, Flett points out that the Trinitarian grounding of mission appeared only partly in the *Final Report* of Willingen. In particular, when it comes to the origin of Willingen's Trinitarianism of mission, Flett insists that the American report developed the Trinitarianism by criticizing the mistakes of previous missions as the result of Christo-centrism, which led to the colonialist expansion of the Western church and an undue distinction between redemptive history and general history (ibid., 161). Considering this, Flett denies that Willingen established God's mission in Trinitarian terms under the direct influence of Barth and Hartenstein. Nevertheless, whether Hartenstein brought a Trinitarian grounding of mission to Willingen in light of Barth's Trinity, since Willingen, the *missio Dei* has become and developed as a new theological watchword to articulate the relationship between mission, church, and world, but with several different meanings.

41. Barth, *CD* 2/2, 3.
42. Ibid.
43. Chung, *Christian Spirituality*, 74–76.

in God's inscrutable justice.[44] God's election and predestination must be taught insofar as the Bible addresses them, while Calvin is not obsessed by these doctrines.[45] Calvin does not confine the sovereignty of God to the doctrines of election and predestination. The sovereignty of God enables Calvin to certainly leave room for God's freedom in dealing with these doctrines.

Calvin emphatically describes justification in Christ through the power of the Spirit as God's decision and act alone, regarding this as the crux of God's eternal election. God's election precedes faith. Faith is not a result of human efforts, but God's freely-given gift in Christ through the power of the Holy Spirit, as we shall see. Calvin highlights Christ as the mirror of election.[46] We can find our election in our relation to Christ alone. Election must also be proved not at once, but eschatologically throughout one's whole life.[47] Calvin encourages us to follow the guidance of the Holy Spirit who, as the Spirit of both God the Father and Christ, helps us be fully convinced of what God has done and will do, although we are incapable of understanding God's eternal election and predestination. Therefore, God's election is God's love in Christ, which can be attained only by the Spirit. It is important to rediscover Calvin's theology of the missional horizon of the Holy Spirit. From the point of the above, the PCK's emphasis on evangelism in relation to individual salvation tends to give priority to human decision or efforts rather than God's act alone—in contrast to Calvin's view. The working of the Spirit also seems to be dependent on individuals' prayers.

Calvin's theology is articulated in a very Trinitarian fashion. But we pay relatively more attention to the Holy Spirit than God the Father and the Son in dealing with Trinitarian aspects of Calvin's theology. This is because Calvin's well-known emphasis on God the Father's sovereignty and Christ's centrality and lesser-known teachings on the Holy Spirit tend to prevent us from regarding Calvin's theology as being fully Trinitarian. However, Benjamin Warfield refers to Calvin as "the theologian of the Spirit."[48] According to Chung, Werner Krusche articulates Calvin's

---

44. *Institutes*, III.23.2.
45. Helm, *Calvin*, 85.
46. *Institutes*, III.24.5.
47. Ibid., III.21.7.
48. Warfield, *Calvin and Augustine*, 484–85, quoted in Chung, *Christian Spirituality*, 4.

theology of the Spirit based on the Calvin's Trinity.[49] Some scholars, such as Chung and Julie Canlis, follow the similar directions with relatively different, respective emphases.[50] Philip W. Butin and J. Todd Billings also highlight the Trinitarian aspects of Calvin's theology, focusing on Calvin's notions of the Spirit, although not systematically developing them as Calvin's theology of the Spirit.[51] However, Chung, following in the footsteps of Krusche, seeks to articulate Calvin's theological scope in a pneumatological framework.

The Spirit plays a crucial role in Calvin's theology, while the Spirit is a passive agent in the PCK's theology. The Spirit is the mediator between creation and redemption in Calvin's view. Calvin describes deliberately that the Spirit is the Creator and Preserver of the world and the God who sent prophets and renews Christians to fit themselves for eternal life, and whom all offices of the church belong to.[52] Calvin takes it for granted that we cannot know God the Father as the Creator and the Son as the Redeemer without the working of the Holy Spirit, because the Spirit is the divine author of Scripture and the initiator of faith. Calvin holds that "the name 'God' in Scripture does not refer to the Father alone."[53] Calvin understands that all three persons of the Trinity were involved in creation.[54] God the Father created the world and the universe out of nothing by the power of Jesus Christ as the eternal Word and the Spirit.[55] God the Father governs the world through the power of the Spirit because the Spirit sustains all things, causes them to grow, and preserves them until the Last Day in terms of providential care.[56] For Calvin, God's providence is essentially *secret,* which indicates God's freedom.[57] Chung, in this regard, contends that Calvin understands the Spirit as the *Spiritus Creator* in terms of providence as God's universal activity.[58]

49. Chung, *Christian Spirituality*, 4–5.

50. For example, Chung develops Calvin's theology of the Spirit related to ethical dimension of faith in terms of cosmos, while Canlis focuses on Calvin's understandings of the Spirit based on the Christian mystical tradition. See Chung, *Christian Spirituality*; Canlis, *Calvin's Ladder*.

51. Butin, *Revelation*; Billings, *Calvin*; Billings, *Union with Christ*.

52. *Institutes*, I.13.14.

53. Ibid., I.13.24.

54. Ibid.

55. Ibid., I.14.20.

56. Ibid., I.13.14., 14.20.

57. Ibid., I.16.1–9.

58. Chung, *Christian Spirituality*, 7, 18.

In Calvin's view, there is coherence between creation and redemption because redemption entails restoration of the whole, corrupted creation. Redemption is essentially Trinitarian in nature because it is God the Father's grace which was achieved by the Son's reconciling office in the Spirit's regenerating power.[59] Calvin underscores the Son's lordship over both the church and the world because the Bible displays Christ as "the Maker of heaven and earth" in terms of creation and the King in terms of redemption.[60] This is possible because the Spirit is the bond of the Father and the Son, as noted above. The Son governs the world through the power of the Spirit, as the Father preserves the world through the power of the Spirit. Billings views Calvin's notion of *imago Dei* as a junction between Calvin's views of creation (or providence) and redemption.[61] On the one hand, the triune God created humans as the *imago Dei* to enjoy being united to God.[62] The fall of Adam has brought the corruption of the image of God so that one could not be united to God, while the image of God still remains in the human beings. On the other hand, God's image was renewed by the Son in the power of the Spirit.[63] Humans, accordingly, can fully restore God's image through the participation in Christ through the Spirit alone.

Calvin's notion of the *secret* or *hidden* work of the Spirit in relation to both providence and redemption seems to be opened toward two interpretations in a broad sense. On the one hand, this notion first might show that the Spirit does not play a role as an active agent ahead of the church out in the world, while the Spirit seems to work as a primary agent in the church. Missional theology, in this regard, treats the Spirit as the primary agent within both the church and the world. The dynamism of the Spirit also tends to be limited to the extent that the centrality of the Word is strictly emphasized in Calvin's theology. On the other hand, this notion at least supports that the Spirit is working in the process of providential care for the whole creation and salvation for the human beings within the world beyond the church. Chung argues that Calvin highlights the hidden work of the Spirit in the reprobate providing "a space for universal inclusiveness of election even toward the reprobate" in spite of his

---

59. *Institutes*, III.11.9.
60. Ibid., I.13.27; 3:9–12.
61. Billings, *Calvin*, 144–61.
62. *Institutes*, I.15.1–4.
63. Ibid., I.15.5.

emphasis on God's election in light of Christ.⁶⁴ Chung brings diverse warrants into discussion from Calvin's biblical commentaries, as well as *Institutes*.⁶⁵ Dennis W. Jowers similarly argues that Calvin includes the Spirit's *extraordinary* work in relation to the unevangelized in his commentaries.⁶⁶

Calvin maintains that union with Christ through the power of the Spirit is at the heart of God the Father's salvific plan, whereas the PCK rarely addresses this. Union with Christ means that, through the power of the Holy Spirit, believers have been accepted in Christ and engrafted into his body by the grace of God. Calvin emphasizes the Spirit as the bond of the Father and the Son and the bond of Christ and the believer in so doing. Calvin certainly states in this light:

> God the Father gives us the Holy Spirit for his Son's sake, and yet has bestowed the whole fullness of the Spirit upon the Son to be minister and steward of his liberality. For this reason, the Spirit is sometimes called the "Spirit of the Father," sometimes the "Spirit of the Son."⁶⁷

Calvin also refers to the Holy Spirit as "the bond that unites us to Christ."⁶⁸ Calvin holds that, "Only the Holy Spirit leads us to Christ."⁶⁹ That is, faith is "the principal work of the Holy Spirit."⁷⁰ Therefore, God's salvific plan is a Trinitarian process in which humans are united to God. As Billings rightly states, "this Trinitarian process unites believers to Jesus Christ by the Spirit in order to serve the Father in gratitude."⁷¹

Calvin also deals with Christian spirituality in very eschatological, communal, and missional terms as compared to the PCK's individual otherworldly spirituality. Calvin understands that Christian spirituality is essentially rooted in the believer's union with Christ in relation to the Holy Spirit. First, Calvin maintains that the believer's union with Christ is the ongoing process of fulfilling the image of God in the *duplex gratia*

---

64. Chung, *Christian Spirituality*, 76. See also *Institutes*, III.2.11.

65. Ibid.

66. Jowers, "In What Sense Does Calvin Affirm 'Extra Ecclesiam Nulla Salus'?" 62–64.

67. *Institutes*, III.1.2.

68. Ibid., III.1.1.

69. Ibid., III.2.34.

70. Ibid., III.1.4.

71. Billings, *Union with Christ*, 65.

(double grace)—justification and sanctification in eschatological terms. For Calvin, justification and sanctification are distinct, but inseparable. On the one hand, justification means that God forgives sinners who are united to Christ thorough the power of the Spirit, and receive Christ's righteousness. Calvin regards this as a gradual progress, insofar as justification is related to Christ's righteousness. On the other hand, sanctification relates to the believers' growing in Christlikeness with the help of the Spirit. Sanctification begins when the Holy Spirit unites believers to Jesus Christ. Accordingly, through this dialectical relationship between justification and sanctification, the Holy Spirit helps Christians spiritually grow in communion with Christ until fully enjoying their communion with God in the kingdom of God.

Second, Calvin offers a picture of the individual's spirituality relating to others within the church in communal terms. The individual believer's continuing spiritual task for union with Christ unavoidably relates to *koinonia*—the communion of the faithful among one another within the church. This is because union with Christ means participation in the body of Christ by the power of the Spirit and Christ is the head of the church. Calvin asserts that Christians cannot enjoy union with Christ "unless we abide in communion with the church."[72] Spiritual growth is impossible apart from the church. Union with Christ is communally manifested through the pure preaching and hearing of the Word of God and the proper administration of the sacraments within the church by the secret working of the Holy Spirit. Furthermore, each member within the church has their own spiritual gift given by the Spirit to serve the common good under the headship of Christ.[73] The sacramental dimension of the church, thus, relates to the missional discipleship in the world in which the Holy Spirit works.

Third, with the above in mind, Calvin develops Christian spirituality in relation to social ethics in missional terms. Calvin, in light of Rom 12:1, considers believers' spiritual act of worship as presenting "their bodies to God as a living sacrifice, holy and acceptable to [him]" to advance God's glory.[74] This leads Calvin to relate Christian spirituality to taking care of people outside the church, along with devotion to God,

---

72. *Institutes*, IV.1.22.

73. Calvin, "Commentary on the First Epistle to the Corinthians," 395–18.

74. *Institutes*, III.7.1.

emphasizing helping and loving one's neighbors.[75] In so doing, Calvin affirms that believers have to love their neighbors because neighbors have "the image of God" in themselves.[76] This notion is partly related to the expected roles of the church and the state based on Christendom of his day, as will be discussed in relation to Calvin's ecclesiology in detail.

Calvin states as to the definition of the term *neighbor*:

> We [believers] ought to embrace the whole human race without exception in a single feeling of love; here there is no distinction between barbarian and Greek, worthy and unworthy, friend and enemy, since all should be contemplated in God, not in themselves.[77]

Billings holds that Calvin regards love of one's neighbor as integral for Christians' lives in union with Christ, relating justice to union with Christ.[78] Billings understands that Calvin views believers' actions of loving both God and neighbor as reflecting "the gift of new life received in Christ through the Spirit."[79] Chung similarly argues that, for Calvin, "Christian spirituality is not to be discussed without regard to Christian commitment for social emancipation and economic justice."[80] Christian spirituality embraces social concerns, justice, and peace, given that the Spirit is both the sanctifier in terms of human life and the *Spiritus Creator* in the cosmic-universal dimension.[81]

CALVIN'S UNDERSTANDING OF THE CHURCH

Calvin's understanding of the church is interrelated with what has been discussed regarding his notion of mission. The church is at the heart of Calvin's theology and life. Calvin attempted to found a new form of church, distinct from both a resurgent Catholicism and a proliferating Anabaptism. From a missional viewpoint, such an attempt had missional impulses. It was from the spirit of the gospel that Calvin was primarily concerned with the ongoing renewal of the church. Calvin's definition of

---

75. Ibid., III.7.5–7.
76. Ibid., III.7.6.
77. Ibid., II.7.55.
78. Billings, *Union with Christ*, 10.
79. Ibid., 108.
80. Chung, *Christian Spirituality*, 13.
81. Ibid., 15–31.

the gospel is as follows: "Christ becomes ours and we are made partakers of the salvation and eternal blessedness brought by him."[82]

Calvin, with a solid basis in the Bible, continually developed his ecclesiology through his theological and practical experiences in relation to both his local ministry in Geneva and his ongoing debates with other contemporary theologians in a systematic, developmental, practical manner. For instance, Calvin's *Institutes* had been revised and expanded in order to reflect Calvin's study and pastoral experiences in various successive editions from 1536 to the last one in 1559. Calvin took seriously the church by addressing it in the longest chapter within the final edition in 1559, while he dealt with the church only in a short chapter within the first edition of *Institutes* in 1536. On the whole, Calvin's theology thus cannot be separated from this focal point—the church.

Calvin places Christ as the Word of God and the head of the church at the heart of his ecclesiology. The concepts of "the body of Christ" and "the Word" play a central role in understanding his ecclesiology. Calvin always understands the church in relation to the Spirit. For Calvin, only the help and leading of the Spirit can lead us to know Christ as the Word of God and participate in the body of Christ. Calvin uses diverse concepts and images to define the church, such as "the church of God," "the mother of believers," "the body of Christ," "the kingdom of Christ," "Christ's Institution," "the temple of the Holy Spirit," "the communion of the saints," "the holy catholic church," "the invisible/visible church," etc. These concepts are closely interrelated. We focus on four ecclesiological concepts in what follows: the body of Christ, the communion of saints, the visible/invisible church, and God's institution.

The Church as the Body of Christ

Calvin posits that the church is the body of Christ and Christ is its sole head in the power of the Spirit. The Spirit helps every believer be engrafted into the body of Christ—the church. This shows that the Spirit links between the individual and communal aspect of faith, which must go hand-in-hand in Calvin's view. The church can have no human head but the headship of Christ, which imparts the gifts of the Spirit in full abundance upon the church. Each member has their own place and gifts to use within the body. The Spirit leads them to enjoy the mutual fellowship and unity in the body of Christ. Calvin also explains the truth of the

82. *Institutes*, IV.1.1.

church in its function in ministry, rule in authority, and practice of the sacraments in relation to the body of Christ in the Spirit.

Calvin emphasizes the administration of sacraments, together with the preaching of the Word, as *notae ecclesia* (the marks of the church) to discern what the true church is.[83] Calvin is concerned with preaching as the Word to be heard and sacraments as the Word to be seen, focusing on Christ as the Word of God. However, we cannot understand these as the Word without the help of the Spirit. The Word and the body of Christ are closely interrelated in the Spirit. For this reason, believers constantly need the help of the church throughout their lives on earth to make their confession of faith more accurate and their lifestyle more adequate to the Word of God as reflected in the mirror of the church.

Calvin contends that believers can identify the true church by the two marks of the church through the help of the Spirit and be properly led to the necessary knowledge Christians should acquire and enjoy.[84] On the one hand, Calvin's emphasis on these two marks as the criteria of the true church seems understandable, given that Calvin intended to reform the existing church in his time. Joshua Ralston argues that they should be understood "as directional signs that point to the core of faithful church life" to achieve visible unity in the church as a community.[85] Ralston holds that Calvin presumes that "no church can be written off completely" "no matter how corrupt."[86] Calvin, in Ralston's view, may be open toward all ecumenical dialogues, as long as the two marks of the church are sufficiently delineated.

Calvin's marks of the *true* church, on the other hand, seem to allow humans to be responsible for deciding whether the church is true or false to the extent that Calvin highlights the *secret* working of the Spirit. At this point, Calvin needs to make the Spirit more explicit in understanding the church and mission. Mikael Welker's notion of the Spirit appears helpful in this regard. For Welker, the broad spectrum of experiences of God's Spirit in today's world leads us to numerous different understandings of the Spirit; various understandings of the Spirit in the Bible show that

---

83. This also shows that the individual's faith necessarily participates in the community of faith because we cannot have faith in God without the Word in the power of the Spirit in Calvin's view.

84. *Institutes*, IV.1.9–10.

85. Ralston, "Preaching Makes the Church: Recovering a Missing Ecclesial Mark," 126.

86. Ibid.

humans can experience God the Spirit, albeit partly.[87] The community of the Spirit is "to grow out of different experiences of God and out of different perceptions of reality" and to "open God's presence with each other and for each other."[88] It also seems that these marks of the *true* church have historically functioned as boundaries to divide churches or denominations. Van Gelder, in this vein, points out that most denominations have used "the formulation of the criteria for the 'true' church in order to justify their claims for legitimacy," testing "for the viability of other denominations."[89] This tendency is likely to resonate with the PCK's narrow, strict understanding of the gospel and the church and ongoing schisms among Presbyterian denominations in Korea.

The above seems to partly shed light on why the PCK's ecclesiology is individual-centered in general and pastor-centered in particular. The PCK misses the ecclesiological dimension of the body of Christ in relation to the Spirit. Fundamentalist missionaries' soteriological focus on the individual's conversion and personal spiritual renewal helped leaders of the early Korean church become aware of the value of individuals and, as such, understand the church as consisting of saved individuals. Most indigenous church leaders, including Kil, regarded missionaries' emphasis on the individual or self as positive because the national crises of a collapsing country were rooted in individual spiritual weaknesses.[90] They were sure that Neo-Confucianism, which played a crucial role as the state religion and ethics, fossilized, corrupted, and weakened the country. It, thus, forced the people to ignore the value of the individual, "exist for the country," and blindly obey the king and parents and the system of "discrimination of against various groups."[91] A narrow understanding of Neo-Confucianism which prioritizes the community over each individual still remains operative as a system of social ethics to support a seniority-based hierarchy of authority within and outside the church in Korea.[92]

---

87. Welker, *God the Spirit*, 7–49.

88. Ibid., 150–51.

89. Van Gelder, "Missional Challenge," 68.

90. Wells, *New God*, 40.

91. Kim, *Protestants and the Formation, 1885–1920*, 113–14.

92. For example, all Korean Protestant churches, regardless of denominations (even Korean immigrant churches in the United Methodist Church in the U.S.), have accepted the Korean style of eldership. Under the influence of the Confucian-patriarchal culture, the PCK leaders also tend to take for granted that the laity should follow

We need to take a close look at Neo-Confucianism, although it is beyond the scope of this section to discuss it in great detail. Neo-Confucianism essentially understands human beings as being related with others in a community to serve *Tao* (the Way of Heaven) or *Tienming* (the mandate of Heaven), focusing on the harmonious development of both individuals and the society.[93] Self-cultivation is necessary in serving the other or society because *Tao* is inherent in human nature. Confucius maintained that one was required to obey the senior or the authority as long as this obedience was related only to serving the mandate of Heaven.[94] The above shows that there remains the possibility of dialogue between Neo-Confucianism and Calvin or missional theology. Both the individuals and the community aim at harmony so as to serve *Tao* in Neo-Confucianism. In a similar sense, individual Christians as bodily parts and the church as the body are mainly concerned with koinonia in the Spirit to serve the headship of Christ in Calvin's ecclesiology.[95] The relation of the self and the other in Neo-Confucianism can be related to the relational understanding of personhood as including otherness in missional theology, based on relational understanding of personhood or the Trinity.

The PCK's lack of notion of the body of the Christ generally leads individual members to relate preaching and sacraments to their personal spheres of faith with little consideration of the working of the Spirit. The PCK treats the role of the pastor as primary for preaching and sacraments in the church in light of Calvin. Ordinary Christians believe that the pastor's personal ability of preaching plays a key role in leadership and church growth. This notion shows that the PCK pays little attention to the work of the Spirit in relation to the pastor's preaching and administration of sacraments. The power of the Word appears to be dependent on the pastor rather than the Spirit. The pastor tends to regard him/her not as a part of the body of Christ, but as the head of the church because of a lack of focus on the body of the Christ in communal terms. Calvin's notion of the one body of Christ, however, underscores that only Christ

---

their decisions by asserting their authority rather than by first listening to lay voices within the church.

93. *Tao* and *Tienming* are regarded as interchangeable in Neo-Confucianism.

94. Makra, *The Hsiao Ching*, 33; Confucius, *The Analects*, 3:6, 11:17, 24.

95. The early Korean translations of the Gospel of John used *Tao* for *Logos*. Most Chinese Bibles also translate *Logos* into *Tao*. In this sense, the word of God or Jesus Christ can be understood in light of Confucian understanding of *Tao*.

has the headship of the church and all members, rather than a pastor or a few leaders, receive spiritual gifts to serve the common good for the whole body through the Spirit.

The Church as the Communion of Saints

Calvin understands the church as the communion of saints in relation to the body of Christ. For Calvin, a believer's union with Christ means that the believer is engrafted into the body of Christ by the power of the Sprit. The Spirit enables the believer to participate in union with Christ and enjoy all benefits from Christ, which are ultimately related to restoring the communion with God. The Spirit links one's communion with Christ to communion with other believers because the church is the body of Christ through the power of the Spirit. Simply put, the Spirit makes church the communion of saints joined together as the body of Christ. Calvin takes into account that the church as the body of Christ is holy because the Holy Spirit makes the church the body of Christ, while the church as a community of people is human. The church needs the true ministry of both the Word and sacraments in the Spirit in order to keep becoming a communion of saints.

Calvin emphasizes that Christ is present in the community of saints as long as the Word is preached and heard and the sacraments are administrated within it and the Spirit secretly works in the whole process. Calvin holds that both the preaching of the Word and the celebration of sacraments are communal, public events by the entire community. Regarding the true ministry of the Word, Calvin highlights not only speaking the Word, but also hearing it as long as the Spirit is working in the process. The preached Word is necessarily accompanied by the community which gathers to hear it. However, it is the only through the work of the Holy Spirit that the Word can be preached and heard.

Baptism means that individuals who newly unite to Christ by faith through the Spirit enter the community "in order to live harmoniously with all believers in complete agreement of faith and love."[96] For Calvin, Christ is spiritually and really present in the Lord's Supper through the secret working of the Spirit, and the community experiences union with Christ and shares a meal of fellowship among its members. The Lord's Supper leads the community "both to purity and holiness of life, and love,

---

96. *Institutes*, IV.15.15.

peace, and concord."[97] Given this, Calvin emphasizes the Lord's supper in terms of his cardinal theology of spirituality, that is, union with Christ. This undergirds Calvin's missional ecclesiology for social sanctification and ethical responsibility. Furthermore, Calvin emphasizes that such mutual love in the Lord's Supper leads all members of the church as the body of Christ to love their neighbors through the acts of concrete charity, in which the Holy Spirit makes them grow and advance in holiness of life.[98]

The Church as the Visible/Invisible Church

Calvin makes a distinction between the visible and invisible church. This distinction does not mean a separation, tension, or contradiction between opposites. It is not identical with a distinction between the true and false church. Calvin relates the distinction of the true/false church to the visible church. By employing the two terms, the visible and invisible church, Calvin intends to show both his emphasis on God's sovereignty in regard to salvation and his primary, practical focus on the *semper reformanda* (continuing renewal) of the church in relation to the visible church. The invisible church retains a critical function challenging the visible, empirical church which has many hypocrites and despisers of God.[99] The Spirit also plays a crucial role in both the visible/invisible church in Calvin's view.

Members of the invisible church are those who are "the children of God by grace of adoption and true members of Christ by sanctification of the Holy Spirit."[100] This essentially means that salvation is the triune God's work only, rather than humans' merit. Calvin emphasizes that the invisible church consists of the elect of God, who are true believers at all times and at all places and invisible to humans. In addition, not all professing Christians in the visible church are members of the invisible church.

On the other hand, the invisible church is accessible to humans only in the form of the visible church. God is united with this visible church through the celebration of the Word and sacraments, which works as long as the Spirit is present in the process. Calvin emphasizes that there

97. Ibid., IV.17.38.
98. See Calvin, "Short Treatise on the Supper of Our Lord."
99. Chung, *The Spirit of God*, 135.
100. *Institutes*, IV.1.7.

is no forgiveness or hope for salvation apart from the visible church.[101] For this reason, Calvin is concerned with local or regional churches in practical terms, despite keeping the single church of Christ in relation to the invisible church. He, thus, admits certain pluralism among different local communities and diverse forms of government according to the circumstances.[102]

The Church as God's Institution

Calvin regards the church as a distinct institution *in the world*, while the PCK tends to treat it as an institution *separated from the world*. Calvin differentiated between the church as the spiritual government and civil government in nature, while these two institutions' functions seemed to be somehow blurred in practical terms.[103] This is partly because both should commonly serve the lordship of Christ, in Calvin's view. Calvin's separation of the two institutions reflects Constantinian Christendom of his day, that is, the state and the church take in charge of political and religious spheres respectively compared to the presence of diverse institutions, including civil societal organizations, in the 21st century. Calvin, from the perspective of Christendom, takes it for granted that civil offices need to be faithful to God.[104] Calvin aimed to establish a new institution for the Reformation, considering need for a religious institution to replace previous roles of the Roman Church in the state. Calvin also treats the civil government in terms of God's providence, whereas he addresses the church in light of God's redemption. The civil government must be responsible for people's (the poor/sick in particular) public welfare with just and peace and help the church worship God and keep sound doctrines. Some scholars view Calvin as an active defender of the right of resistance against unjust rulers who are against God's will and law, whereas absolute civil obedience is generally regarded as Calvin's position.[105]

---

101. Ibid., IV.1.4.
102. Ibid., IV.1.9.
103. Ibid., IV.20.1–3.
104. Ibid., IV.20.6, 10.
105. See Chung, *Christian Spirituality*, 119–26; Pettegree, "The Spread of Calvin's Thought," 213–16; Welker, "Calvin's Doctrine of the 'Civil Government,'" 209–210; Camion, "The Right of Resistance in Jean Calvin and the Monarchomachs," 1–25.

Calvin understands the church to be "the external means" by which "God invites [people] into the society of Christ."[106] The church is the external means by which believers are helped to maintain and advance in their faith and truly experience the benefits of salvation in Christ through the Holy Spirit. For this reason, education and discipline together become the chief methods used by the church to enable it to truly function as an external means.[107] Moreover, he notes in light of God's providence that the institutional church provides an external, historical medium of salvation. God uses ministers, sacraments, and organizations instrumentally by the power of the Holy Spirit. In Calvin's view, individual Christians should perceive themselves as involved in the world and the church should be a distinct institution grounded in the Word of God and have an impact on the world through its diverse ministries. Calvin, in the same vein, notes that the church is a public place and an organized gathering of believers in the world. Calvin regards the church as a public institution in order to be involved in and have an impact on society and the world, given that the Spirit is working as the hidden power in relation to God's ongoing creation in the world.

CONCLUSION

This chapter has outlined the understandings of the PCK and Calvin regarding mission and the church. We addressed these implicitly and explicitly related to the factors of both the Spirit and context. Van Gelder proposes that "the church is always both forming and reforming," focusing on *the Spirit* and *context* as the two primary factors regarding missional congregations.[108] The church is always forming in order to become contextualized in missional terms, while it is always reforming to maintain its identity in confessional terms.[109] The Spirit maintains "a dynamic and healthy tension between change and continuity, and between mission and confession."[110] The PCK seems to lack such a tension, maintaining the *status quo*. This is because it does not take seriously its mission and identity in relation to the Spirit and its context. At this juncture, it is helpful for the PCK to constructively revisit Calvin's notions of mission and

---

106. *Institutes*, IV. Title of Book IV.
107. Ibid., IV.1.5; IV.10.28–30.
108. Van Gelder, *The Ministry*, 54.
109. Ibid., 54–55.
110. Ibid., 54.

the church. It has its root in them in confessional terms, which resulted from Calvin's deliberate consideration of the working of the Spirit and his context, as seen above.

The PCK generally understands mission to be its activity, although it partly admits that mission is God's. Its primary concern is with not what the church is, but what the church does. The second coming of Jesus and church growth appear to function as an impetus for the PCK's active engagement in mission. The PCK regards itself as the primary agent of mission. The PCK takes it for granted that church growth means the expansion of the kingdom of God. The PCK does not fully understand evangelization in Trinitarian terms, while its emphasis on evangelization as mission is based on its focus on Christ as the Word of God. Undoubtedly, it tends to pay little attention to Calvin's pneumatology, limiting the work of the Spirit to the personal sphere and within the church. It does not consider the church in relation to the Trinity. The PCK, as seen above, does not seem to embrace them completely with consideration of their close, inner relations, although it officially accepts Calvin's ecclesiological concepts. Through its experiences of local contexts, the PCK, rather, has developed its own functional ecclesiologies: the church as (1) an institution, (2) a self-supporting church, (3) a spiritual-renewal-driven church, (4) a lifeboat, and (5) a growth-driven church. These ecclesiologies have contributed to the PCK's growth. Relatively speaking, these ecclesiologies seem to lack Calvin's emphasis on the communal aspects of the church. Additionally, the PCK's ecclesiological tendency of being separated from the world is at odds with Calvin's primary concern for the church as God's instrument for God's interaction with the world.

Calvin paves the way for a theology of God's mission by highlighting God's Trinitarian interaction with the church and the world, although he does not fully develop his pneumatology and missiology. His primary interest lies in what the church is. Calvin takes seriously the work of the Holy Spirit throughout his whole argument in relation to the doctrine of salvation, the Scriptures, the church, and the Christian spirituality and life, although his pneumatology is not fully developed. For Calvin, the Spirit alone leads the church to exist for both communion with Christ and communion with other believers. God also uses the church as a missional instrument in order to fulfill God's salvific mission through the mediation of Christ and in the power of the Holy Spirit by not only conducting the true ministry of the Word and sacraments in the world, but serving the neighbor and the world. The next chapter addresses the research methodology.

3

Methodology

THIS CHAPTER PROVIDES A detailed account of how the research was conducted. Accordingly, it deals with the key research question and methodology, sensitizing concepts, the research process, the role of the researcher, and ethical considerations.

KEY RESEARCH QUESTION AND METHOD

This research proposed to explore the following question: For the PCK congregations which have been actively involved in their neighborhoods, what are the understandings and practices of their listening to their neighbors? Related sub-questions are as follows: (1) Why do they listen to their neighbors? (2) What helps them to listen better to their neighbors? (3) What do they learn from this listening process? and (4) What commonalities, if any, exist between such congregations within the PCK?

The selection of the research methodology was driven by the nature of the primary research question. The key research question and its sub-questions, as noted above, seek to accomplish the following: (1) exploring the ways and phenomena of congregational listening to the neighborhood in terms of local mission, (2) describing the congregations' understandings of their listening to their neighbors, and (3) constructing a substantive theory of their listening experiences in relation to their neighborhoods. Charmaz's constructivist grounded theory was suitable for the inquiry related to addressing these questions. This is because the purpose of grounded theory is to develop a theory for an action or process that is *grounded* in the viewpoints of the participants, especially in situations where little is known about a topic or where a new outlook is required. The researcher's worldview incorporated Charmaz's argument that all theories cannot be separated from a researchers' worldview.[1] Therefore, researchers and research participants co-create theories.

This constructivist grounded theory study entails a methodology in which theory is *grounded* in data such as: observations, interviews, conversations, written reports, texts, their interpretations, and the like. The researcher, along with research participants, participates in constructing a theory in this process. This is because the resulting theory is the researcher's interpretation of the research participants' understandings of phenomena of the study.[2] A theory is similarly constructed through the researcher's "past and present involvements and interactions with people, perspectives, and research practices."[3]

What the researcher brings to the data influences what is seen within it.[4] For Charmaz, constructivist grounded theory retains the rigor of the traditional grounded theory method while it fosters openness and reflexivity and encourages empathetic understanding of the participants, meanings, actions, and worldviews. Theoretical analyses in constructivist grounded theory are *interpretive* renderings of a *studied* reality rather than representing objective reporting. Therefore, Charmaz's constructivist grounded theory was chosen for this study in acknowledgement of the subjective nature of the research and the multiple realities of those involved in the study. Moreover, it was assumed that the studied reality was co-created by the research participants and the researcher.

SENSITIZING CONCEPTS

According to a constructivist grounded theory, *sensitizing concepts* provide a theoretical foundation for the development of a theory. These concepts do not provide bench marks or "prescriptions of what to see," but "suggest directions along which to look."[5] Charmaz regards these as "points of departure to form interview questions, to look at data, to listen to interviewees, and to think analytically about the data."[6] The following sensitizing concepts gave me a sense of how my empirical data might

1. Charmaz, *Constructing Grounded Theory*, 129–30.
2. Ibid., 130–31.
3. Ibid., 10.
4. Ibid., 15.
5. Blumer, "What is Wrong with Social Theory?" 7.
6. Charmaz, *Constructing Grounded Theory*, 17.

fit within conceptual categories. I provide sensitizing concepts in what follows, which shaped this study in terms of theoretical, biblical, and theological perspectives.

Theoretical Perspectives

This section addresses hermeneutics of the other and Open Systems Theory (OST) in terms of theoretical perspectives.

Hermeneutics of the Other

Mission is based on engagement with the other as long as mission is committed through the medium of language, which essentially is social. The church needs a missional hermeneutics to understand the other as its interlocutor in order to understand mission as dialogue. The church historically has not treated the other as its interlocutor, regarding the other as heathen, uncivilized, and lost. No dialogue can be possible between the church and people in the world, given such understandings of the other. In this regard, we need to attend to a hermeneutics to understand the other.

This first led me to focus on Gadamer's hermeneutics in relation to the other because Gadamer regards dialogue as the basis for coming to an understanding in his book *Truth and Method*.[7] Gadamer posits that understanding occurs in the process of a *fusion of horizons* between the interpreter and text or between the speaker and the listener. Put differently, understanding comes from a fusion of horizons between one's own horizon and the other's horizon.[8] This is possible because we are located within tradition, language, and the history of effect. Gadamer regards the human being as a linguistic being, based on the Heidegerian ontological paradigm—being in the world.[9] We can never know ourselves or the world without linguistic mediation in Gadamer's view. Gadamer understands language as "the universal domain which mediates past and present."[10] As such, understanding each other can be possible. There is a temporal distance between the speaker and listener or the text and reader

---

7. Gadamer, *Truth and Method*, xxxi, 300–305, 359–61, 443, 561.

8. Ibid., 300–305.

9. Ibid., 435–68. In particular Gadamer precisely notes that "man's [sic] being-in-the-world is primordially linguistic" (440).

10. Chung, *Public Theology*, 15.

in the process of interpretation, and it can be overcome by the fusion of the horizons between the two, as noted above.

In contrast, Levinas contends that we cannot understand the other fully.[11] Levinas seeks to reject the self/self-consciousness-driven ontological philosophy of the West and instead develop an ethics of the other, pointing to the Holocaust as the product of ego-centered western philosophy. Levinas usually uses the capitalization of the singular "Other" rather than the plural "others" to emphasize concrete face-to-face encounter with another person and avoid generalizing the other. Levinas sharply criticizes that all western philosophical traditions, including modern philosophy, involve totalitarianism because these have continued to confine the other within the self's ontological frame of its own sameness by destroying "the radical alterity of the Other."[12] What we need in the face of the other is not objective searching after truth, but recognition of otherness. We come to have the idea of *infinity* in meeting the other. In other words, "the other is associated with the Infinite," and "the face of the other is the expression of the Infinity."[13] The face of the other is infinitely foreign and transcendent. Levinas regards the other as "the poor, the stranger, the widow, and the orphan," emphasizing God's solidarity with them, as Chung argues.[14] Thus, it is ethical and religious for Levinas to recognize and communicate with the other.

Levinas paves a way to conceptualizing hermeneutics of the other in light of God's saying through the other's face. Levinas, in *Otherwise than Being: Or Beyond Essence*, holds that language came into being through human face-to-face relations. Language presupposes a discourse with the other.[15] "Language comes to me through the other," and "words are enacted already within the primordial face-to-face of language."[16] The face of the other naturally leads us into the absolute openness of *infinity* as long as the other cannot be *I*. Levinas relates this notion to God since he is also a Jewish Talmud scholar. God speaks to us through others, and, as such, God shows Godself to us in the face of others, although God is

---

11. Levinas, *Totality and Infinity*, 43. In light of phenomenological hermeneutics, Levinas emphasizes that we cannot reduce "the other" to the ontological hermeneutical category of "the same."

12. Ibid., 35–36.

13. Chung, *Cave and Butterfly*, 185.

14. Ibid., 195.

15. Levinas, *Otherwise than Being*.

16. Chung, *Cave and Butterfly*, 195.

always transcendent. Levinas also holds that God's saying (what God is saying) is limited to God's said (what God has said), considering that human discourse is ongoing. Furthermore, one's discourse with the other is essentially ethical rather than ontological in the face-to-face encounter with the other because it is the process of understanding our responsibilities and obligations *toward* them rather than our consciousness *of* them. This refers to Levinas's contribution to the hermeneutics of the other in light of God's act of speech through the world and in the otherness of the other.

Open Systems Theory

To more fully understand the congregation's relationship with its neighborhood in terms of God's mission, a congregation needs to take seriously Open Systems Theory (OST). A variety of organizational perspectives can be used to study the church because the church can be regarded as an organization. According to Van Gelder, "organization is essential to the church's existence."[17] Mary Jo Hatch argues that the way of understanding organizations is multi-perspectival.[18] Given this, OST can be defined as a theory of organization that views organization as a system which continuously interacts with its environment.[19] I regard a congregation as an organization within an open system since the church is a Spirit-led community in a particular context. Organizations, like open systems, receive inputs, transform these inputs in certain ways, and return outputs to their environments. OST was first proposed under the name of "General Systems Theory" by the biologist Ludwig von Bertalanffy in the 1950s.[20] The *open systems* perspective based on General Systems Theory was developed within different theoretical areas during the late 1960s: Thompson's organizational theory (rooted more in the bureaucratic/structural tradition) and Katz and Kahn's social psychology (rooted more in the human relations tradition).[21] The open systems perspective has dynamically developed in a variety of streams by critically reflecting prior organizational notions within and outside OST.

17. Gelder, *The Essence*, 157.
18. Hatch, *Organization Theory*, 3–23.
19. See ibid., 36–100; Van Gelder, *The Ministry*, 134–52. According to Van Gelder, OST, which emerged in the late 1960s, has been primarily concerned with the relationship between organizations (or communities) and their environments.
20. Hatch, *Organization Theory*, 37.
21. Van Gelder, *The Ministry*, 134–35.

From the late 1960s to 1970s, theorists were mainly concerned with *organizational survival* in an organization's interaction with its environment, focusing on "gathering sufficient resources to survive."[22] Theorists emphasized that an organization needed to take seriously its *goal attainment* during the 1970s and 80s, pointing out that organizational survival alone cannot be a true reason for an organization's existence.[23] They emphasized a need for *strategic planning*. Other organizational theorists, however, realized that goal attainment and strategic planning could not fully address the rapidly changing postmodern context. Another accommodated theory emerged, stressing reengineering and continuous improvement by the 1980s. This theory aimed at *a higher level of efficiency* and *productivity* through an organization's reengineering and total quality management with the careful consideration of internal operations. However, this theory tended to pay relatively little attention to the external environment. A new stream emerged as a fundamental shift centered on transforming organizational culture in the 1980s and 90s. This approach held that "the culture of the organization" was understood as "a whole," and leadership was treated as "an activity of *sensemaking* in shaping and reshaping the organizational culture."[24] In particular, leadership primarily needs to develop vision. Peter Senge argued for understanding an organization as a learning system in the 1990s.[25] He emphasized a system perspective for understanding organizations, along with feedback loops. Various postmodern approaches have emerged and been developed under the influence of information technology, new science, chaos theory, and the like since the 1990s.[26]

An open system is one where the organization has contact with the environment, its flows, interactions, and information, from the perspective of OST. Organizations are strongly influenced by their environment. The organizational environment consists of other organizations that exert a variety of forces of an economic, political, or social nature. Organizations, as open systems, are integrated wholes whose properties cannot be reduced to those of smaller units; instead of concentrating on basic building blocks or substances, every organism is an integrated *whole,*

---

22. Ibid., 137.
23. Ibid.
24. Ibid. Emphasis in original.
25. Ibid., 138–39.
26. Ibid., 139.

and thus, a *living system*.²⁷ Another important aspect of systems is their intrinsically dynamic nature. All the components of an organization are interrelated and, as such, changing one variable might impact many others. An organization as an open system has a conceptual frame of "inputs, transformation, and outputs" in relation to its environment.²⁸ In brief, OST views an organization as a complex set of dynamically intertwined and interconnected elements, including inputs, processes, outputs, feedback loops, and the environment. Any change in one element causes changes in other elements. The *fit* and/or the *gap* must be considered between subsystems within an organization or between an organization and its external environment in the process.

Biblical Perspectives

My primary concern was to explore *the dynamics of congregations' listening to their neighbors*, focusing on PCK congregations which have been actively involved in their neighborhoods in terms of mission. Considering this, I paid special attention to the biblical notions of the neighbor and the other, listening to the neighbor and the other, the kingdom of God in relation to the church and mission, and the church as a Spirit-led community.

Biblical Notions of the Neighbor and the Other

From the perspective of the Old Testament (OT), the Hebrew word most often translated as "neighbor" is *rea* (רֵעַ),²⁹ which has a wider variety of connotations: friend, lover, and the usual sense of neighbor. It might be generally used to refer to anyone who is not an immediate kinsman or an enemy. It was legally used to refer to any fellow member of the covenant with God, in other words, fellow Israelites. However, Jesus broadens the meaning of *neighbor* to include even the enemy. One of the best remembered parables of Jesus is that of the Good Samaritan who stops to help an injured man when no one else would do so. Less well remembered is the fact that this parable was told in response to the question "Who is my neighbor?" Jesus' answer suggests the broadest possible interpretation for *neighbor*, such that it even includes members of unfriendly tribal groups.

---

27. Hatch, *Organization Theory*, 37–38.
28. Van Gelder, *The Ministry*, 135.
29. The literal Hebrew word for "neighbor" (Lev 19:18) is not *rea*, but *reyacha*, which explicitly means "your fellow Jew."

This would be consistent with his command to love one's enemies. In line with this, Jesus puts loving our neighbors, along with loving God, at the center of God's commandment (Mt 22:34–40; Mk 12:28–34; Lk 10:25–38). In this regard, the church's concerns for the neighbor cannot be separated from mission.

Biblical Listening to the Neighbor and the Other

God is the One who listens, in terms of listening to the other/neighbor. "I have observed the misery of my people who are in Egypt; I have heard their cry on account of their taskmasters. Indeed, I know their sufferings."[30] The Bible also says, regarding the importance of listening that, "[he] who answers before listening—that is his folly and his shame."[31] Many theologians argue that the Bible is composed of people's stories about God and their experiences with God.[32] God has told his stories through people's stories. Accordingly, we can listen to God's stories by listening to people in the world, though partly and ambiguously. God also listens by entering into unique settings and private perceptual worlds that give God the ability to hear the predicaments of those who wish to talk with him. One such perceptual world is that of the outcast, which is one way to classify the life of Jesus. Frank Lake writes that Christ must be a "listener to every item of painful shame that is recounted, so that its power to bind the soul in the iron chains of condemnation and alienation is manifestly overcome."[33] It was Jesus who listened to both God and people in the world. Jesus used the act of listening in ways that created love and fostered healing (Mk 5, 9).

The Kingdom of God

The concept of the kingdom of God has been used within the PCK in relation to understanding both the church and mission since the early missionaries came to Korea.[34] The kingdom of God is at the center of

---

30. Ex 3:7 NRSV; See also Ex 6:5; 2 Sam 22:7; Ps 34:6, 15, 17; 10:17.
31. Pr 18:13 NIV.
32. Brown, Davaney, and Tanner, *Converging on Culture*.
33. Lake, *Clinical Theology*, 52.
34. Underwood, *The Call of Korea*, 5. As the early missionaries to Korea believed that the extension of the church meant the extension of the kingdom of God, Horace Underwood, the missionary father of the PCK, regarded the phenomenal growth of the Korean church as "the progress of [God's] kingdom." In other words, for him,

Jesus' preaching. It is the core of the gospel, the realization of the redemptive reign of God. On the one hand, Jesus' proclamation of God's kingdom is the accomplishment of God's promise to Israel in the OT; on the other hand, it is another promise to the final eschatological kingdom of God. Put simply, the kingdom of God has both *already* but *not yet* dimensions. According to Van Gelder, we cannot "build, extend, promote, and [or] establish" God's kingdom; rather, we must "receive, enter, seek, and inherit" it (Lk 18:17, 24–25, 29–30; Mt 6:33, 25:34).[35] However, most Korean Protestants believe that to *build* and *extend* the kingdom of God is their missionary calling under the strong influence of fundamentalist missionaries to Korea.[36] Evangelization and mission are regarded as the most important tasks to do so. The PCK's "Twenty-First Century Confession of Faith" points out many present-day problems in the shadow of the explosive church growth and emphasizes the life-centered mission approach in terms of God's mission; however, it still regards church growth as one of the PCK's ultimate values in terms of mission.[37]

However, the church cannot build or extend God's kingdom from the biblical perspective because this is God's work. The Holy Spirit is the primary agent for this work. The author of the Book of Acts demonstrates that the Spirit leads all missionary activities and creates the church by relating mission to proclamation of the already-present and still-coming kingdom of God. The church looks towards the kingdom of God, while the church is not God's kingdom. The church as the eschatological community of salvation waits for the kingdom of God and makes a pilgrimage towards it. The church, the herald of God's kingdom, also proclaims the coming kingdom of God to the world. Thus, the church is "an *anticipatory sign* of the definitive reign of God: a sign of the reality of the reign of God already present in Jesus Christ, a sign of the coming completion of God."[38] The church must also be constantly aware that its goal is not in itself, but can only be found in the kingdom of God. Therefore, all the church is to do is serve the reign of God in a humble manner. All Christians have to do is participate in God's redemptive ministry in the world.

---

increasing the number of believers meant *the extension of God's church*, which meant *the progress of God's kingdom*.

35. Van Gelder, *The Essence*, 87.
36. See Underwood, *The Call of Korea*.
37. See The Presbyterian Church of Korea, *Constitution*.
38. Küng, *The Church*, 96. Emphasis in original.

The Church as a Spirit-led Community

We need to look at the holy and human, spiritual and social nature of the church in the New Testament (NT) in terms of the church as a Spirit-led community. The NT holds that the Spirit creates and builds up the church. The Spirit makes the believer a part of the body of Christ, and the church is the temple of the Spirit. However, the church is composed of humans situated in a particular context in another sense. The church consists of the people made free by the creative freedom of God in the Holy Spirit. All members, not a few, receive charisms (spiritual gifts) to serve the church and each other by the Spirit in terms of the church as a *charismatic* structure.[39] Therefore, the church must avoid emphasizing them since charisms are not something special. The church created by the Spirit is structured according to charismata given freely for mutual and communal benefit. All believers are essentially equal in the church, regardless of ecclesiastical order.

The church needs communal discernment in order to seek the will of the Spirit as well as the common good and unity of the church because all members of the church become and remain one body of Christ by the Spirit. Küng contends that Paul relates the image of a body, which meant *human community* in the Hellenistic terms of Paul's day, to the crucified, resurrected, and ascended Christ.[40] The church becomes a unity that transcends diversity, as the church becomes united as one body through partaking in the sacrament of the crucified body of Christ (1 Cor 10:16–17). The church as the body of Christ is to live as a unified community in sacrificial love and fellowship. We have many members with their respective different functions in the one body of Christ, without losing interdependence among all the members.

Theological Perspectives

This section addresses the ecclesiologies of Calvin and missional ecclesiology in that order.

Calvin's Ecclesiology

This part is articulated in relation to my discussion concerning Calvin's ecclesiology in chapter 2, in which I understand the body of Christ, the

---

39. Ibid., 163ff.
40. Ibid., 204–35.

communion of saints, the visible/invisible church, and God's institution as Calvin's primary ecclesiological notions. I pay special attention to Calvin's *Institutes*, Book 4, which is mainly concerned with the church, given that the PCK's ecclesiology is rooted in the work of Calvin, to some extent in Trinitarian terms. Relatively speaking, the PCK's *Constitution* deals with ecclesiology mainly in relation to Christology, with little consideration of the Trinity, while *Institutes* addresses the church in terms of the close relationship between Christology and the Trinity. Butin asserts that Trinitarian controversies in Calvin's day led Calvin to continuously revise *Institutes* throughout his life.[41] For this reason, I pay careful attention to Calvin's ecclesiology in relation to the Trinity.

Calvin relates his primary concern for the Word to the Trinity in his ecclesiology. That is, Calvin construes faith and the church in a very Trinitarian fashion. Leaning on Gregory of Nazianzus, Calvin emphasizes *perichoresis* in order to address the Father, the Son, and the Holy Spirit as three distinct persons without losing the emphasis on the unity, whereas Calvin's Trinity is based on the Western Church's God-the-Father-centered Trinity in light of Augustine.[42] He deals with several key theological themes: God's glory, sovereignty, election, freedom, grace, Christ's Word and Lordship, and the Spirit's power and sanctification. According to Calvin, "God by the power of his Word and the Spirit created heaven and earth out of nothing."[43] God's election is God's love in Christ, which we participate in by the work of the Spirit. The church is also God's people called by God in Christ through the Spirit.

Missional Ecclesiology

Missional ecclesiology is primarily concerned with three essential dimensions, aiming to participate in God's mission in the world: (1) God's Trinitarian mission, (2) each church's local context as a field of God's action, and (3) the church as a Spirit-led community. The missional church

---

41. Butin, *Revelation*, 26–38; In the following two books, arguing against today's criticisms of Calvin's emphasis on union with Christ, Billings tries to understand Calvin's theology by taking seriously Calvin's original thoughts regarding union with Christ. However, as compared with Butin, Billings pays relatively little attention to the Trinity and Calvin's socio-historical context. See Billings, *Calvin*; Billings, *Union with Christ*.

42. *Institutes*, I.13.17.

43. Ibid., I.14.20.

is a missiological ecclesiology and ecclesiological missiology.[44] A missional ecclesiology invites us to see the church differently, beginning not with the church as we see it, but through the lens of the Triune God's mission in the world. A missional view of the church would remind us that whatever is true of the church is true because it is first and foremost true of God in Christ, who through the work of the Spirit calls the church into being. God's act of self-sending into the world defines the Church. As the Father sends the Son the world, so the Church also is sent into the world to be the community of witness to God's gracious action. Mission is no longer the church's activity in light of missional ecclesiology.

Missional ecclesiology primarily focuses on God's Trinitarian mission. It has emphasized God the Father's sending the Son, the Spirit, and the church to the world in light of the Western Church's Father-centered Trinity since its beginning. Later, missional ecclesiology has accepted the Eastern Church's emphasis on *perichoresis*, the "interrelationships" between the Trinity, to view God's mission in relational terms.[45] This relational perspective of the Trinity helps us realize that our fellowship with God precedes our participation in God's mission. To some extent, God's existence as a social community provides the basis for the social nature of the church.[46]

Missional ecclesiology also pays special attention to the contextuality of the church. It construes the church as situated in a historical, social, local world. The church, likewise, is also a product of a particular culture in a particular context. Missional ecclesiology holds, in light of Küng's ecclesiology, that "the church's essence is always embodied in some

---

44. Van Gelder, *The Essence*, 27–44.
45. Van Gelder, *The Ministry*, 88.
46. I view Barth, Moltmann, and Zizioulas, *inter alia*, as the primary theologians who have influenced the formation of missional ecclesiology. In order to stress the *unity* of the three persons in the Trinity, in light of Luther and Calvin, Barth employs the Greek term *perichoresis*, which was used to understand the communion of the three divine persons by Greek Church Fathers. Relatively speaking, while Barth emphasizes the unity of God, both Moltmann and Zizioulas base their understandings of the Trinity on *God's relationality*. To emphasize the *difference* of the three persons, Moltmann accepts wholly John Damascene's development of the concept of eternal *perichoresis* of the three persons, centering on *the circulatory character* of the eternal divine life. Zizioulas maintains the precedence of person over substance. Like Moltmann, he also regards *perichoresis* as primary in understanding the Trinity. In contrast to Moltmann's emphasis on the threeness as the premise of *perichoresis*, Zizioulas's understanding of *perichoresis* begins from God's unity. See Barth, *CD* 1/1; Moltmann, *The Trinity*; Zizioulas, *Communion*.

tangible, visible form that is shaped by its particular time in the history and its place in some specific human society."[47] It requires the church to understand and interpret context in order to faithfully witness the gospel toward the world. Missional theologians attempt to cultivate new ways of life through participation in particular, cultural, social interactions with the world, considering that a culture means something cultivated literally. Simply put, the missional nature of the church is always contextual.

The church also is not a building or a collection of individual Christians, but a social community which is led by the Spirit in the view of missional ecclesiology. The church does not mean a place or association, but a Spirit-led community. Moreover, the Trinity's *perichoretic* relationship of the three Persons helps missional ecclesiology to inform the social nature of church and its leadership.[48] This social notion of the church enables us to understand the church as a Spirit-led community of *koinonia*—"holy living, mutual support, and sacrificial service."[49] In this vein, Latini regards the church's missional vocation as "participating in Christ's ongoing ministry of reconciliation unto *koinonia*" by understanding *koinonia* as *gathering*, *upbuilding*, and *sending* in light of the Barthian Trinity.[50] The development of biblical and theological understanding of the Spirit's role through the missionary movements of previous centuries also leads us to rediscover the church as the Spirit-led community in the world. Thus, the church is not simply an association, being made by the free choices of the individuals, but a community of the people of God who are led by the Spirit.

Furthermore, missional ecclesiology emphasizes evangelism in terms of the reign of God. The church exists to witness the gospel in the world. However, missional ecclesiology does not portray the gospel as something static, or a message for individual salvation. Missional theologians regard the gospel as God's invitation to bear witness to God's kingdom, which consists of his people, considering that God's kingdom or God's reign is at the heart of Jesus' gospel. As long as the gospel is God's word in relation to God's kingdom, the gospel has an essential dimension of criticizing cultures, principalities, powers, and peoples, not to mention the church. The already-but-not-yet nature of God's kingdom continues

---

47. Guder, *Missional Church*, 86.
48. Ibid., 82.
49. Ibid., 145.
50. Latini, *The Church and the Crisis of Community*, 180. Emphasis in original.

to call the church to be an eschatological community in the world. Thus, evangelism is not a proclamation of individual salvation, but the Spirit's invitation into an eschatological community and salvation, accordingly, is "a social reality of transformed relationships."[51] The church always needs decision-making processes in witnessing the gospel because the church is a community. These processes do not focus on following a dominant opinion in the community, but on being led by the Spirit. The church has already begins its public witness to the gospel in the process.

RESEARCH PROCESS

Charmaz holds that researchers can shape and reshape their data collection and, subsequently, refine their collected data. In so doing, they are able to adopt a flexible approach to data collection rather than a rigid prescription of methods. This flexibility of methodology has resulted in grounded theory researchers collecting data through the use of a wide variety of data collection methods. Data for this study were primarily collected through the use of in-depth individual interviews and focus group discussions. Overall, this study worked through mostly overlapping phases: data-collection, note-taking, coding, memoing, sorting, and writing.

Selection of the Congregations

I selected three PCK congregations which had actively engaged in their neighborhoods for over five years through theoretical, purposeful sampling. Charmaz states that "theoretical sampling means seeking pertinent data to develop your emerging theory" and, moreover, theoretical sampling is conducted to "elaborate and refine" theoretical categories.[52] This selection of three PCK congregations happened through a three-stage discernment process. Nominations included the congregations which were studied from the perspective of congregational relationship with the neighborhood in terms of mission, and which were recommended by the board of national mission ministry and the board of social service ministry within the PCK in the same category. Once names of twelve congregations were submitted, a preliminary list was created.

---

51. Guder, *Missional Church*, 97, 182.
52. Charmaz, *Constructing Grounded Theory*, 96. Emphasis in original.

Meanwhile, I received the help of one person in charge of social service ministry within the PCK and my fellow pastors who had been involved in local mission and social service. I ranked twelve congregations from the highest to the lowest according to their frequency of being recommended. I originally planned to send a research invitation letter by both email and post to all congregations in the preliminary list. However, those who helped me make the list advised me that I should first contact the lead pastor or the pastor in charge of local mission in each congregation by phone, considering the cultural context of ministry. I followed their advice, contacting pastors in order to explain the purpose, expectation, timeline of the study and the reason why the congregation was in the list. In this manner, three congregations were preliminarily selected.

I emailed a letter to the lead pastor and the pastor in charge of local mission and/or social service in each congregation, stating the purpose and expectation of the research project. A phone interview with one of them was made, clarifying the purpose of the study, the expectations of the congregation's participation, and determining their availability within the given timeline of the research. After the phone interviews were completed, three congregations (Heavenly Creek, New Community, and Holy Hill) were finally selected. Then, schedules were arranged and logistics set up for the following extended research visits: September 5–9 (Heavenly Creek), September 12–16 (New Community), and September 19–23 (Holy Hill) in 2012.[53]

The participants of in-depth personal interviews and focus group interviews, which were the primary methods of this study, were selected in the following way. I received consultations of the lead pastor or associate pastor in charge of local mission and/or social services to the neighborhood within each congregation, considering the context of each congregation in the process. Purposeful sampling was used to recruit all participants who were involved in the congregation's local mission and/or social services to the neighborhood for over three years. I asked each congregation regarding in-depth personal interviews to include the lead pastor, the associate pastor in charge of local mission and/or social services to the neighborhood, and one male and female lay participant. By doing so, I conducted six interviews (including one email interview with the lead pastor) in Heavenly Creek, four interviews (including one email interview with the associate pastor) in New Community, and five

---

53. Names of congregations have been given pseudonyms, in accordance with the study's proposal and informed consent.

interviews in Holy Hill.[54] The grand total of participants was fifteen, including two interviews by email.

I conducted two focus group interviews in each congregation. Thirteen people in Heavenly Creek, ten in New Community, and ten other people participated in group interviews in Holy Hill. On the whole, thirty-three people participated in focus group interviews.

Data Collection

Data were collected from June through December 2012. In fact, data collection and data analysis were conducted simultaneously in terms of grounded theory. The five following types of data were collected for each congregation in terms of data sources: a congregational profile, an on-site ethnographic visit over an extended weekend, in-depth personal interviews (six in Heavenly Creek, four in New Community, and five in Holy Hill), two focus groups, and my journal. Personal interviews and focus group interviews were the primary sources of data, while the other data sources were supplementary. I created a profile of each congregation before the ethnographic visit in attempting to place the congregation within the larger context of geography and time. This profile included the following: demographics of the neighborhood in which the congregation was located; a three-year history of the congregation's membership, budget, and giving; social services to the neighborhood; an overview of the mission, vision, and ministries of the congregation; and notes from both phone and email conversations with the lead pastor and/or the associate pastor in each congregation.

As a participant-observer, I engaged each congregation in an on-site visit. I participated with and observed members of each congregation in their natural setting and attended as many activities as possible over the extended research visit. The following served as the baseline for each visit: worship, congregational activities, and social services and activities in relation to the neighborhood, while these activities varied from one congregation to another. Field notes were gathered from the activities as well as from general observations and impressions both while visiting the congregational site and the greater area. I tried to note things regarding personal interviews and focus group interviews, such as the identity

---

54. I could not interview the lead pastor of Heavenly Creek or the associate pastor of New Community during my on-site visit due to their sudden, official business. Accordingly, I conducted personal interviews with them by email.

of each speaker, body language and gestures, and environmental issues throughout the process of interviews and conversations.[55]

In each congregation, I conducted in-depth interviews with the lead pastor, the associate pastor in charge of local mission and/or social service, and one male and female lay participant who were involved in the congregation's local mission and/or social services to the neighborhood for over three years. I conducted two additional interviews with one male elder and one female lay leader respectively in Heavenly Creek. I conducted one additional interview with one male lay leader in Holy Hill. I utilized a protocol (see appendix A) for interviewing them. This protocol was developed on the basis of sensitizing concepts. I undertook field tests with the protocol in order to ensure its clarity and appropriateness for the purpose of the research before interviewing the participants. I conducted personal interviews of one male pastor and one lay female Christian for the field testing of this protocol. This process helped me realize that the pastor appeared familiar with both its contents and expressions while the lay Christian needed a more detailed explanation regarding those of the protocol. Accordingly, I provided a more detailed explanation for lay interview participants during later on-site interviews. Both felt that the two questions in the protocol were similar, so that I conflated them into one question. I revised the protocol based on their feedback. I formalized the interview protocol and the primary and open-ended follow-up questions in advance. I shared these with the interviewees a month before the interview. I explained the purpose and expectation of the study to the interviewees before every interview and distributed an informed consent form to be reviewed and signed (see appendix C). I kept field notes and memos on interviewees' attitudes and emotional gestures or expressions during the whole process of these interviews. With the advanced permission of the interviewees, I also audio taped all interviews by using an MP3 voice recorder. Each interview took about 40–45 minutes to complete.

Two focus groups similar to the in-depth interviews were hosted at each site. I conducted two focus groups, which consisted of those who were involved in the congregation's local mission and/or social services to the neighborhood for over three years, being sure to use gender-inclusive language in the interview process. All interviews were audio-taped via an MP3 voice recorder. Each interview took about 60–90 minutes to

---

55. Although I wanted to utilize the scribe for interviews, in terms of cultural context of each congregation, lead pastors and/or associate pastors politely refused to allow me to employ this option. In the same vein, they refused to be video recorded.

complete. In addition, I recorded my observations in my field notebooks and kept a field diary to chronicle my own thinking, feelings, experiences, and perceptions throughout the research process.

Data Analysis

I followed Creswell's steps of data analysis based on Charmaz's steps of coding data: organizing and preparing data (transcripts, field notes, images, etc.) for analysis, reading through all data, coding the data, summarizing themes and descriptions, interrelating themes and descriptions, and interpreting the meaning of these.[56] I first transcribed all interviews in Korean. Because English is my second language, I asked an expert translator who knew and spoke both Korean and English to translate all Korean transcripts of interviews into English. In terms of an audit trail, I asked two fellow students who studied theology in the M.Th. program at Luther Seminary and who were familiar with Korean Christianity to check the process of coding and data analysis. For example, they examined all coding processes by asking "Are coding strategies applied correctly?" and "Is the process of categorizing appropriate?" I asked the translator and two auditors to sign consent forms (see appendix E) to keep data confidential. I also gathered multiple data, such as congregational profiles, observations, and articles regarding the researched congregations, for the purposes of triangulation.[57] I undertook constant comparisons that aimed to code subsequent interviews or data from other sources with the emerging theory in mind.

I utilized the qualitative analysis program NVivo 10 software program for coding and analyzing data. This program was helpful in coding, organizing, sorting, and analyzing complex non-numerical or unstructured data. In particular, this program helped me capture web pages and online PDFs related to the study. For instance, I captured web pages of three congregations and converted these to PDFs in order to use these as data. Patterns and themes were more easily identified and different categories and nodes—containers of codes—were developed as part of the process of analyzing data through the NVivo 10 program. I made concepts and theories coherent with relative ease. Once individual site analysis was completed, the findings were compared with data from

---

56. Creswell, *Research Design*, 173–201.

57. Triangulation means that multiple forms of diverse and redundant types of evidence are used to check the validity and reliability of the findings.

other sites in an effort to discover commonalities among the three PCK congregations. The aforementioned five sources of data from three sites were triangulated with theme coding, blind readers, and NVivo 10.[58] Nevertheless, I had to decide what to code and how to conceptualize.

The coding procedure applied in this study closely followed the steps suggested by Charmaz. The data were analyzed using four levels of coding: (1) initial coding (line-by-line coding, *in vivo* codes), (2) focused coding, (3) axial coding, and (4) theoretical coding.[59] At all stages of the coding process, the data were searched until recurring themes and codes reached a point of saturation and I was satisfied that analyzing the data further would not contribute anything new to what was already discovered. Triangulation of the data also occurred at all stages of the research project with multiple sources of verification used to confirm findings.

---

58. The five sources are the following: a congregational profile, an on-site ethnographic visit over an extended research visit, in-depth personal interviews, two focus groups, and my journal.

59. Charmaz, *Constructing Grounded Theory*, 42–71. (1) *Initial coding* is the process of examining each sentence of the interview transcriptions, observation notes, biographies and other written material to label each line with a name or code. The goal of this step in grounded theory is to get a closer look at what participants said in interviews or what they did during observations. Line-by-line coding also involves highlighting and collecting *in vivo* codes. *In vivo* codes represent specific terms used by the participant that are used to ascribe meaning to their thoughts and actions. These codes are then examined to condense their meaning and action. They are then coded in ways that relate directly to the data and emerging categories; (2) *Focused coding* is intended to bring more focus to the data by selecting codes that help combine multiple ideas and concepts ultimately reducing and refining the data. Interview data are examined for recurring codes and code themes. Some themes become saturated very quickly so that by the time all the interviews are completed, a small bit of focused coding has already taken place. The resulting list of codes and themes act much like a lens, bringing fuzzier codes, general descriptions, and other bits of information into a coherent level of focus; (3) *Axial coding* involves organizing and reconstituting large amounts of data in new ways in order to add meaning and clarity to the emerging data. Rather than being a linear interview-by-interview process, coding of the interviews involves an iterative and ongoing process within, and between, interview analyses. These steps create interwoven activities that allow the theory to emerge from the data, adding more and more clarity and definition to the relationships between emerging constructs. Memo writing and free writing help reduce codes in the initial coding and focus coding stage and later aid in making connections between codes in the axial and theoretical coding stages; (4) At the stage of *Theoretical coding*, relationships between codes are revealed and corresponding hypotheses about these relationships begin to emerge and the first constructs of the grounded theory begin to take shape.

I undertook the following steps, based on Creswell's suggestions regarding reliability/validity strategies, to check reliability and validity of research procedures and findings:[60]

(1) Check transcripts to make sure that they do not contain obvious mistakes during the transcription.

(2) Make sure that there is not a drift in the definition of codes or a shift in the meaning of the codes during the process of coding.

(3) Crosscheck codes.

(4) Triangulate different data sources of information (interviews, observations, and document analyses) by examining evidence from the sources and use it to build a coherent justification for themes.

(5) Clarify the bias the researcher brings to the study.

(6) Use an external auditor to review the entire project.

The findings of the study were "presented in descriptive, narrative form rather than as a scientific report" in the following chapter.[61] I interpreted all results of this research, from the missional perspective as discussed earlier. Then, I described implications of all results of this research.

ROLE OF RESEARCHER

I have regarded myself as a participant-observer, interviewer/focus group facilitator, and constructivist theorist through the whole study, although these roles are closely inter-related. First, I played a role as a participant-observer. Strictly speaking, it seemed hard for me to observe what was happening in processes and activities during my on-site visits while participating in these. Nevertheless, I tried to reduce my impact by fully participating in processes and activities as much as I could. My observations were also aimed at describing and recording what I observed. I observed the physical environment, the interactions between people, worship services and diverse ministries, and languages used within each congregation by using the field notes. I tried to maintain an *emic* perspective (an insider's view) rather than an *etic* perspective (an outsider's view) in the process, keeping in mind Clifford Geertz's thick description.[62]

---

60. Creswell, *Research Design*, 190–200.

61. Ibid., 200.

62. By accepting Max Weber's notion that "man is an animal suspended in webs of significance he himself spun," Geertz tries to understand culture in those webs and

Second, I played a role as interviewer and focus group facilitator in relation to individual and focus group interviews. I tried to maintain "a balance between making the interview open-ended and focusing on significant statements."[63] I asked questions that invited the interviewees to think about the topic. I also sometimes used probe questions to help the interviewees to articulate ideas or understandings.[64] Reflexive listening was my primary way of responding to the interviewees. I helped them feel comfortable during interviews by making eye contact or other interpersonal connections. I, in the same vein, set up circle seating and provided some snacks for the focus group interviewees to create a warm and friendly environment. By so doing, I helped them freely call out their ideas. As facilitator, I invited and facilitated a discussion by asking focus group questions (see appendix B). I sometimes trimmed my list of questions or provided an open space to deal with emergent ideas, attending to the rhythm and pace of each group interview.

Third, I have regarded myself as a constructivist theorist throughout the study. Charmaz's grounded theory holds that the role of the researcher is central to the generation of a theory through this study. The researcher can be regarded as a co-constructor of a theory with the research participants. Not only did I collect the data, but I interpreted the data. In this process, I named codes and categories in order to create a theory by generating insightful questions and conducting the constant comparisons of data, depending on my point of view.

ETHICAL CONCERNS

I had to pay careful attention to potential ethical issues in the process of the research. First, I attempted to maintain neutrality in the investigation and tried to avoid biases. I consulted with professors and others experienced in research to check for leading questions or any potential bias that might result from the way the questions were asked. I could

---

regards the analysis of culture as an interpretive science "in search of meaning" rather than an experimental one searching for law. In doing ethnography, Geertz comes up with Gilbert Ryle's philosophical term "thick description." For Geertz, doing ethnography is a thick description to establish rapport, select informants, transcribe texts, take genealogies, map fields, keep a diary, and so on. See Geertz, *The Interpretation of Cultures*, 1–30.

63. Charmaz, *Constructing Grounded Theory*, 26.

64. For instance, I asked, "Would you explain further?" or "Would you give an example?"

check potential biases in my interview attitude as well as in the questionnaires of the interview protocol by means of field tests prior to the interviews with the participants of the research. In particular, I had to consider, regarding focus group interviews, that I might easily impose my opinions on them in the interview process because I was a pastor and my participants were lay members. I kept trying to check my attitudes and verbal/nonverbal expressions and not force interviewees to answer every question in order to avoid this. I, moreover, let participants know the purpose and procedures of the interview in advance. I kept listening to participants' own answers in the actual interview process after offering questions to the participants.

Second, I considered Korean traditional and congregational culture, in which Korean congregations are generally pastor-centered. Letters detailing the purpose and the content of the personal interview/focus group conversation were emailed ahead of time to the senior pastor of each of the three congregations as research participants. I conducted personal interviews and group focus interviews after receiving the consent from the lead pastor. I also maintained use of terms of respect with the participants in the interview process because honorific expressions were necessary with those who were old, had authority, or were not familiar in terms of Korean culture. I was careful to translate the personal interview questions and focus group questions into Korean because Korean has more expressions of respect than English has.

Third, I needed to arrange proper psychological and physical environments for the participants. I designed an interview environment where the participants felt comfortable answering the questions in the most natural way. Regarding the place and time of the interview, I respected their opinions through earlier communications with them. I obtained permission from them by asking them to sign a consent form (see appendix C and D) before starting the interview and focus group meetings. The consent form highlighted the purpose and methodology of the study and clarified how the information would be used. I assured confidentiality by promising that I would not identify them and their congregations by name in the report or in any conversations with other people. In this sense, I use pseudonyms for them and their congregations to protect their anonymity. I assured them I would protect their privacy and kept conveying this protection after completing the research project. I kept these secret from other people, although some of them expressed complaints and criticisms of their own congregations and pastors. I will let them know how to access these results if they want to have access to the results of the research. All raw data will be stored in a lock box and destroyed after ten years.

Finally, I needed to keep a neutral position regarding data collection, analysis, and interpretation. For this reason, I employed a translator for translating the data regarding interviews in Korean into English. I employed two auditors to double-check the process of coding and data analysis in order not to manipulate them in order to meet my expectations or agenda. Via a consent form (see appendix E), I asked the translator and auditors to keep all data confidential. I checked my own field notes and observations soon after each visit was done. A copy of the overall findings will be made available to the lead pastor in each congregation. It will note that data from this research will be presented in, but not limited to, the researcher's dissertation, as well as additional scholarly articles, papers, presentations, and publications that might arise.

CONCLUSION

This chapter was primarily concerned with the research methodology. It discussed the key research question and method, sensitizing concepts, the research process, the role of the researcher, and ethical considerations. It provided the following sensitizing concepts in light of Charmaz's constructivist grounded theory: hermeneutics of the other, OST, biblical notions of the other/neighbor, biblical notions of listening to the other/neighbor, the kingdom of God, the church as a Spirit-led community, Calvin's ecclesiology, and missional ecclesiology. I researched three congregations (Heavenly Creek, New Community, and Holy Hill) following the research process which Creswell recommends, with consideration of Charmaz's coding process. The next chapter addresses the data analysis and research findings.

4

Research Findings and Analysis

THE PREVIOUS CHAPTERS PROVIDED an introduction to this study. They briefly dealt with the PCK's understandings of mission and the church in comparison with Calvin and justified the methodology used in conducting this research. This chapter presents the profiles of the three participant congregations and the findings from the data. It also identifies and discusses emergent categories evidenced in the interviews. The profile of each of the three congregations includes: (1) a brief historical sketch, (2) a brief description of the physical setting and environmental context, (3) an introduction to the congregation's social services for their neighbors, (4) a brief discussion of their worship services and ministries, (5) a brief discussion of their organization and leadership, (6) a brief discussion of challenges they face, and (7) a brief demographic description of personal and group interview participants. I address each profile in a descriptive manner but loosely follow the order of the above seven points, based on interviews and observations of research sites.[1] We start with Heavenly Creek according to the order of my visits.

PARTICIPANT PROFILES

This section addresses the profiles of the three research congregations (Heavenly Creek, New Community, and Holy Hill), including personal interviews of participants and focus groups that were conducted.

---

1. I use quotation marks and block quotes to designate quotations from transcripts of interviews or data provided by the ministries studied to indicate that the researcher is using their words. For the sake of confidentiality, I do not use the exact titles or names of sources.

Heavenly Creek

I visited Heavenly Creek from September 5–9, 2012. I conducted six personal interviews and two focus groups (five persons and nine persons respectively). I interviewed the lead pastor, a pastor in charge of the Community Service Center, an elder, and one male and two female lay volunteers. Overall, four interview participants were male and two were female. One male lay participant and one female lay participant, who used to be volunteers, were full-time staff for the Community Service Center. All group interview participants were lay volunteers, consisting of thirteen females and one male.

Heavenly Creek has stood in the tradition of loving God and serving its neighbors since it was founded as a daughter congregation of a larger nearby congregation in a major city in Korea in 1926. It opened an evening school for those who could not go to school during the day in the mid-1930s. Its practical social welfare services were begun by the third lead pastor, who was appointed in 1947. He encouraged members to turn their attention to the congregation's neighbors. Korea faced the Korean War (1950–53) between North and South Korea, which brought massive suffering in both psychological and material terms around that time. Many factories were built around Heavenly Creek after the war.

A lot of people with the hope for economic success moved from rural areas to the region where this congregation is located. Most of them were farmers and the uneducated. Heavenly Creek established a bible school and a technical school to provide them educational opportunities. It also organized the Industrial Evangelism Department as a department—an *extraordinary* mission—for evangelizing those who worked in factories. Many leaders, including some elders, were known to have begun to attend Heavenly Creek through the *medium* of the bible school, the technical school, and/or the Industrial Evangelism Department in the 1960s. Accordingly, the congregation believed that faith was closely related to interactions with its neighbors.

Heavenly Creek was selected as one of the PCK's pilot congregations to pursue the development of social mission programs in 1981. Heavenly Creek established the Community Development Institute, sponsored by the General Assembly of the PCK, which aimed to promote continuous local community development projects. The Institute was renamed the Community Service Center in 2001. This change in name was because the literal meaning of the Community Development Institute seemed to limit its programs to activities for developing the local community while excluding social welfare services. This renaming was also related to the rapidly changing local context of Heavenly Creek. Its surrounding areas used to be typical industrial areas which consisted of small-and medium-sized factories. However, many new apartments began replacing factories in the early 1990s. This resulted from state-led urban renewal projects. The neighborhoods of Heavenly Creek have quickly developed since then in economic and cultural terms.

About 400,000 people lived in its larger community and about 19,000 people lived in the neighborhood of Heavenly Creek, as of 2012. Heavenly Creek implemented new cultural programs, such as music classes, while developing its previous programs for the poor and the marginalized. Heavenly Creek built a new building for its Community Service Center to provide additional space in 2005. It expanded and remodeled the main chapel with a seating capacity of about 1,200 people in 2008. Heavenly Creek as of 2012 has three main buildings, including an education hall. From my observation, congregational leaders were always ready to open all buildings to serve neighbors, although the Community Center was primarily used for this purpose. Heavenly Creek also opened its parking lot to its neighbors during the week days. This did not seem easy in an urban setting in Korea because parking costs were generally expensive in cities and it was demanding to take care of the parking lot.

Heavenly Creek provides eight worship services (one Wednesday, one Friday, four Sunday for adults, one for young adults, and one Sunday afternoon) and dawn prayer meetings every day (except Sunday). Approximately 5,500 adults currently attend the Sunday service. Heavenly Creek has gradually grown. The lead pastor did not want to officially count the number of worship attendants, while emphasizing the vision for church growth in terms of personal evangelism. He seemed to intend to encourage members to get more involved in personal evangelism, rather than emphasize only church growth. The atmosphere of two worship services which I attended seemed vigorous. The worship style was typically preaching-centered. Neighbors were frequently mentioned during the worship.

Heavenly Creek wants the Community Service Center to aim at improving the residents' quality of life, evangelizing them, and living together with them in order to realize the kingdom of God on this earth. This Center provides diverse education and social welfare services, such as the following: Korean language classes, after-school activities for kids, classes for the elderly, music classes, a library, free daily lunch services for the elderly, daycare centers, a center for children with severe disabilities, scholarships for poor students, a private non-profit credit union to help people in economic difficulties, an activity called "the bazaar of love," and repairing of homes of low-income households, etc. In financial terms, the state partly began to support some programs a few years ago, while most programs were mainly undertaken through its own budget and funding. The Center used to conduct a survey every five years to investigate the local and regional situation and identify the diverse needs of the residents. Feedback was used in the process of almost all programs. Based on these processes, Heavenly Creek tried to assess its services and relationships with the neighborhood, seek alternatives, and develop programs. Furthermore, volunteers were officially asked to not relate their service to their personal evangelism. This is because the leadership of Heavenly Creek did not want their community services to be regarded only as *tools for evangelism*.

As of 2012, fourteen full-time pastors, nine part-time pastors, and seventeen elders served Heavenly Creek. The lead pastor was installed in 2007 and upheld his predecessors' emphases, focusing on *worship, evangelism, education, outreach,* and *fellowship* as the five indicators. The predecessors tended to view Heavenly Creek's social services only in relation to social mission, while emphasizing overseas mission and evangelism. In contrast, the present lead pastor weaved these five indicators in light of *holistic mission*, which he came to gain through his study of missiology in a doctor of ministry program. For this reason, most interview participants seemed to understand their activities in light of mission. For the lead pastor, holistic mission included social involvement and excluded political dimensions in relation to the theology of God's mission, while accepting the emphasis on fervent evangelism from the church-growth line, in which the majority of Korean Protestantism was rooted.

Many members regarded his leadership as active and positive. From their standpoint, the lead pastor wisely overcame a few crucial crises which Heavenly Creek faced in the process of transition of leadership by using his leadership in an appropriate manner and providing his pastoral vision and teaching. To lead a huge organization, the lead pastor seemed to properly utilize a traditional pastor-centered and top-down approach, while complementarily using strategic delegation of leadership. For instance, he entrusted one pastor with the leadership of the Community Service Center. To communicate with volunteers, the pastor in charge of the Center took part in monthly meetings of all volunteer organizations related to the programs and the activities of the Center.

The website of Heavenly Creek introduced its mission as follows: "Our mission is to become those who follow Jesus by realizing Jesus' three primary ministries—'evangelization,' 'education,' and 'healing and caring'—on this earth." The website also highlighted "love" in regard to the inner relationship of Heavenly Creek and being "together with the world" in regard to its outer relationship. "Our neighbors," "God," "social (or community) service," "open congregation (in terms of the relationship with the neighbor)," "love," "for our neighbors (or regions)," and "together with our neighbors" were buzz words within Heavenly Creek.

From my standpoint, Heavenly Creek is facing the following challenges. First, Heavenly Creek needs to take into consideration how to relate its congregational growth to its relationship with the neighborhood, because it has been steadily growing in numbers while the needs of its neighbors have been also increasing. Second, given the first challenge, Heavenly Creek needs to deal with how to develop better internal communication. Third, Heavenly Creek needs to pay more attention to the poorer residents who would be not able to afford living in a redeveloped neighborhood, while focusing on new middle-class residents due to state-led urban renewal projects.

New Community

I visited New Community from September 12–16, 2012. I conducted four personal interviews and two focus groups (three persons and seven persons respectively). I interviewed the lead pastor, a minister in charge of the family library, and one male and one female lay volunteer. Overall, three interview participants were male and one was female. All group participants were lay volunteers, consisting of seven females and three males.

From my observation, New Community was a small congregation in number but a strong congregation in terms of its work related to the neighborhood. New Community was begun as a *minjung* congregation to realize the primary spirit of *minjung* theology, that is, *for the marginalized* and *the oppressed* in 1986. Most founding members, as educated Christians, used to live in Seoul, the capital of South Korea. They searched for where to serve. The current lead pastor was told that the present site needed special care, because it was regarded as one of the poorest areas in Korea at that time. Many small factories began to be built in its neighborhoods, which used to be rural. On the one hand, the founding group of New Community went to serve local residents for spreading Christian culture and creating sound citizenship, rather than aiming at the growth of New Community itself. On the other hand, New Community was suspected as being *bbalgangyi* (communist) by the rich and other Christians in the neighborhoods.

Remarkably, New Community was committed to trying to live for and with the *minjung* (the marginalized and the oppressed) in that region in response to the *minjung*'s stories. The founding group of New Community first started a daycare center a few months prior to founding the church in 1986. They thought that children were neglected and did not have enough care in difficult living conditions, because parents worked at factories until late in the evening. Two lay leaders opened a small library for parents as well as children in 1989, because they became aware that children's problems were directly connected with the problems of the local community. Later, this library became a larger library (called "Exciting Family Library") through the help of civil societies and the civic government. It was natural that New Community opened the first local children's center in that region in 1990. This is because, as children grew, they needed afterschool programs.

Korea was supported by the International Monetary Fund (IMF) in 1998. The so-called "IMF era" was a decisive factor in breaking up families who worked at small factories. At this juncture, New Community established the Family Support Center in order to prevent the dissolution of poor families. New Community also provided counseling program services for mothers to solve the problem of child abuse through the Family Support Center and anger management programs and cultural programs for children, such as violin classes. New Community became aware that many poor families dreamed of leaving this community after becoming successful. New Community realized the importance of community ministry beyond the boundaries of the church and family. New Community has attempted to take care of the whole community in an ecological sense since 2000, with the conviction that there is no hope without the transformation of the whole community.

New Community was located amongst old houses as of 2012, while new apartment complexes were on the other side of the street. These apartment complexes were constructed due to urban renewal projects, which had exploded throughout Korea over two decades. Approximately 15,000 people currently reside in the neighborhood of New Community and its larger community numbers about 450,000 in population. The main building of New Community was constructed as a three-storey red brick building in 1996, which is currently used for worship and the day care center. It looks like an old-fashioned building. Nevertheless, the building was *kind of new* and *fortunate* for the members of New Community, because the previous main building was a Korean traditional one-storey building. This previous building is currently used for programs for the elderly. The Exciting Family Library is located in the local community center. This library is regarded as one of the most historic libraries, because it resulted from the small library movement led by civil societies of the region. The children's center has rented a floor of a building near New Community.

New Community provides three worship services (one Wednesday, one Friday, and one Sunday) and dawn prayer meetings during every season of the church year. Approximately forty adults attend Sunday worship as of 2012. I was surprised at the fact that this small congregation had done great things that other large congregations could not do. All attendants sat on chairs without legs at floor level during the worship service. The worship style was typically preaching-oriented. To some degree, the lead pastor's preaching seemed to be informative. New Community provides a study gathering called "Café Humanities" for the public instead of worship service one Wednesday a month. This gathering includes an open Bible study.

New Community still puts priority on low-income residents and seniors living alone in the neighborhood, although the influx of new middle-class residents has increased. New Community believes that it and the community can grow together, while many congregations in the area are isolated from the community. New Community provides diverse educational, social, and cultural services and programs, such as a day care center, a children's center, Family Support Center, family library, center for the elderly, and village school, etc. The day care center, the children's center, the Family Support Center, and the family library have been partly supported by the state since the late 1990s. On the one hand, the financial support of the state seemed to be undeniably helpful for New Community in economic terms. On the other hand, this seemed to limit New Community's freedom in terms of administration, which used to be enjoyed. New Community has a Local Mission Committee for the systematic management of all programs and services once a month. New Community's limits of human and material resources led to early cooperation with civil societies since the late 1990s. For instance, New Community undertook the business of creating what is known as an "urban village" together with a civil society in 1998. New Community occasionally conducted research and dialogue with its neighbors in the daily lives of its members for the spread of Christian culture and the development of the local community.

Leadership consisted of the lead pastor and one associate minister, who was primarily in charge of the family library. New Community understood all programs and services as "local mission." New Community was not concerned with overseas mission, unlike the other two research participant congregations. New Community had a relatively democratic leadership, as compared to the other two research participant congregations. For instance, my study of New Community was not decided until the meeting of all members accepted my request of the study, while it was decided by the lead pastors within the other two congregations. However, regarding the vision and plan of New Community, the lead pastor's leadership seemed to be operative as a decisive factor. The lead pastor was one of the founding members. On the one hand, he wanted to critically develop the essential vision of New Community as a *minjung* congregation in regard to taking care of the marginalized. On the other hand, he acknowledged weaknesses regarding ecclesiology in general and worship in particular within *minjung* theology and the *minjung* church. He also pointed out that *minjung* congregations paid little attention to the rapidly emerging era of civil societies in the 1990s which created networks with local organizations and civil society beyond their fences. The lead pastor dreamed of being a pastor of a village rather than a congregation and *eco-systematically* creating a village community of justice, peace, and life within a city.

"Local mission," "together with the neighbor," "creating a village," "a small congregation," "caring," and "network" were buzzwords within New Community. From the viewpoint of the study, New Community is facing the following challenges. First, many members feel a sense of fatigue because of their long-term service related to the neighborhood and lack of human resources. For New Community, this must not be a new issue. In this regard, many interview participants hoped for a sustainable level of New Community's quantitative growth in an appropriate manner and, as such, they would need to put more effort into personal evangelism. Second, New Community seems to need to control the pace of creating or undertaking new activities and agendas.

Holy Hill

I visited Holy Hill from September 19–23, 2012. I conducted five personal interviews and two focus groups (four and six participants respectively). I interviewed the lead pastor, a pastor in charge of the social welfare foundation, a male lay leader as manager of the social welfare foundation, and one male and two female lay volunteers. Overall, four interview participants were male and one was female. A lay leader as manager of the social welfare foundation was hired when the foundation was established in 2007. The total number of group interview participants was ten, consisting of two male elders and eight lay volunteers (two males and six females).

Holy Hill has regarded itself as a *local* congregation since it was founded in 1954. Holy Hill has its essential reason to exist *for the only love of neighbor* in the world in light of the gospel. Holy Hill has tried to be a congregation *for* and *with* its neighborhood. From its early days, Holy Hill has been interested in serving and sharing by focusing on the joys and sorrows of the people in the neighborhood, which has been well known as a representative industrial area in Korea. Holy Hill opened a school for the elderly in 1987. Holy Hill then practiced social services for its neighbors step-by-step, such as a school for babies and blood donations. Holy Hill organized the Regional Services Department to oversee a variety of community service activities separately in 1998. Holy Hill founded a social welfare foundation to better serve its neighbors through the specialization of its community services in 2006.

When I visited Holy Hill, the construction of the main building was in full swing. There were few complaints about it from the neighborhood. This is because there has been a good relationship between Holy Hill and its neighbors. The reason for this construction was also to ultimately serve the neighborhood. Holy Hill planned to create a cultural center for local residents. Practically and symbolically, Holy Hill would open parking space to the neighbor and not put up a fence. In detail, libraries and cultural space, such as a coffee shop, and chapel with more than 2,500 seats and a 600-seat cultural venue will be located on the first floor for easier accessibility for the residents. This is based on the following simple reason. The lead pastor said that "the reason why a local congregation does not exist between mountains but between regions or towns is that Christians ought to live together with their neighbors by serving and sharing communities."[2]

The region surrounding Holy Hill was urbanized due to industrialization in the 1960s and 70s. This region was established for the purpose of the aggregate export industry. Many people moved to this region for the sake of economic success. Most residents used to work in nearby factories. Over the decades, urban renewal projects led to a change in Holy Hill's neighborhood. Newly built apartment complexes replaced old houses. Approximately 57,000 people currently resided in the neighborhood of Holy Hill and its larger community was around 430,000 in population.

Holy Hill provides nine worship services (two Wednesday, one Friday, four Sunday for adults, one for young adults, and one Sunday afternoon) and dawn prayer meetings every day. Approximately 2,800 adults currently attended the Sunday worship service. Holy Hill has gradually grown. Holy Hill was primarily concerned with personal evangelism based on the priority of the gospel and overseas mission, in addition to social services for its neighbors. However, it avoided aggressive evangelism and church growth programs without social services for the neighbor. The atmosphere of the two worship services that I attended seemed warm and vigorous. The worship style was typically preaching-centered. Neighbors were frequently mentioned during the worship.

Holy Hill believes that the church has the responsibility for the community to participate in social welfare. Holy Hill used to be involved in diverse social services. In the process, Holy Hill came to realize that its neighbors felt uncomfortable to come to the church and they had suspicion about the purity of Holy Hill's service. This is because there were negative views of aggressive evangelism of Korean Protestantism and services as means for church growth in Korea. Considering this, Holy Hill founded a welfare foundation. Holy Hill donated a considerable amount of money for the foundation. However, it did not use its name for the name of the Foundation for the comfort of its neighbors. To serve the marginalized people systematically, it also hired specialists appropriate for each social welfare program.

This welfare foundation provided diverse programs and services such as a nursery, programs for people with disabilities, hobby classes, beauty services, volunteering in hospitals, support for students skipping

---

2. This was recorded in the interview.

meals, after-school classrooms, and the like. A Christian civic organization requested Holy Hill to open a food bank service. Holy Hill utilized the partnership with local government to do so. Holy Hill also persuaded restaurants in big factories to participate in the service by donating their surplus food. Holy Hill supplied packed lunch boxes for over twenty small congregations to their neighbors. Furthermore, through a movement of both donation and prayers, more members of Holy Hill had helped support people with disabilities, eyesight surgery for North Koreans, and refractory patients beyond the region since 2003.

Eleven full-time pastors, seven part-time pastors, and twenty-eight elders currently serve Holy Hill. The lead pastor was installed in 1993, focusing on *worship, discipleship, education, mission, social service,* and *fellowship* as six goals. Holy Hill's purpose statement is as follows: "Holy Hill is a good congregation which shares love with each other in the church and practices mission in the world." The lead pastor studied missiology in a doctor of theology program. He knew about the current trends of missiology, including the missional church conversation in North America. He also emphasized "holistic mission," as did the lead pastor of Heavenly Creek. He held that the gospel and social welfare should be in harmony, like "the two sides of the same coin" and must coexist.[3] The lead pastor understood his role to be a "distributor" of the love of God and Word. To do so, he was primarily concerned with communicating with the neighbors by paying attention to the situations of the neighborhood. Many members and volunteers respected the lead pastor.

For Holy Hill, "local congregation," "a congregation with the region," "no fence," "welfare," "steady," "expertise/expert," "love," etc., were buzz-words. From the perspective of my observation, Holy Hill is facing the following possible challenges. The first challenge would be related to how to deal with internal communications between hired experts of social welfare and volunteers which come from Holy Hill. This is related to possible conflicts between expert-based and volunteer-based approaches. How will the experts deal with the original purpose of the welfare foundation without losing their focus or interest in quality? How will volunteers get more involved in social welfare services with consideration of the original purpose of the welfare foundation? Second, Holy Hill needs to pay more attention to the poorer residents who would not be able to afford their redeveloped neighborhood.

---

3. This was recorded in the interview.

DATA ANALYSIS

Constant comparative analysis of the data was utilized in the process of coding and analysis for saturation of the data and also linking of the subcategories to the core categories. I continued to compare codes and identify the similarities and differences in order to facilitate the development of concepts. In doing so, I asked the following questions:

(1) What is happening and what is going on?

(2) How do the participants come to this experience?

(3) How do the participants' understandings of listening to the neighbor develop?

(4) What are the important influences on this process?

(5) How did they engage in the making of meanings?

(6) What were their understandings of the main concepts, ideas, and experiences?

(7) What mechanisms accounted for this knowledge?

I followed the following coding process suggested by Charmaz, as noted in the previous chapter: (1) initial coding (line-by-line coding, in vivo codes), (2) focused coding, (3) axial coding, and (4) theoretical coding.[4] Charmaz claims this process is flexible rather than linear and rigid.[5] She states that "if we wish, we can return to the data and make a fresh coding."[6] This resonates with the coding process of this research. I also kept writing analytical memos throughout the whole process of coding until the first draft of the research.[7]

I moved rapidly through the data in the initial line-by-line coding. I coded the data descriptively rather than interpretatively in this process. I endeavored to maintain the language of the participants. The codes were related to their own thoughts, personal/congregational histories, events, actions, feelings, needs, desires, visions, environmental contexts, etc. As a result, I created 185 nodes and 2089 codes by using NVivo 10.[8] Interestingly, recurrent codes were identified and patterns of relations between them began to become apparent, both across and within individual tran-

---

4. Charmaz, *Constructing Grounded Theory*, 42–71.

5. Ibid., 2, 9, 15, 61, 71.

6. Ibid., 71.

7. Ibid., 80–95.

8. A *node* is a container for coding or a location of the coded text in NVivo 10.

scripts from the outset of coding the data. For example, all participants referred to their neighbors as the poor, the marginalized, the unprivileged, low-income-earning people, and the like. At the same time, they regarded their local environment as poor, marginalized, underdeveloped, etc. Their understandings of church were naturally related to a church for such kinds of people.

I then moved to focused coding, which was used to capture, synthesize and understand the main themes—categories—in each interview script. All of the categories were continuously reworked in a recursive fashion, moving among the interviews, the initial codes, and the categories in the process of focused coding. I then began axial coding, which aims to relate main categories and their sub-categories in the process of focused coding of the first-person interview script. This is because Charmaz does not seem to explicitly separate focused coding from axial coding as do Strauss and Corbin.[9] Instead, Charmaz tends to include axial coding in focused coding.[10] These two coding processes resulted in paring down the categories to the following nine main ones: (1) definitions and notions of church, (2) definitions and notions of neighbor, (3) definitions and notions of God, (4) mission and evangelism, (5) programs, (6) ways of serving the neighbor, (7) leadership, (8) relationship with the neighborhood, and (9) the process of listening to the neighbor.

Theoretical coding was then used to reorganize the data and the categories above to develop a theory explaining the main concern of the research participants from an analytical perspective. According to Charmaz, theoretical coding aims to "move [the researcher's] analytical story in a theoretical direction."[11] I theoretically sorted previous categories and integrated my analytical and conceptual memos in the process. In so doing, I came to consider the category of "the process of listening to the neighbor" to be the core category. This seemed to fit the purpose of the study.

The primary conceptual categories of "knowledge/view," "motive/purpose," "attitude," "skill/method," "outcomes," and "leadership" were emergent from the analytical process and were found to constitute the

---

9. Charmaz, *Constructing Grounded Theory*, 60–63.

10. Ibid., 61–63. Charmaz warns that axial coding applies too rigid and formal of a frame to the data analysis. Instead, she recommends a less formalized approach of reflecting on categories and sub-categories and to establish connecting links between these to make sense of the interview data.

11. Ibid., 63.

phenomenon of listening to the neighbor from the participants' perspective. An overview of these categories and their subcategories is provided in table 1. The next section addresses these primary categories and subcategories in more detail.

Table 1: The Primary Conceptual Categories

Primary Category	Sub-Category
Knowledge/View	Church, Neighbor, Mission, Context
Motive/Purpose	Better Serving the Neighbor, Making Their Local Communities Better, Carrying Out Mission
Attitude	Maintaining Humility, Remaining Open, Maintaining Empathic Attention
Skill/Method	Using Personal/Organizational Relationships, Providing Open Spaces, Utilizing Feedback/Media
Outcomes	Learning from the Neighbor/Process, Mutual/Reciprocal Communication and Relationships, New Missional Events
Leadership	Primary Role of the Lead Pastor, Internal Communication

Overviews of personal interview participants and focus groups are respectively provided in table 2 and 3 prior to turning to the next section.

Table 2: Overview of Personal Interview Participants

Participant	Age	Gender	Congregation
A	50s	M	Heavenly Creek
B	40s	M	Heavenly Creek
C	60s	M	Heavenly Creek
D	50s	F	Heavenly Creek
E	40s	M	Heavenly Creek
F	60s	F	Heavenly Creek
G	50s	M	New Community
H	40s	M	New Community
I	40s	M	New Community
J	40s	F	New Community

K	50s	M	Holy Hill
L	30s	M	Holy Hill
M	40s	M	Holy Hill
N	50s	M	Holy Hill
O	60s	F	Holy Hill

Table 3: Overview of Focus Groups

Focus Group	Number of Participants	Gender (M/F)	Congregation
A	5	1/4	Heavenly Creek
B	8	0/8	Heavenly Creek
C	3	0/3	New Community
D	7	3/4	New Community
E	4	4/0	Holy Hill
F	6	0/6	Holy Hill

Excerpts from interviews, along with my observation, are provided below and show that the findings of the study are clearly grounded in the raw data. I use the most appropriate excerpts to explain those findings.

Knowledge/View

Knowledge/View emerged as a category in response to the participants' perceptions of listening to the neighbor. They facilitated primary knowledge/view before their listening to the neighbor. In other words, they did not begin to participate in the process of listening to the neighbor in an epistemological perspectival vacuum. They expressed their understandings of listening to the neighbor by mainly utilizing the following knowledge and views: church, neighbor, mission, and context. The participants' understandings of mission and context appeared to influence their understandings of church and neighbor, as we see below. As sub-categories, these four concepts constitute the category of *knowledge/view*.

Church

Church was identified as a subcategory of *knowledge/view*. This category has four primary properties according to the frequency: a church for the neighbor, a church with the neighbor, a church different from the majority of churches in Korea, and a church of Christ. The first three categories seem to be contingent on the last category, as we see below.

First, all personal interview participants and all four focus groups most frequently understood their congregations as *a church for the neighbor*. Their congregations' long histories of serving their neighbors naturally led them into this notion of church. Accordingly, they held that their congregations existed to serve their neighbors. This is evidenced in the following excerpts:

> They called my congregation "our church," "a church which works for our community," or "our church for our community," although they weren't those who went to church. (Participant E)

> We have helped our local community.... All we have to do is help our neighbors in this community. (Participant K)

Second, all personal interview participants and all focus groups also regarded the church as *a church with the neighbor*. Participants understood their congregations as *a part of their context and larger community* in relation to this perception. This was apparent in the following excerpts:

> With initiative, this congregation goes and lives together with the region ... and because members of local congregations come from their neighborhoods, they have to live without losing their identities and being isolated from their neighbors. (Participant K)

> These days, the meaning of local mission is changing ... local mission means that the church has to go together with its neighbor. (Group C)

All congregations seemed to come to develop such a notion of church with the neighbor through the process of serving their neighbors. For example, Participant H said that his congregation earlier focused on becoming a church for helping its neighbors, and added a notion of church together with its community according to the socio-cultural change in its environment since the early 2000s. This notion was shown more frequently in New Community than in Heavenly Creek and Holy Hill.

Third, all personal participants and all focus groups described their congregations as *a church different from the majority of congregations* in Korea. They commonly evaluated other congregations as self-centered in terms of ecclesiology and one-way in terms of evangelism and mission. In a broader sense, they did not regard other congregations as churches either for or with their neighbors. This understanding led them to consider their congregations as relatively good and/or true. Examples abound as follows:

> Christianity has been seriously stagnant. This is because the church hasn't had good influences on unbelievers. However, we have heard that Heavenly Creek has done good works . . . from the neighbors. (Participant C)

> Now, the Korean church has only a big dream of church growth through evangelism . . . sees people as the objects of evangelism . . . because it has no role for its local society, it is criticized and isolated from the society, and people have fear about evangelism . . . Conversely . . . making contact point between the local society and us . . . when people feel that the presence of the church is good not only for us but also for the region . . . people may open their hearts to accept Jesus Christ with delight. (Participant G)

> In that sense, this region is blessed because God has given Holy Hill to this area and because Holy Hill has done good activities, which other congregations wouldn't have had undertaken . . . For some congregations, helping their neighbors is a method for evangelism, which isn't regarded itself as the end but as a tool . . . they expect church growth and tangible results by running a big social welfare center. (Participant L)

Finally, all personal interview participants and all focus groups expressed their congregations as *churches of Jesus Christ*.[12] Relatively speaking, they mentioned God a few times and rarely mentioned the Spirit while referring to church. From my observation, even those who did not mention explicitly the church in relation to Christ seemed to presume their congregations as churches of Christ.

> Because Jesus regarded creating a community as the core of his life, we aimed at creating a community from the beginning . . . and this community cannot but exist between villages. (Participant G)

12. Except Participants B, D, and J.

> Those who don't know Jesus Christ can be regarded as our neighbors, because we are a community of Christ. (Group E)

This notion of a church of Jesus Christ seemed to lead all participants to consider the above three ecclesiological notions. This is because the way Jesus related to his neighbors in the Bible seemed to cause them to understand their congregations as churches both for and with their neighbors. That is to say, Jesus lived both for and with his neighbors, though his life seemed somewhat simplified in this regard.

Neighbor

All personal interview participants and all focus groups perceived their neighbors as *people in need*, *local residents*, and *those who need the gospel*. First, all participants had a common understanding of neighbors as *people in need* as follows:

> Our neighbors are those who are poor and needy. . . . Holy Hill regards those who are poor and needy as neighbors in this region, because the least is biblically taught as our neighbor. (Participant M)

All participants seemed to take for granted that their congregations had to put priority on taking care of people in need in terms of church for the neighbor.

Second, all personal interview participants and all focus groups regarded their neighbors as *local residents* or *communities* as follows:

> The neighbors of [our congregation] are the local community in which it is included. (Participant E)

> First, physically, the residents in this area centered around this church would be our neighbors. (Participant F)

> [Our neighbors] are local residents. (Group F)

This perception is relatively in consonance with the understanding of a church *with* the neighbor. This perception seemed to enable research participant congregations to consider newly-arrived middle-class people as their neighbors and admit their members as neighbors to other residents.

Third, all personal interview participants and all focus groups perceived their neighbors as those who needed the gospel. They understood the gospel in relation to the love of Jesus or God, salvation, and/or the kingdom of God, which were interrelated. For example, they categorized their neighbors as those who did not believe and know Jesus (Group F), those who needed salvation (Participant B), those who needed the kingdom of God and the gospel (Participant H), and the like. We take a more careful look at the gospel in terms of mission below. In fact, the above three notions of neighbor seemed to be closely interrelated. For example, Participant A said that "[Our neighbors] are local residents who don't attend [our] congregation, need the love of God and the gospel to be heard, and whom we have to serve."

Mission

Mission was identified as a subcategory of *knowledge/view*. All personal interview participants and all focus groups understood their activities, including listening to the neighbor, in light of their understanding of mission. *Witnessing the gospel* and *missio Dei* were primary properties of mission.

First, *mission* is mainly concerned with *witnessing the gospel* as follows:

> Some Christians don't want to tell the fact that they go to church or that they have churchly offices. So . . . we, believers, have to play a role as light and salt in the world. We have to show that we are Christians through our deeds. (Participant C)

> We'd better witness [the gospel] through our lives. Actually, they don't understand faith through the Bible. Rather, they come to church through looking at the language, activities, and lives of those who go to church. (Participant E)

In fact, all participants' understandings of the gospel varied. They understood the gospel as love, salvation, and/or the kingdom of God in a broader sense. They tended to emphasize the gospel in relation to *both* spiritual *and* bodily needs and *both* personal *and* communal aspects. They believed that they had to bear witness to the gospel through their deeds in their daily encounters with their neighbors. Those who mentioned the kingdom of God in regard to the gospel tended to emphasize the need for *building* or *expanding* it.

Relatively speaking, Heavenly Creek and Holy Hill put their priority on spiritual and personal aspects of the gospel, whereas New Community was primarily concerned with bodily needs and community in terms of the gospel. For example, participants of Heavenly Creek and Holy Hill tended to relate the kingdom of God to personal salvation, while participants of New Community seemed to look at the kingdom of God in relation to their lives within their larger community. It is surprising that participants of New Community did not explicitly use the term "love," which was normally used in Heavenly Creek and Holy Hill in relation to the gospel or in other aspects of mission. For example, they preferred to use the term "togetherness" instead of "love," even when other participants of Heavenly Creek or Holy Hill could have related their understandings or activities to love. New Community took seriously Jesus' togetherness with the oppressed and the marginalized in terms of the gospel. New Community somehow seemed to avoid using the term "love," in that many congregations in Korea had a tendency to utilize it in order to justify their one-way evangelism.

Second, *missio Dei* was identified as another property of *mission*. All personal interview participants and all focus groups acknowledged that God was the subject or agent of their mission and social services as follows:

> I think salvation of all human beings is God's obvious purpose, and God is using the Community Service Center and Heavenly Creek for this purpose. (Participant B)

> I think I see through their offspring the fact that God intervened in their efforts, probably while the church was being constructed, as the church was being expanded, and as the church was being revived. . . . He loved our church members and they were able to get by, but God was truly tenaciously taking care of them . . . . But I get the feeling that the boundaries of this love are widening and flowing. (Participant F)

> New Community gains new energies via cooperation with civil societies and gives it back to its local community. . . . I think this is God's way of [mission]. (Group C)

Most participants, however, perceived God's mission in relation to the Father, rather than in light of the Trinity. In particular, many participants did not mention the Spirit until I asked a question regarding the Spirit, while Jesus was mentioned relatively often, despite no direct questions regarding Jesus.[13] Most participants, except pastors, tended to

---

13. What follows is the total word frequency regarding the three divine persons in all interview scripts: God (173 times), Jesus and/or Christ (eighty-four times), and the Spirit (fifty times). God and the Spirit were explicitly questioned once in the interview process, while Jesus was not directly addressed as an interview question topic.

relate the activities of the Spirit to the personal sphere of belief such as personal heart and minds, rather than mission.

Furthermore, Heavenly Creek and Holy Hill placed their emphasis on the *centripetal* dimension of God's mission—from the world toward the church.[14] They believed that personal salvation, along with concern for their neighbors' social welfare, was important and the church had to play a primary role for it. In contrast, New Community seemed to consider God's mission to be *centrifugal*—from the church toward the world.[15] It tended to believe that God's primary concern was in the world and, as such, the church had to be primarily concerned with participating in God's mission in the world rather than in the church.

Context

All personal interview participants and all focus groups acknowledged that their local contexts led them to their identities and mission. In their view, the research participant congregations had been primarily concerned with the poor and the marginalized in that they were located in underdeveloped areas such as industrial areas. A good example of this is as follows:

> The factories have largely disappeared here, but they say there were a lot of factories . . . at first, in the beginning. And so although it was a few people in homes, it was mainly missions for the industry. So I think that this is a church whose purpose, from its inception, was to serve its neighbors. (Participant F).

For the same reason, all three congregations had provided their neighbors with social services mainly for caring. All three congregations also took seriously the importance of *space*, because their neighbors were too poor to have enough space for their lives. This aspect somehow caused them to deal with *providing open spaces* as a skill/method in the process of listening to their neighbors, as we see below.

The recent changes to their contexts, such as an influx of middle-class residents, led all research congregations to develop relevant programs and/or alternative approaches to these environmental changes

---

14. Johannes Blauw suggests the distinction between *centripetal* mission in the Old Testament and *centrifugal* mission in the New Testament in order to describe the missionary nature of the church. See Johannes Blauw, *The Missionary*, 44–80.

15. Ibid.

according to each congregation's material and personal capacity. An example regarding this is as follows:

> So since apartment buildings began to be built here, they opened a music school. Previously, it hadn't really been practical, but it became possible when the apartment complexes came in and the residents could afford lesson fees, albeit at a modest level. (Group A)

New Community developed ways of collaboration with civil societies, considering its lack of personal and material capacity.

Motive/Purpose

Motive/purpose was articulated as a category as a result of what motivated the participants to listen to the neighbor. These two concepts explained why participants listened to their neighbors. On the one hand, the research uses the concept of *motive* as what individual participants valued and what drove them to act and behave in certain ways on a personal level. On the other hand, I also employ the concept of *purpose* as a goal or aim for which participants exist or act on a congregational level. However, these two appeared to be inseparable. "Better serving the neighbor," "making their local communities better," and "carrying out mission" were clustered as the subcategories of *motive/purpose*. The first primary category—knowledge/view—in particular, its subcategories of church and mission, seemed influenced the category of *motive/purpose*, as we see below.

Better Serving the Neighbor

All personal interview participants and all focus groups took it for granted that they should listen to their neighbors in order to better serve them. This is the most dominant notion in relation to the category of motive/purpose. They tended to regard *paying attention to their neighbors' needs* as *listening to their neighbors*. They did not want their services to satisfy only themselves. This notion was apparent in the following excerpts:

> The most important thing is to catch the voices, expectations, and/or interests of the residents as soon as possible. . . . That's the key point to us. (Participant B)

> They take requests from the local residents to select target houses—from heads of local areas, and so on, and also from the

members of our church who feel that they really want to help fix up this or that house in the neighborhood. (Group A)

Those who aimed to serve their neighbors could seemingly do nothing but listen first before speaking to their neighbors. This shows that their relationships with their neighbors had essentially an *asymmetrical* dimension. That is to say, their neighbors did not listen to them in the first place. All three congregations' long-term involvement in serving their neighborhoods naturally led them to get used to first paying attention to their neighbors so as to meet their neighbors' needs. For example, Participant I said that his congregation started a daycare for children, then as children grew, it opened an afterschool program for them, and then it started a library for its local community which lacked cultural infrastructure.

Furthermore, the category of *better serving the neighbor* seemed to be influenced by the first primary category of *knowledge/view*. In particular, participants' understandings of church, neighbor, and mission caused them to try to better serve their neighbors. Participants' understandings of their congregations as churches for their neighbors enabled participants to focus on better serving their neighbors. Their primary notion that their congregations was distinct from other general congregations in Korea seemed to enable them to search for better serving their neighbors. Their understanding of neighbors as people in need also tended to lead them to take for granted their concerns for better serving the neighbor. Mission as witnessing the gospel in relation to God's mission seemed to prompt participants to aim at better serving their neighbors. This is because they believed that they had to bear witness to the gospel through their lives related to their neighbors.

Making Their Local Communities Better

All personal participants and all focus groups wanted to listen to their neighbors for making their local communities better places. They thus emphasized that the church as a part of its larger community needed to communicate with its neighbors to do so. They considered listening to be a primary aspect of communication with their neighbors. It seems apparent that the research participants or participant congregations regarded listening as a critical part of their communications with their neighbors and their neighbors as equal conversational partners. Put another way, as equal conversational partners, both research congregations and their neighbors took part in making their communities better. Examples are as follows:

> [Our congregation] commissioned specialized research institutions [to determine local residents' thoughts]. They visited every home to ask diverse survey questions regarding local residents' requests, viewpoints on [our congregation], the problems of this region, etc. (Participant D)

> [We] are concerned with how to communicate with those who live together with us in this same space for the [common] good. (Participant I)

> [In] the process of the [housing] redevelopment project for [our congregation's] neighborhood, residents couldn't look for a meeting place to cope with this project. [When they asked our congregation to offer a place for the meeting,] our congregation opened a space for them to do so. (Participant N)

Research findings also clearly show that they first tried to communicate with their neighbors in order to serve. This communication seemed to be two-way. Examples are as follows:

> It always works in that way. I have dialogues with [my neighbors] . . . come to know their needs. . . . As a result, I make a program. (Participant G)

> We didn't think about it before . . . we were told about it. In so doing, we had conversations with moms of kids in different kinds of difficult situations. (Participant L)

All three congregations frequently had communication with local governments and/or civil society organizations for the sake of making their local communities better. Most of them took seriously the importance of respecting or acknowledging each other for communication. This notion presumes a *symmetrical relationship* between congregations and their neighbors. However, this relationship, too, seemed to have an *asymmetrical starting point* as long as congregations primarily aim at serving their neighbors. This is because listening to their neighbors relatively tended to precede communicating with them, although listening seemed inseparable from such communication.

The notion of *making the local community better* apparently seemed to be influenced by the first primary category of knowledge/view. Their poor and underdeveloped context in terms of culture and economy led them to listen to their neighbors for improving their communities. This seemed very natural because most members of the three research congregations were residents in such poor areas. The category of *making the local community better* was seemingly contingent on the notion of a church both *for* and *with the neighbor*. The notion of a church with its neighbor had relatively more influence on this category, as participants regarded their neighbors as co-residents rather than people in need. Participants took for granted having dialogue or communication with their neighbors in this regard. All research congregations took into consideration involvement in making their communities better in light of the gospel and God's mission. They believed that Jesus was involved in improving his community and God had been involved in making human communities better in God's way.

CARRYING OUT MISSION

All personal interview participants and all focus groups tried to communicate with their neighbors for *ultimately* carrying out mission. This subcategory appeared to be a broad, but essential purpose, while the above two subcategories seemed to be regarded as direct purposes. Participants did not want to reduce their intention of communicating with their neighbors as only a means for church growth. They instead expected this communication process to serve the purpose of carrying out mission. Examples are:

> [God] wants His love to be practiced toward [our congregation's] local residents. (Participant A)

> [God] wants [our congregation] to get along with the poor within its area . . . and to witness the kingdom of God and the gospel. (Participant H)

> I pray that they will meet the Lord someday, but don't force them to do so. (Participant O)

This purpose was diversely expressed according to their understandings of mission. In other words, the expressions of the purpose were linked with *mission* as one of the first primary category's (*knowledge/view*) subcategories, which had *witnessing the gospel* and *missio Dei* as primary properties. For example, some participants communicated with their neighbors for the sake of their neighbors' personal salvation. Even these cases showed that participants did not want to treat their neighbors as objects of their evangelism. This is because in terms of God's mission, they believed that it was only God that could convert their neighbors. Some participants related their communication with their neighbors to the primary aim of loving them. Some participants regarded their communication with their neighbors as a process of *building* or *expanding* the kingdom of God. This shows that participants seemed to have motives or purposes based on their own understandings of mission.

Attitude

The category "attitude" emerged from the data in response to the volume of commentary that was evident in regard to how to treat the neighbor in the process of listening. This category has the following subcategories: *maintaining humility, remaining open,* and *maintaining empathic attention*. These categories are very interrelated because research congregations essentially aim to serve their community.

Maintaining Humility

This attitude among the three subcategories was the most frequently addressed. All personal participants and all focus groups commonly acknowledged that they tried to be *humble* in order to serve and communicate with their neighbors. *The Oxford English Dictionary* defines *humble* as "marked by the absence of self-assertion or self-exaltation; lowly: the opposite of *proud*," "modest, [or] unpretentious" in terms of attitude.[16] *Merriam-Webster Dictionary* refers to it as "not proud or haughty," "not arrogant or assertive," "reflecting, expressing, or offered in a spirit of deference or submission."[17] Such meanings of "humble" provided me with perspectives for categorizing participants' attitudes toward their neighbors as *maintaining humility*. The expressions "serving" and "service" also tend to be naturally related to *humility* in terms of Korean culture. Many participants used honorific suffixes to refer to their neighbor or neighbors in Korean. In this sense, they seemingly tried to be humble vis-à-vis their neighbors as follows:

---

16. *Oxford English Dictionary*, s.v. "humble," http://www.oed.com/view/Entry/89298?result=3&rskey=4eHd9y& (accessed April 15, 2013).

17. *Merriam-Webster Online*, s.v. "humble," http://www.merriam-webster.com/dictionary/humble?show=0&t=1366316366 (accessed April 15, 2013).

> We should approach to our neighbors without making them uncomfortable and showing off [what we have done for them]. (Participant D)
>
> The threshold of the church shouldn't be high. (Participant O)
>
> We, our congregation, have to be humble in order for our neighbors to feel comfortable. . . . I am primarily concerned with it. The school for the elderly is multi-religious . . . it seems very humble. (Group B)
>
> Pastors are open to communicate . . . we have to be humble in order to communicate with our neighbors. We need to humbly approach them. (Group E)

This attitude seems to mean that participants wanted to first consider their neighbors' feelings rather than their own. They intentionally sought their neighbors' interests in their services. They did not treat their neighbors as objects for their satisfaction related to their services. They did not want to exercise control over their neighbors through helping them. Put differently, they did not want their services for their neighbors to intentionally or unintentionally force their neighbors to come to their congregations. This meant that their intention of listening to their neighbors naturally made their attitudes humble.

The attitude of maintaining humility also included the dimensions of *respecting* neighbors' positions. For example, Participant J regarded communicating with the neighbor as "thinking once in the other's position."[18] This was in particular evident in terms of their relationships with their local governments or civil society organizations. This attitude was also somehow related to the attitude of *learning* from the other. For example, one participant mentioned that he tried to treat students whom he served as better than himself and learn from them in the process of communication, regardless of their age.[19]

Remaining Open

All personal interview participants and all focus groups expressed several references to "remaining open" in Korean in terms of relationship and conversation, although they can be all translated only as "open" in English. These references meant that participants were open to whatever

---

18. This was recorded in the interview.
19. This was recorded in the focus group interview.

their neighbors spoke. This open attitude did not mean that participants had to abandon or give up their own viewpoints in listening to their neighbors. This attitude, rather, meant that they were *ready to listen* to whatever their neighbors said with respect. In this sense, participants had tried to listen to and pay attention to the neighbor with an open mind, as follows:

> Our congregation as a faith community should always live together with the poor with an open mind and all members keep awake in order to listen to and respond to the requests of our neighbors. (Participant H)

> I need to take more interest in and open my ears to the neighborhood . . . get ready to meet the alderman or the representative of the local government, whenever they come. (Participant K))

> The door of our congregation has been always opened [in terms of communicating with its neighbors.] (Participant O)

The attitude of *remaining open* is related to participants' *skill/method* of "providing open spaces" in order to listen to their neighbors, as we see below. The latter seemed to result from a direct reflection of the former.

Many participants, in the same vein, emphasized *recognizing* and *acknowledging* otherness. Here are a few examples:

> So, apart from whether you believe in Jesus or not, from the standpoint of mutually understanding that there are people on this earth with these thoughts, and people on this earth with those thoughts, I believe we should not be hostile toward one another even if others believe in other religions. . . . I don't think that just because this is the case I should reject a certain god that another person believes in, or that person's life itself. I believe that we must recognize one another and coexist with one another. (Participant F))

> I think we can communicate with those who are similar . . . the other who is different from me . . . different from me in many different conditions . . . it is faith that we accept this other. (Participant G)

This attitude seemed to include the attitude of being ready to listen to whoever the other is and trying to accept whatever the other requests. For instance, Participant C tried to listen to a female shaman's request for fixing her house, although he knew that her house was probably used for worshipping gods. Shamans are generally regarded as enemies of Christianity or Satan's children in Korea. The attitude of remaining open thus appeared to have a dimension of *flexibility* to be interrupted or change existing plans in the process of listening to the neighbor.

Maintaining Empathic Attention

All personal interview participants and all focus groups treated *maintaining empathic attention* or *attentive empathy* as crucial in the process of listening to their neighbors. The reason why I chose the expression *empathic attention* is that it emphasized the need for paying attention to both their neighbors' physical needs and emotional pain with empathy rather than judgment in this process. The Oxford English Dictionary defines "empathy" as "the power of projecting one's personality into (and so fully comprehending) the object of contemplation" in psychological terms.[20] Simply put, empathy can be regarded as sensitive to the other's feelings. The Oxford English Dictionary defines "attention" as "earnest direction of the mind, consideration, or regard" in relation to attitude.[21] This means to attend to the comfort or pleasure of the other. The reason why I bind *empathy* and *attention* in one category "empathic attention" (or attentive empathy) is that participants focused on both their neighbors' mental and material needs with empathy.

Participants seemingly agreed that this dimension of *empathic attention* was needed. They thought that most of the marginalized or the poor really wanted to hide their emotional pain, and that their neighbors had the tendency to feel ashamed of their poverty or current social status. For this reason, participants were not concerned with listening to only their neighbors' verbal expressions, but also feelings beneath them. They tried to wait until their neighbors were ready to share their stories. They wanted to be empathic listeners while their neighbors spoke about their pain and weaknesses. Examples are:

> We very often cried when visiting [the elderly] to fix their homes. (Participant C)
>
> [Communicating with our neighbors] is to apprehend their mental and economical state and situations. (Participant H)

---

20. *Oxford English Dictionary*, s.v. "empathy," http://www.oed.com/view/Entry/61284?redirectedFrom=empathy& (accessed April 15, 2013).

21. Ibid., s.v. "attention," http://www.oed.com/view/Entry/12802?redirectedFrom=attention#eid (accessed April 15, 2013).

> Mission . . . isn't that we judge them, but that we accept and listen to their lives and listen to their pain. (Participant N)
>
> I am one who plays a role as listener because people want to speak. I am aware that I'd rather listen to them when seeing that they want to speak. They seem to get many things simply through this. (Group B)
>
> They [who aren't cared for by their parents] don't want us to give something [material], but listen to them. (Group F)

Participants thus were empathically concerned with both material and mental dimensions related to their neighbors' needs.

Taken together, the three sub-categories of attitude, that is, *maintaining humility*, *remaining open*, and *maintaining empathic attention*, simultaneously worked together in the process of listening to the neighbor. These three cannot be sharply distinguished from one another, as seen above. We cannot think of one of them without consideration of the other two in listening to the neighbor. Participants tended to understand humility in relation to openness and empathy. Openness also began with humility and empathy toward the other. Empathic attention somehow meant that participants were truly open to feel the pain of their neighbors in the process of humbly listening to them. Furthermore, the category of attitude seemed to be influenced by the above primary categories of *knowledge/view* and *motive/purpose*, but not *vice versa*.

Skill/Method

The category "skill/method" has the following three subcategories: using personal/organizational relationships, providing open spaces, and utilizing feedback/media. The reason these categories are identified as skill/method is that this research is not primarily concerned with personal listening, but congregational listening to the neighbor. The category of *skill/method* is contingent on the above primary categories: *knowledge/view*, *motive/purpose*, and *attitude*.

Using Personal/Organizational Relationships

All personal interview participants and all focus groups acknowledged that their personal and/or organizational relationships helped participants listen to their neighbors. These relationships were operative as a medium for listening to participants' neighbors as follows:

[We] have had relationships with organizations, such as schools and community centers, and continued to communicate with them. (Participant B)

Have conversations with those whom I met on the way of coming and going, while exercising, or through other parents of the schools [where my kids go to]. (Participant J)

Recently, one of the representative programs is "Food Bank." . . . God provided us with it, [which was] a chance. The representative of the "Sharing and Joy" came and asked us to help small congregations in order to needy people in this region . . . the Food Bank program came to begin. (Participant K)

They take requests from the local residents to select target houses, from heads of local areas, and so on, and also from the members of our church who feel that they really want to help fix up this or that house in the neighborhood. Requests are brought to the center with those kinds of people acting as the grapevine, and the center then sends out people to inspect the houses and so on, and I think that such services will also act as our outreach channels. (Group A)

. . . through the pastor [of a big neighboring congregation], heads of *Tongs* or *Bans* [subdivisions of a city in Korea]. (Group D)

In particular, many participants seemed to think that their congregations' long-term relationships with their neighborhood via their local services led their neighbors to offer *trust* between their congregations and their neighbors. Their neighbors knew that their services were not directly used simply as a means for church growth and, as such, did not doubt these research participant congregations' authenticity or sincerity related to their services. Participants took for granted that their neighbors expect them to listen to them. Organizational relationships were relatively official conduits of listening to their neighbors, while private relationships were somehow unofficial channels in the process of listening.

Using these relationships to listen to their neighbors was contingent on the above three primary categories: knowledge/view, motive/purpose, and attitude. In detail, their relationships were the result of their knowledge/view regarding church, neighbor, mission, and context. Their motive/purpose for listening to their neighbors led them to use their relationships with their neighbors in the process of listening. Using personal/organizational relationships can be understood as exterior, synthetic expression of their attitude toward their neighbors in the process of listening.

Providing Open Spaces

All personal interview participants and all focus groups considered *providing open spaces* as important in regard to listening and communication. "Open" appeared to include the meanings of *breaking down walls, lowering thresholds,* or placing no limitations in both physical and psychological terms. Participants also referred to the concept of "spaces" in both physical and psychological terms. They similarly tended to understand social service programs as spaces between their neighbors and themselves. Examples are as follows:

> . . . heard our neighbors' praise [about us] through diverse programs [which we provided]. (Participant A)
>
> Personally speaking, the church should have no threshold [boundaries]. (Participant N)
>
> If churches open many cultural centers, cafes, sports centers . . . residents naturally come there and communicate with one another. . . . We can listen to them. (Group B)
>
> When I came to church, I thought of some people [I saw] in the church as members . . . [they] weren't our members. . . . Neighbors felt free to come and go to the church. (Group D)
>
> We have always left the door open. For example, our congregation has run a counseling program for long time. (Group E)

Providing open spaces seemed to be influenced by participants' knowledge/view, motive/purpose, and attitude regarding their listening to the neighbor. For example, providing open spaces resulted from participants' reflections of their context and mission. Their motive/purpose led them to offer open spaces to their neighbors in the process of listening. This is closely related to the attitude of remaining open. In addition, providing spaces meant that research participant congregations showed their empathy and consideration for their neighbors' poor status. Their neighbors did not usually have enough spaces to live and some of them were hardly able to pay for even the rent in their urban setting.

Utilizing Feedback/Media

All participants talked about the importance of utilizing feedback (including surveys and conferences) or media, such as newspapers, websites, and social networks, in order to listen to their neighbors.[22] Media was mostly used for accepting feedback, along with providing information regarding what their congregations were doing. The primary purpose of feedback aimed at improving existing programs and services for the neighborhood. This process was also open toward the neighbor's other opinions which were not directly related to its primary purpose. Regarding feedback, participants used both oral and written feedback. Examples are as follows:

> We have utilized feedback to listen to the reflections of the residents who have taken participated in events which our church has provided. (Participant A)
>
> Community consciousness research or surveys of residents' needs were conducted to evaluate our existing programs and whether or not our congregation should keep providing, or if we received other requests from them [residents] . . . what kind of programs would available . . . these were the processes of getting feedback. (Participant E)
>
> [We] sometimes conducted researches of this region . . . held conferences regarding [using] facilities. (Participant M)
>
> So we made an all-round survey, taking the Korean Language School of a Theological Seminary in [a city in Korea] as our model. (Group A)
>
> . . . we conducted research. (Group D)

Several participants also used diverse media to listen to the neighbor.[23] Such participants tended to understand that media would play a more central role in listening to their neighbors. All research participant congregations also had used their own websites for both themselves and their social services and programs in order to listen to their neighbors. Examples are:

> Before, the paper had some neighborhood characteristics. From an aspect of listening to the voices of neighborhoods, M News

---

22. Except Participants C and O.
23. They were Participants B, D, E, F, G, and J, and Groups A, B, and C.

was a little better.... Now there are many pages. But the number of pages used to be small.... Because of this it really had the feel of a neighborhood newspaper. (Participant F)

Then, he opened a space for learning about the business related to the society on Facebook. I took part in it and encouraged him.... Those who were interested in what he suggested came to join in Café Humanities to discuss. (Participant G)

Relatively speaking, New Community seemed to utilize media more actively than Heavenly Creek and Holy Hill.

Utilizing feedback/media was directly related to participants' knowledge/view. For example, feedback questions seemed to depend on their knowledge/view regarding church, neighbor, context, and mission. This subcategory was also concerned with serving their motive/purpose in the process of listening to the neighbor, as seen above. Utilizing feedback/media seemed to be contingent on their attitude toward their neighbors. This process could be caused by maintaining humility, as long as it focused on accepting neighbors' viewpoints. It could be regarded as a result of remaining open, as long as it sought to accept neighbors' opinions outside feedback questions. It seemed to reflect the attitude of maintaining empathic attention in that it focused on reflecting neighbors' mental and physical needs.

Outcomes

The category "outcomes" was emergent in response to the result of listening to the neighbor. This category contains the following three subcategories: *learning from the neighbor/process, mutual/reciprocal communication and relationship*, and *new missional events*. They were dependent on one another. In other words, one did not seem to work without the other two. The first two sub-categories seemed to be consistent results of the listening process, while the last sub-category tended to be inconsistent results of listening to the neighbor. However, they can be understood as new missional events. The previous primary categories resulted in the category of *outcomes*, while the latter tended to provide the former with new information, view, knowledge, direction, and so on.

LEARNING FROM THE NEIGHBOR/PROCESS

Learning from the neighbor/process was identified as a subcategory of the category *outcomes*. This is because all personal interview participants and all focus groups mentioned that they learned from their neighbors and/or the process of listening to them. Many participants were sure that their neighbors also were learned and/or transformed through the process of communication. Examples are:

> [the Spirit] led me to learn from Jesus [in the process of communicating with the neighbor]. (Participant H)

> What did the children need? Although programs were important. . . . What was true love [for them]? Consoling [them] and feeling empathy [for them]. (Participant N)

> . . . saw their [the elderly's] transformation, I became aware that I would be able to continually challenge and do something, although I'm getting older. (Group B)

> When I first visited children's homes [which weren't cared by their parents due to economic incapability or absence of parents], [they] didn't open their hearts or open even their doors. . . . Now, they opened their mouths and began talking with me . . . they wished somebody would have listened to them . . . then they don't want us to give something, but listen to them. That's all. (Group F)

Learning from the neighbor/process appeared to influence a *mutual/reciprocal communication and relationship* and *new missional events*, and *vice versa*. For instance, participants' mutual relationship with their neighbor could be understood as a dimension of their learning from their neighbors or the process of listening to their neighbors. This category also seemed to be directly contingent on the primary category of attitude—maintaining humility, remaining open, and maintaining empathic attention. For instance, participants could learn from the neighbor/process because they maintained humility toward their neighbors in the process of listening. This subcategory also appeared to be influenced by the other primary categories: knowledge/view and motive/purpose. For instance, their views of God led them to interpret that God could teach them through their neighbors. Their purpose of making the local community better helped them learn from their neighbors and the process of listening. Conversely, what participants learned from their neighbors or the process of listening transform or develop their knowledge/view, motive/purpose, attitude, and skill/method.

Mutual/Reciprocal Communication and Relationship

All personal interview participants and all focus groups expressed that they reached a *mutual/reciprocal communication* and *relationship* through the process of listening to the neighbor. In this regard, communication and relationship seemed to be closely related. The examples of this category are as follows:

> My friends [whom I take care of] are friends with intellectual and developmental disabilities. I first thought they couldn't communicate . . . they can't express . . . they know this person likes me, these people don't like me, treat me in a bad manner, or respect me. I have seen these . . . they come to me to express a sense of intimacy. . . . I am aware that God's love is witnessed in our relationship. Recently, some of them have been getting better, so their non-Christian parents have given me positive reflections. (Participant E)

> [Communication] may not mean that we come to church and have dialogues. Communicating means understanding each other, putting myself in the other's place, considering the other first. . . . I delivered lunch boxes to the elderly, this delivery is just delivery not communication. . . . When I go inside and know the other's situation, understand the current heart of the other, I, too, open my heart. We can communicate each other. (Participant J)

> . . . not a world only for them [or] a league only for them [but] permeating each other with one's own identity. (Group C)

Participants listening to their neighbors were an essential part of communication with their neighbors. Participants understood that their relationships with their neighbors became more mutual and reciprocal. For example, their neighbors seemed to ask for help without hesitation. They and their neighbors also expected further communications with each other. The research congregations' personal or organizational communications with their neighbors thus seemed to lead many neighbors to draw near and be opened toward them in relational terms. This subcategory was closely interrelated with the other two: learning from the neighbor/process and new missional events, as discussed earlier. In this sense, the relationship between this subcategory and the other primary categories seemed to be almost the same as the category of *learning from the neighbor* was related to these categories. The former was a result of the latter, while the former enabled the latter to transform and develop.

New Missional Events

All three congregations shared a similar experience related to the process of listening to the neighbor. All personal interview participants (except Participant F) and all focus groups shared unexpected events through the result of this listening process. I identified these unexpected events with a category of "new missional events." Examples are as follows:

> Later, the female shaman whose house we fixed recommended others and those who came to her to go to our congregation if they wanted to go to church. As a result, a person came to our congregation. (Participant C)

> *We didn't think about it [Stump Ministry] before* . . . we were told about it. In so doing, we had conversations with moms of kids in different kinds of difficult situations . . . had several meetings with the manager of the Welfare Center and those who were interested in youth . . . invited those who were well-known about this issue and know-how . . . we have undertaken it [Stump Ministry] since the beginning of this year.[24] (Participant L)

> *It was really unexpected, and our church had never actually planned it* when we founded the school, even the pastor himself. Had it not all come by way of conducting some survey on the local residents, while circulating a newspaper? This knowledge indicates that there were many illiterate people among us. And thus it followed that we committed to serving the regional community once again—once again for the local residents. Then it would also open the way for evangelism.[25] (Group A)

In a narrower sense, it was surely apparent that they did not always experience missional events via listening to their neighbors. I, however, understand that *learning from the neighbor/process* and *mutual and/or reciprocal communication* and *relationship* could be regarded as missional events in a broader sense. These two sub-categories also seemed to pave the way for missional events. Those who experienced missional events

24. Emphasis added.
25. Emphasis added.

had a tendency to be opened to new missional events. The relationship between this subcategory and the other primary categories seemed to be almost the same as the other sub-categories of *outcomes* were related to those primary categories, as discussed earlier.

Leadership

The primary category "leadership" emerged from the data. Leadership seemed to be involved in all stages of the listening process. Leadership consisted of the following two subcategories: *the primary role of the lead pastor* and *internal communication*.

The Primary Role of the Lead Pastor

The data evidenced that the lead pastor played a primary role in the whole listening process. All personal interview participants and all focus groups mentioned explicitly and implicitly that their lead pastors had a significant impact on their listening to their neighbors. Their lead pastors provided them with teachings, perspectives, visions, ideas, encouragement, and the like. *Inter alia*, most participants mentioned that their lead pastors' teachings regarding how to relate to the neighbor encouraged them to listen to the neighbor. We can see this as follows:

> I think we shouldn't accuse them of their lives, but accept, pay attention to, and listen to their sorrows and suffering . . . it is the mission that the lead pastor emphasizes. (Participant N)

> [The lead] pastor always, tons of times, says to us, "Always do [your neighbors] a favor, or share." I thus try to do even what brings disadvantage and accept disadvantage. (Group B)

It seems natural for all participants to take seriously their lead pastor's leadership. This is because they, regardless of the styles of their congregations' organizations and leaderships, had a common agreement that the lead pastor was at the heart of leadership as follows:

> I think it is important to focus on the lead pastor, embrace the perspective of his pastoral ministry. (Participant A)

> Anyway, the lead pastor founded this congregation. . . . We have been educated through the lead pastor's preaching, since it was founded. (Group C)

> I feel like the Session has supported the lead pastor's primary interests of ministry, too. (Group E)

All three lead pastors seemingly tried to become a good example of attitude toward their neighbors by maintaining humility, remaining open, and maintaining empathic attention. This was apparent because all three lead pastors also played a role as key listeners and communicators in terms of organizational relationships with their local governments and civil society organizations. They readily accepted what they learned from the listening process to their neighbors. They provided their congregational members with their theological interpretations regarding new missional events.

Internal Communication

Internal communication was identified as a subcategory of leadership. All personal interview participants (except Participants F, J, and O) and Focus Group A, B, C, and D talked about their internal communications throughout the listening process. Given the primary role of the lead pastor, *internal communication* tended to be pastor-oriented. They took for granted such a tendency. Personal dialogue and regular group meetings were the two primary tools for internal communications. The following examples illustrate this category:

> each program has a monthly meeting of volunteers and an evaluation meeting per semester to discuss one another's thoughts. The pastor in charge of [our congregation's local service] participates in such meetings. He listens to all they say . . . since we do our work according to [the lead pastor's pastoral policy], he accepts what can be accepted to such extent. (Participant D)

> [What the leadership emphasizes] is preferably continuous dialogue and organizational structure of communication. (Participant H)

> So I told this to our pastor, and he said "What percentage of people in the region really are illiterate? Could you make a survey? A young mother in her thirties really is illiterate?" So we made an all-round survey . . . that's how we came to open our own school. (Group A)

This category seemed to be contingent on the primary role of the lead pastor. This is because the lead pastor also played a central role in the process of internal communication. For example, Participant A said that "it is important to focus on the lead pastor, embrace the perspective of his pastoral ministry," as noted earlier.[26] Relatively speaking, internal communications tended to be related to the primary categories of attitude, skill/method, and outcomes, while the primary role of the lead pastor was concerned with the primary categories of knowledge/view and motive/purpose.

Considering the above, leadership appeared to have significant relationships with impact on other primary categories, that is, *knowledge/view, motive/purpose, attitude, skill/method*, and *outcomes*. Leadership seemed to play a key role in providing congregational members with *knowledge/view* and *motive/purpose* in the process of listening to their neighbors. Conversely, the latter appeared to shape the role and contents of leadership. Leadership was concerned with maintaining good *attitudes* appropriate to the process of listening to the neighbor and had an impact on deciding *skills* or *methods* for better listening. *Attitude* and *skill/method*, likewise, influenced leadership when leaders took part in listening to the neighbor. *Leadership* and *outcomes* seemed to influence each other. On the one hand, leadership influenced *outcomes* to the extent that *knowledge/view, motive/purpose, attitude, skill/method* had effect on *outcomes*. One the other hand, *outcomes* drew new changes and new perspectives to *leadership*. Leadership provided information and perspectives related to listening to the neighbor prior to listening, helped members to keep focused while listening to the neighbor, and reflect on outcomes after this listening.

DEVELOPING A GROUNDED THEORY

We discovered the following six primary categories: "knowledge/view," "motive/purpose," "attitude," "skill/method," "outcomes," and "leadership." The first category of *knowledge/view* contains "church," "neighbor," "mission," and "context" as subcategories. Church and neighbor influenced each other, as did mission and context. The first two subcategories were influenced by the last two.

The second category of *motive/purpose* contains "better serving the neighbor," "making their local communities better," and "carrying out mission" as subcategories. The first two subcategories seemed direct and concrete, whereas the last one appeared indirect, but essential. The first

---

26. This was recorded in the interview.

subcategory, on the one hand, showed the *asymmetrical* dimension of the relationship between the research congregations and their neighbors; on the other hand, the second subcategory was related to the *symmetrical* aspect of this relationship.

The third category of *attitude* consists of the following subcategories: "maintaining humility," "remaining open," and "maintaining empathic attention." These three subcategories influenced one another. The fourth category of *skill/method* contains the following subcategories: "using personal/organizational relationships," "providing open spaces," and "utilizing feedback/media."

The fifth category of *outcomes* includes "learning from the neighbor/process," "mutual/reciprocal communication and relationship," and "new missional events." The first two subcategories, on the one hand, appeared to be consistent results of the research congregations' listening to their neighbors compared to the last subcategory, which was inconsistent. On the other hand, the first two could be understood as new missional events as long as their listening to their neighbors was ongoing and missional. Three subcategories seemed to depend on each other in this regard.

The sixth category of *leadership* consists of "the primary role of the lead pastor" and "internal communications." The latter appeared to be contingent on the former.

The research findings showed diverse relationships among six primary categories.

1. The category of knowledge/view influenced all other five categories, whereas the categories of leadership and outcomes only had an impact on the category of knowledge/view.
2. The category of motive/purpose influenced the categories of attitude, skill/method, outcomes, and leadership, while it was contingent on the categories of knowledge/view, outcomes, and leadership.
3. The category of attitude was influenced by the categories of knowledge/view, motive/purpose, outcomes, and leadership, whereas it had an impact on the categories of skill/method, outcomes, and leadership.
4. The category of skill/method influenced the categories of outcomes and leadership, while all others, including the category of outcomes and leadership, had an impact on this.

5. The category of *outcomes* resulted from all other categories, while the former tended to shape the latter anew by bringing new information or insights.
6. Both the category of leadership and all other categories seemed to have an influence on each other.

The research findings, furthermore, indicated that listening to the neighbor could not be defined by a fixed, static concept, but displayed an ongoing process as long as the research congregations sought to get missionally involved in their neighborhoods. However, it did not appear to be a *simple linear* process, but an *intricate, multifaceted*, and *integrated* process. This process seemed to be distinguishable into the three distinct, but inseparable phases: *pre-listening, present-listening*, and *post-listening*. I regarded *knowledge/view* and *motive/purpose* as the phase of pre-listening, *attitude* and *skill/method* as the phase of present-listening, and *outcomes* as the phase of post-listening. Leadership was involved throughout all phases of listening. These three phases were continually *sequential* as well as *cyclical*. This process also tended to be *developmental* because the category of outcomes seemingly included aspects of learning and provided all other categories with new information or insights.

Based on the above, I propose the following theory (see figure 1): (1) the process of the church's listening to the neighbor is a missional activity as long as it is a part of its missional engagement in its neighborhood and God is the subject of this. In addition, this process is also based on the fact that outcomes of this process could be regarded as missional events, as seen above. (2) The process of listening has six categories: *knowledge/view, motive/purpose, attitude, skill/method, outcomes,* and *leadership*. (3) This process has three distinct, inseparable phases (pre-listening, present-listening, and post-listening) and is sequential, cyclical, and developmental. (4) It is an intricate, integrated, multifaceted, and ongoing process, given the diverse relationships among the primary categories.

Figure 1: The Process of Listening to the Neighbor

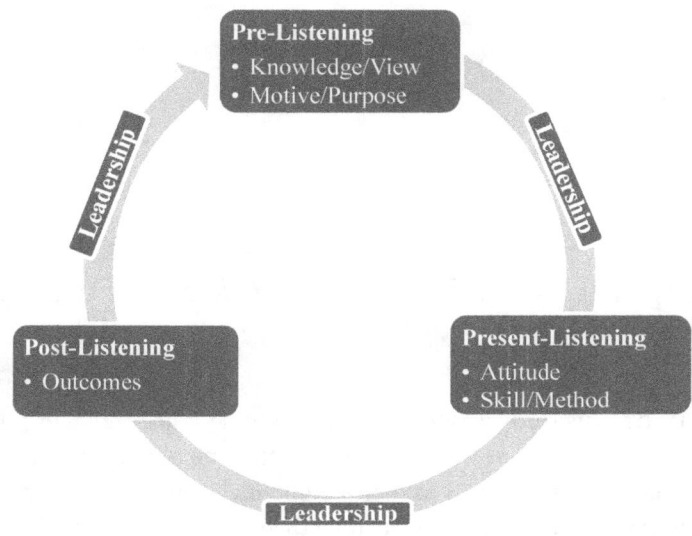

CONCLUSION

This chapter dealt with the participant profiles of Heavenly Creek, New Community, and Holy Hill, and the analysis of data. As a result of analysis, we reached the following research findings: (1) the research congregations' listening to their neighbors was a missional activity as long as it was a part of their missional involvement in their neighborhoods and God was the subject of this. (2) This was an intricate, integrated, multifaceted, and ongoing process. (3) This process had six primary categories (knowledge/view, motive/purpose, attitude, skill/method, outcomes, and leadership). (4) It had the following three phases: pre-listening (knowledge/view and motive/purpose), present-listening (attitude and skill/method), and post-listening (outcomes), whereas leadership appeared to be involved throughout the whole listening process. (5) It was also both sequential and cyclical while also being developmental. I concretize the emergent theory of listening to the neighbor in what follows by undertaking a dialogue between the research findings and the sensitizing concepts and relevant literature.

5

Theoretical Reflections on the Research Findings

THE AIM OF THIS study was to develop a grounded theory that explained how PCK congregations which had served their neighbors via local mission/social services listened to their neighbors. Chapter 4 presented the data findings and analysis allowing for a theory to be constructed regarding the aim of this study. This chapter draws on the data and relevant literature to discuss, reflect, and develop the theory further. It also undertakes a dialogue between the results of data analysis and theoretical sensitizing concepts presented in chapter 3. This chapter also deals with other literature related to the results of the data analysis in the process.

GADAMER AND LEVINAS: HERMENEUTICS OF THE OTHER

This section addresses hermeneutical reflection on the research congregations' understandings of the other/neighbor. In so doing, we focus on Gadamer's and Levinas's hermeneutics of the other.

Gadamer and Listening to the Other

Gadamer contends that understanding is produced through the conversation between the text/reader or speaker/listener. Gadamer assumes that we cannot converse with the other without the medium of language, which is inherent in all human beings.[1] The logos inherent in being, through which we participate, is "bound up with language."[2] He also

---

1. Gadamer, *Truth and Method*, 417.
2. Ibid., 417.

understands that language is essentially relational. Gadamer takes into account that hermeneutics essentially entails one's conversation with the other or the text. Listening to the other is necessary in the process of conversation. Gadamer understands that human relations essentially cannot be possible without the process of understanding and, as such, the mediation of the conversation, as we shall see.

Gadamer posits that hermeneutics aims at coming to an understanding through a conversational encounter with the other. Gadamer, in this regard, employs a game metaphor to explain the meaning of *coming to an understanding*. The subject of the game is not the players, but its play. The game accordingly has its meaning within the ongoing interplay of players. However, the game does not have the only true or correct meaning, but rather, continually produces relative meanings according to particular players and particular situations. Players who participate in the game within a particular situation have shared meanings in the process. They can be somehow regarded as a community of such shared meanings. This game metaphor sheds light on Gadamer's notions of conversation and hermeneutics, such as the primary roles of pre-understanding, fusions of horizons, relativity and temporality of understanding, and human belonging together within shared meanings.

When the research congregations listened to their neighbors, they started this process with their own *knowledge/view* regarding *church*, *neighbor*, *mission*, and *context* as discussed in chapter 4. Gadamer calls this "prejudice" (fore-understanding).[3] Gadamer asserts that human beings cannot help but enter into any dialogical situation with their own prejudices, because they are conditioned by their own individual and social histories or historical horizons of traditions. These horizons are bound up in such dimensions as gender, age, religion, socio-economic class, education, and so on. *Prejudice* literally means fore-judgment, indicating all the assumptions required to make a claim of knowledge. Gadamer regards prejudice as neither positive nor negative in understanding the other. Instead, prejudice is an inevitable feature of all human understanding. Gadamer views prejudice as the starting point and the very source of our knowledge. This indicates that research participants approached their neighbors based on their pre-understandings of them and their contexts. Participants' pre-understandings of mission and church were operative in the process. Such pre-understandings worked to

---

3. Ibid., 268–306.

shape the motive/purpose, attitude, skill/method, outcomes, and leadership in the process of listening to their neighbors. Outcomes appeared to constitute new pre-understandings for the next process of listening. Their neighbors, too, tended to get involved in the research congregations' services and relationships with their own positive pre-understandings of the research congregations and their mission.

Gadamer takes for granted that human relationships are essentially produced only through conversations, as noted above, insofar as one's being is elementarily linguistic. Gadamer also emphasizes that listening to the other is required as long as a conversation is necessary in the process of understanding. Relationships between the research congregations and their neighbors, in this sense, must be produced through conversations, whether these conversations were actively undertaken or not. The research congregations' listening to their neighbors would seem very natural to Gadamer. The results of the data analysis also evidenced that research participant congregations were primarily concerned with listening to their neighbors in the process of their interactions with them.

Gadamer contends that a conversation is possible in that both parties consider each other to be their conversational partner. They are *equal* in this process. This notion leads Gadamer to discuss listening to the other with openness toward the other. We need to take a careful look at Gadamer's concept of *a fusion of horizons* to understand this more fully. Our understanding is essentially possible because we are historically within a tradition and ground in a *historically-effected consciousness*. We, thus, bring our epistemic horizon to the other to understand the subject matter (or truth) of the conversation. We cannot transpose ourselves into the horizon of the other to understand what the other says, because human beings do not have an objective epistemic horizon. The Gadamerian concept of *fusion* presumes that there is a distance or otherness between conversational partners. Our understanding, in detail, starts with acknowledging the horizon of the other, as well as our own horizons. This also means one's "acknowledging the otherness of the [other]."[4] As a result of this fusing of horizons, a new expanding horizon emerges for all parties related to the process of understanding. This leads to new possibilities and new levels of understanding that did not exist before the conversation began. This also means that understanding necessitates that all horizons will change. Therefore, listening to the other is involved

---

4. Ibid., 302.

in openness to the other by opening up spaces and even accepting some things that are against us.

Gadamer *partly* credits the Buberian notion of the I-Thou relation in terms of mutual relationship.[5] However, Gadamer points out that such a notion fails to acknowledge that I and Thou are "situated within a tradition."[6] The I-Thou relation seems to limit mutual relationship to a narrow inter-subjectivity between the two. This is because the I-Thou relation does not embrace the tradition, which includes broader bonds across society. What is worse, one who does not consider the subject matter of the conversation in light of tradition may dominate this relation by claiming that he/she understands the other.[7] Gadamer claims that this may be the case in "charitable or welfare work."[8] Therefore, "the openness to tradition characteristic of historically effected consciousness" leads to openness with each other and a "genuine human bond."[9] Both parties are *equal* and *symmetrical* as long as they seek to come to an understanding.

I, in a similar sense, conducted interviews by addressing participants as his equal conversational partners. I was open to participants' understandings regarding the research topic, continuing to search for new possible interpretations. Most research participants, too, understood to some degree their neighbors as their conversational partners, while some participants in the research congregations did not. They showed *openness* to their neighbors in terms of their *attitude* and *skill/method*. They tried to listen to their neighbors with an open mind and provided them with open spaces in both physical and psychological terms. Most research participants understood their congregations as "an open congregation," "a congregation without wall," "a congregation with a lower threshold," and the like.[10] Their understanding of openness is to allow their neighbors to speak to them and be willing to learn something new from their neighbors or in their listening process.

---

5. David Vessey argues that Gadamer critically accepted the Buber's I-Thou accounts of intersubjectivity. See Vessey, "Gadamer's Account of Friendship as an Alternative to an Account of Intersubjectivity," 61–67; However, Gadamer does not mention explicitly Buber in dealing with the I-Thou accounts in *Truth and Method*. See Gadamer, *Truth and Method*, 351–353.

6. Ibid., 354.

7. Ibid.

8. Ibid.

9. Ibid., 355.

10. These originate from interview transcripts.

Gadamer maintains that every conversation is primarily concerned with the subject matter (or truth) of the conversation rather than conversational partners, as he shows through the game metaphor. Both conversational partners have shared meanings in the process of conversation, which is a reciprocal interplay. They participate together in the community of such meanings. Gadamer holds that this conversational relationship leads both partners to a mutual relationship—solidarity. Gadamer considers *coming to an understanding* in a conversation to be "transformed into a *communion* in which we do not remain what we were."[11] Conversation partners *belong to* such a communion because they equally participate in the subject matter of the conversation.

Gadamer asserts that neither side can dominate the conversation to come to an understanding. Listening to each other means that both conversation partners are open to each other, "belong to and with each other [and] belong to and with the subject of their discussion."[12] From this point of view, *outcomes* as a primary category within the research findings, such as learning from the neighbor/process, mutual/reciprocal communication and relationships, and new missional events, did not result from participants' or their neighbors' monologue, but dialogues between them and their neighbors. Outcomes were not possessed by one party, but were shared practices or meanings between both parties. In a word, outcomes were social constructions shared by both. The research congregations and their neighbors who participated in their social services seemed to be regarded as a community of these shared meanings or practices.

The emergent theory of listening to the neighbor in this study seems to fit to a great extent the Gadamerian hermeneutics, because both are open to further growth. A conversation necessitates listening to the other, as long as it seeks to come to an understanding and a reciprocal relationship. Gadamer views the process of coming to an understanding in a conversation as the process of making sense of the subject matter or meaning of the conversation in a particular situation. Understanding, thus, is continually interpretive, temporal, and developmental in terms of the hermeneutical cycle. The theory says that listening to the neighbor is

---

11. Ibid., 371. Emphasis added.

12. Ibid., xv–xvi, 355. In this regard, Gadamer emphasizes that the German terms *gehören* or *hören*, equivalent to "listen to" in English, include the meaning "to obey." Once we listen to what the other says, we belong to its subject matter.

a process of a sequential, cyclical, and developmental process, just as the Gadamerian hermeneutics suggests.

Participants entered into the process of listening to their neighbors with their pre-understandings about themselves and their neighbors. Listening to the neighbor led research participants and congregations to reach the following *outcomes*: "learning from the neighbor/process," "reciprocal/mutual communication and relationship," and "new missional events." Congregations' listening to their neighbors, in the Gadamerian sense, inseparably embraces openness toward a new horizon. Doubtlessly, this is a learning process. This process empowered reciprocal/mutual communication and relationship between congregations and their neighbors. This listening process furthermore led congregations to engage in new missional relationships, which were not expected to happen. These events brought not only better relationships with the neighbors, but also a more positive attitude of openness to congregations in regard to their communication with their neighbors. Therefore, mission is concretized and changed within a particular situation through congregations' interactions with their neighbors.

Levinas and Listening to the Other

Gadamer's hermeneutics seems to explain well the reciprocal and mutual aspects of research participant congregations' relationships with their neighbors. It assumes that these congregations and their neighbors are equal in the process of conversation and both need to listen to each other. However, it does not adequately address that they tended to listen to their neighbors before their neighbors listened to them or when their neighbors were not interested in relating to them. Their listening to their neighbors in this regard seemed to be *asymmetrical*, unlike Gadamer's reciprocal listening. Levinas's hermeneutics of the other more appropriately deals with such cases because Levinas emphasizes asymmetrical listening.

The data analysis indicated that the research participants tended to view their congregations as churches both *for* and *with* their neighbors. Levinas seems to support the notion of church for the neighbor, while Gadamer would likely support the notion of church with the neighbor. Levinas understands the relationship between the self and the other as asymmetrical. What we first do in the encounter with the other is relate ourselves to the other rather than understand the other. We first pay attention to the other and the otherness of the other. Such attention leads us to be responsible for the other and to serve the other. There are asymmetrical and unequal relations between the self as listener and the other as speaker. This is because the other's speech takes primacy in these relations and the self plays a role mainly as listener. Levinas thus seems to support that the church essentially exists for the other and should be primarily a listener in relations to its neighbors.

Levinas posits that the other is not simply another self or a being who is the same as the self. The other transcends the self's conceptual categories. This is because the other is not an object to be observed, measured, or understood. Levinas distances himself from the totalizing tendencies of western philosophy based on an ontological frame. The other is other than being. Western philosophy prioritizes knowledge of the self with regard to the other and ontology, which is concerned with the unity of being over the ethical relationship. The other is reduced to an object of knowledge and the otherness of the other is not given attention. However, Levinas highlights that the otherness of the other transcends the horizons of the self-centered thought and the conceptual and logical structure of language.

The metaphor of face is at the heart of Levinas's hermeneutics of the other in terms of the emphasis on radical otherness—*alterity*.[13] There are various reasons why Levinas uses the *face* to emphasize the otherness of the other. The face indicates the particular individual in front of the self. This face is too unique and specific to be generalized into the ontological categories of the self. The face of the other has transcendent and infinite dimensions. Levinas regards the face as the most naked part in the body, as compared with other parts covered by clothes. The face has absolute vulnerability in its nakedness.[14] Levinas symbolically relates the face of the other to the face of "the poor," "the orphan," "the widow," "the stranger," and the like.[15] When encountering the face of the other, we have no time to think about who or what the other is, and, instead, we recognize an urgent command to respond. Levinas explains such a command coming from the face by drawing on the primordial expression:

---

13. Levinas, *Totality and Infinity*, 187–219.
14. Ibid., 74–77.
15. Ibid.

"you shall not commit murder."[16] The face of the other *speaks* to us and invites us into a relationship in this way.[17]

Levinas relates the face of the other to a trace of God, in that the face is both infinite and transcendent. Levinas takes issue with Buber's horizontal and reciprocal notion of the I/Thou relation because it does not grasp the transcendent dimension of the other, i.e., alterity. Levinas regards God as "otherwise than being."[18] God is not a being of thematization and objectification. Levinas explains this by using the concept of "*illeity*."[19] *Illeity* is a neologism derived from the French *il* for "he" or "it," and from the Latin *ille* for "that one there, at a distance."[20] *Illeity* reflects that while certain Jewish prayers begin addressing God as *Thou*, these end by calling God *He*.[21] Levinas denotes *illeity* as "outside thou and the thematization of objects."[22] *Illeity* illustrates that God passed by and then there is a trace of God in God's absence. Levinas holds that we can experience only a trace of God and our experience of God cannot be represented and generalized. It highlights the *irreversibility* of both time and one's asymmetrical relation with God. In this light, Levinas relates the *illeity* of God to the *illeity* of the other. The face of the other is the limit of the self's experience of the other. The self cannot know what is hidden in the other, behind and beyond the other's face. The other is infinite and transcendent, as is God. We, in this regard, can listen to the voice of God in indirect ways of listening to the face of the other—the poor, the widow, the orphan, the stranger, etc.

Levinas holds that there is the third party alongside one's relationship with the other. This means that I, too, am the other to someone. The third party, as a person who is not the other, simultaneously relates to me while I relate to the other.[23] The third party is responsible for me. The entry of *a third party* allows me to "become an other like the others."[24] This entry causes imbalance to become balanced and reciprocity to become possible, and, as such, "[others] have responsibility for me just as

16. Ibid., 199.
17. Ibid., 198.
18. Levinas, *Otherwise than Being*.
19. Levinas, "Trace in the Other," 345–59.
20. Levinas, *Ethics and Infinity*, 177.
21. Chung, *Cave and Butterfly*, 199.
22. Levinas, *Otherwise than Being*, 12. Emphasis in original.
23. Levinas, *Totality and Infinity*, xli.
24. Ibid., 160–61.

I have for them."[25] The presence of a third party indicates that there are many others beside the other. There are lots of third parties beyond the relationship between I and the other. Simply put, Levinas's notion of the third party presumes that there are always others beyond myself and the other. Levinas maintains that the presence of God as *illeity* in the face of all human beings enables third parties to enter one's relationship with the other and, thus, enables us to live together for others with responsibility in the society.[26] However, we cannot experience God's presence, but only God's traces in the face of others because God as *illeity* is "not present [but] has always already past."[27]

We can understand, in this light, that there were third parties beside the relationships between the research congregations and their neighbors who were engaged in their social services. This may mean that each of them can be both the other to someone and a third party in encountering one's relation with others in the Levinasian sense. For instance, many personal interview participants said that new members came to their congregations because they heard from others about those who benefited from social services of those congregations. Other neighbors seemed to function as a third party in this regard. Local governments or civil society organizations sometimes appeared to play a role as a third party in terms of the participant congregations' relationships with their neighbors. As third parties, the research congregations also sometimes entered relationships between their local governments or civil society organizations and their neighborhoods. This was possible due to God as *illeity* in our relationships with others in the Levinasian sense. Most participants referred to the entry of the third party which helped them as God's working in process. The Holy Spirit, from a missional perspective, may help the research congregations through third parties when they serve their neighbors. Thus, we may understand the Holy Spirit as the essential third party because the Holy Spirit worked not only between the research congregations and their neighborhoods, but also between them and their local organizations or civil society organizations.

Research participants tended to acknowledge that there seemed to exist asymmetrical relations between them and their neighbors in the Levinasian sense. This resulted from the fact that they aimed at serving

---

25. Smith, *The Argument to the Other*, 172–74.
26. Levinas, *Otherwise than Being*, 146–65.
27. Ibid., 148.

their neighbors. They tended to consider themselves as being *one for the other*. All of them agreed that caring for their neighbors was one of their primary responsibilities. They took this for granted because they believed that it reflected the primary teaching of Jesus. Some participants mentioned that they listened to the voice of God by listening to their neighbors. For example, one interview participant said,

> On the one hand, voices of the neighbors would be hollow sounds; however, on the other hand, they sounded like a voice of God. For this reason, [listening to] voices of the neighbors is important in order that the church may be more concerned with its neighbors rather than its greed.[28]

They seemed to accept that God sometimes spoke to them through voices of their neighbors, as Levinas argued earlier.

Both Levinas and Gadamer take seriously the otherness of the other and listening to the other, while Gadamer's notions of these do not seem to be radical enough for Levinas. Gadamer holds that the other's otherness is always open toward possibilities of fusing the self's horizon because the self and the other stand on the same ground—language—and Gadamer seeks coming to understanding in the encounter with the other. In contrast, Levinas's otherness does not allow such possibilities because it is based on abysmal separation between the self and the other and Levinas is concerned with relating to the other in the encounter with the other. Their different approaches are related to their notions of language. Levinas seemingly regards language as a product of human face-to-face relation, whereas Gadamer tends to treat language as the medium of human relation. Language means an essential ontological basis to Gadamer and, as such, language is related to thinking, comprehending, and understanding.

Gadamer takes for granted that we cannot have relationship with the other without conversation because there cannot be relationship without understanding what the other said. In contrast, Levinas claims that relationship is already begun when encountering with the other. This is because relating to the other is prior to understanding the other. Levinas also views the western notion of language based on ontology as concerned with conveying concepts and limited to including only what the other is saying. Levinas instead holds that language is based on face-to-face relation and, as such, includes the expression of the face, eye gaze,

---

28. This was recorded in the interview with Participant B.

gesture, signs, and so on.[29] Levinas claims that the face speaks beyond the words spoken. Levinas, later, develops the concepts of the *saying* and the *said* in *Otherwise than Being: Or Beyond Essence* via *Totality and Infinity: An Essay on Exteriority*. The saying is regarded as the manifestation of the face of the other in the self's encounter with the other, whereas the said points to and thematizes the saying, and always bears its traces.[30] Levinas emphasizes that the other's face first *speaks* to the self in the encounter with the other. Therefore, listening to the other is a primary response to the other.

Listening to the other is more important to Levinas than Gadamer. Strictly speaking, Levinas does not often explicitly use the expression "listening to the other." However, we can understand a primary response to the other as listening to the other to the extent that Levinas continues to highlight the other who speaks to me. The other is the one who speaks to the self and, as such, the self is not a speaker but a listener in relation to the other. Levinas is primarily concerned with listening to the other as *attentiveness* to concreteness of the other. This listening means to pay attention to the otherness of the other. Paying attention to the other's otherness means to *sense* what the other signifies in the face. Levinas argues that sense precedes meaning and makes meaning possible, and Levinas takes primacy in *sense* over *meaning* in relation to the other.[31] Levinas, in this vein, articulates the concept "listening eye" so as to listen to the face of the other.[32] This is because the poor, the widow, the orphan, and the stranger are usually *silent* and *voiceless*.

Maintaining empathic attention as a subcategory of attitude in the research findings seems similar to Levinas's notion of listening to the

---

29. Levinas, *Totality and Infinity*, 182. Levinas argues as follows: "Language does not group symbols into systems, but deciphers the symbols. But when this primordial manifestation of the Other has already taken place, when an existent has *presented* himself and come to the assistance of himself, not only verbal signs but all signs can serve as language. But speech itself does not always find the welcome that ought to be reserved to speech. For it involves non-speech, and can express in the sense that implements, clothing, and gestures express."

30. Levinas, *Otherwise than Being*, 5–16, 34–51, 75–81, 183–84.

31. Levinas, *Basic Philosophical Writings*, 33–64. Levinas addresses "Meaning and Sense" in a chapter of this book, which was originally published as an article in 1964.

32. Levinas, *Otherwise than Being*, 30, 37–38. Levinas uses the other and the neighbor as interchangeable terms more explicitly in this book. He used to refer to the other mainly as "the weak," "the poor," "the widow," "the orphan," "the stranger," and the like in his previous books.

other as paying attention to the otherness of the other. Levinas's listening is primarily concerned with *paying attention* to the other's vulnerability, misery, suffering, etc. This listening is inseparably related to "taking care of the other's need."[33] The research participant congregations, likewise, placed their priorities on paying attention to the poor and marginalized conditions of their neighbors from their early periods. They continued to pay primarily attention to the needs of their neighbors. They developed their *listening eyes* to listen to even the *voiceless speeches* of their neighbors. For example, one congregation published a newspaper to address its neighbors' stories, which were collected by its volunteer reporters. It listened to a young mom who could not read the newspaper, while delivering these newspapers to its neighbors. It conducted research and a survey to listen more carefully regarding her story. It finally opened a school for reading Korean. All participant congregations had a similar tendency to pay attention to their neighbors' needs in this regard. However, empathic dimension of attention seems opposite to Levinas's listening. Empathy can be regarded as one's ability of identifying oneself with others and their situation, while Levinas understands that one cannot stand in the other's position because the other is transcendent.

Levinas's listening to the other has something to do with *learning* from the other because the other is totally different and transcendent. The face of the other continues to bring the alterity and the idea of infinity to us. Levinas regards that "to have the idea of infinity" as "to be taught."[34] What one has to do in conversation with the other is "welcome his [sic] expression and receive teaching from the other."[35] Welcoming the other and the other's otherness, thus, requires being opened toward the other and teachings of the other. It also requires being humble toward the other. One, here, cannot choose such openness toward the other, but it is given by the other, due to the asymmetrical relationship between the other as speaker and oneself as listener.

Levinas's listening as learning seems to be related to the following research findings: maintaining humility and remaining open (subcategories of attitude) and learning from the neighbor/process (a subcategory of outcomes). They seem to emphasize humility, openness, and learning with little consideration of the other's necessary response to their service

---

33. Ibid., 74.
34. Levinas, *Totality and Infinity*, 51.
35. Ibid., 51.

or compensation. However, each of them has some nuanced understandings of humility, openness, and learning. On the one hand, the research findings presented that maintaining humility and remaining open resulted in learning from the neighbor/process. On the other hand, the Levinasian notion of listening as learning seemingly includes dimensions of attitude, skill, and results as to learning. Learning, welcoming, and being open seem to be interchangeable to Levinas. Research participants seem to treat humility, openness, and learning in both active and passive terms, whereas Levinas contends that they are only passively given by the other's otherness.

In conclusion, there seem to be similarities and differences between Gadamer and Levinas. Both value listening to the other. They also pay attention to relational aspects of this listening process. However, there are differences between them. Gadamer posits that the listening process aims at coming to mutual understanding, which is possible because of linguistic mediation. He treats the other as an equal conversational partner and conversation as for the common good between conversational partners. A congregation, in this regard, exists to live together with its neighbors. However, Levinas maintains that listening to the other is necessarily required to serve the other. The self plays a role mainly as listener, while the other plays a role as speaker. The self is responsible for listening to the other, and listening goes *beyond the linguistic dimension*. Levinas regards the other or the neighbor to be the weak, the orphaned, the widowed, the stranger, etc. In the Levinasian sense, a congregation exists to live *for* its neighbors. These two notions regarding the church are apparent within the research results. The participant congregations first regarded themselves as congregations for their neighbors. They, then, became aware of being congregations together with their neighbors through their relationships with them.

OPEN SYSTEMS THEORY: ORGANIZATION AND ENVIRONMENT

OST essentially assumes that organizations are always rooted in particular environments and, as such, are involved in processes of exchange of material, resources, and information with them. OST posits that organizations are open systems which exist for purposes and reasons and are dependent on their environments. OST is primarily concerned with organizations' interaction with their environments. This concern needs to be addressed in terms of the following two dimensions: how to both learn/adapt to and change/control the environment. The degree of turbulence and uncertainty in the organizational environment has a major influence on the internal operations of organizations because organizations seek equilibrium and stability within their environments. There must be a *fit* between organizations and their environments in the face of rapidly changing contexts.[36]

Katz and Kahn articulate organizations' relationships with their environments as a systematic model of cyclical process of input-throughput (transformation)-output.[37] Therefore, improving fit between the environment and the internal components of an organization helps to increase effectiveness and performance in transforming inputs to outputs. Organizations must develop appropriate structures and leadership to cope with their turbulent, complex, and rapidly-changing environments. The research congregations' listening to their neighbors can be regarded as a process of both seeking fit between the research congregations and their environments and preparing ministries and structures in responding to challenges due to environmental changes, as we see below.

The research findings evidence that the three research congregations as open systems have been strongly influenced by their environments. We have seen that *context*, as a subcategory of knowledge/view, has influence on understanding one's congregation, neighbor, and mission, as well as other primary categories (motive/purpose, attitude, skill/method, outcomes, and leadership). Research participants definitely understood their congregations as *local* congregations which have been located in industrial areas and involved in their larger communities. Their definite notions of church seem different from the PCK's general notions of church, which often pay little attention to their locality and interactions with the larger communities. Such locations have influenced all three congregations to get involved in social services for their neighbors. This is because their neighbors in industrial areas have been low-income workers, the uneducated, the poor, the marginalized, poorly-cared-for children, and the like. The research congregations provided their neighbors with open spaces because they were considerate of their neighbors' poor living conditions.

---

36. Hatch, *Organization Theory*, 77–90.
37. Ibid., 121–23.

The research congregations developed their social services by interacting with their environments and larger communities. These services have resulted from adapting and recontextualizing in the face of challenges due to rapid industrialization and urbanization. All three congregations have changed their services according to changes taking place in their environments. For example, they first placed their primary focus caring for the poor and the marginalized in their neighborhood. Recently, urban renewal projects have brought rapid changes to their residential environments and an influx of middle-class residents in economic and cultural terms. These environmental changes have led these congregations to provide more culture-relevant programs.

The research congregations seem to be able to understand the process of listening to their neighbors through the lens of Katz and Kahn's input-transformation-output model in regard to understanding their contexts.[38] They received information of their contexts, together with human/material resources, as inputs from their environments regarding their neighbors as a primary part of their environments. Their leadership interpreted such information by using their pre-knowledge/view regarding church, neighbor, mission, and context and considering their motive/purpose.

Understanding contingency theory and resource dependence theory might enable the research congregations to deal with uncertainties and complexity from their environment.[39] Contingency theory presumes that there is no one best way to structure and manage an organization. Contingency theory seeks to respond appropriately to an organization's on-going environmental changes. Organizations need to be more flexible in changing their structures and approaches. However, Hatch points out that "uncertainty lies not in the environment, but in the individuals who consider the environment when they make organizational decisions."[40] This means that organizations, although even in the same environment, differently interpret and cope with challenges from the environment. It seems apparent for the research congregations to show different interpretations and approaches to their neighborhoods, although they were located in very similar environments—poor, urban, and industrial areas—and had a common listening process toward their neighbors. For

---

38. Van Gelder, *The Ministry*, 135.
39. Hatch, *Organization Theory*, 77–80.
40. Ibid., 78.

example, Heavenly Creek regarded its ministries to serve neighbors as *service for local society* compared to New Community's *local mission* and Holy Hill's *social wellbeing service*.

The respective resources of the research congregations, from a perspective of resource dependence theory, seemed to lead them to deal differently with their similar situations. For example, Heavenly Creek and Holy Hill tended to utilize their inner human resources because they are big enough to supply volunteers. In contrast, New Community seems to optimize its outer relationships with civil societies. This might be the case as it relates to resource dependence theory. Resource dependence theory holds that organizations are dependent on and shaped by available resources from their environments.[41] Congregations need to be aware of resources they need to draw from their environment to carry out their mission. To understand their environments, as Van Gelder emphasizes, congregations need to take into consideration "population trends, demographic profiles, transportation patterns, residential location of membership, organizations serving the community, business development and employment, and so on."[42]

The research findings also lead us to think about organization survival and goal attainment theories from an OST perspective. Research participants tended to understand their congregations by comparing other normal congregations in Korea as to *church* as a subcategory of knowledge/view. They understood other congregations as closed systems or systems only for seeking their survival. Such congregations seemed to have lacked interaction with their environments or interest in inputs from outside without consideration for outputs toward their environments. Research participants took for granted that they paid little attention to their neighbors and were not accorded with their environments and larger communities.

Goal attainment theory, conversely, seems to be appropriate to explain how the research congregations related to their environments. They had obvious *motives* and *purposes*, as the research findings evidenced, such as better serving the neighbor, making their local communities better, and carrying out mission. They undertook *strategic plans* to achieve these. For example, they appointed pastors in charge of taking care of their neighborhoods and prepared their buildings and facilities for their

41. Ibid., 80–83.
42. Van Gelder, *The Ministry*, 143.

social ministries. The following primary categories of attitude and skill/method can be understood in this sense. The research congregations did not address their social services as strategic plans for church growth, while many other congregations in Korea did. However, we can see that such approaches of not relating their services to church growth seem to result from their strategic planning in a broader sense. The research congregations have tried to listen to their neighbors in order to serve their neighbors. They do not aim at gaining immediate, tangible achievements through their social services. Instead, they deal with their social services in the sense that God is subject of their ministries and their relationship with neighbors. They somehow seem to be able to overcome limits of goal attaining approach in coping with challenges due to rapidly changing contexts because they have continued to listen to their neighbors within such contexts.[43]

The emergent grounded theory of the listening process in this study also seems to have similarities and differences in relation to the perspective of reengineering and continuous improvement. According to Van Gelder, this perspective emphasizes "reengineering" and "total quality management" so as to "insure higher levels of efficiency and productivity."[44] The emergent theory similarly shows that the research congregations' listening processes have internal communication processes for continually improving the quality of their services. However, the above perspective pays relatively little attention to organizations' external environments, while focusing on the organizations' internal operations.[45] In contrast, the research congregations' listening processes include both continuous enhancement of their internal operations and attention to their environments. This is because this process essentially is a process of paying attention to their environments via neighbors.

OST's notion of organizational boundaries can help congregations form their identities in relation to their larger communities and environments. Congregational life is related mostly to managing boundaries. Van Gelder suggests four types of congregational boundaries: location; building or facilities; the religious heritage and the biblical and confessional values; and organizational history and core ministry values.[46] All

---

43. Ibid., 137.
44. Ibid.
45. Ibid., 138.
46. Ibid., 144–45.

three research congregations are located in poor, urban, and industrial areas. They have naturally been involved in serving their poor and marginalized neighbors within their respective locations. Their buildings and facilities have been used for services toward their neighbors. They have a similar tendency to consider how to use or build their buildings or facilities in relation to their neighbors. For instance, Holy Hill has been constructing its new main sanctuary for both holding its worship services and providing its neighbors with cultural events.

The PCK's emphasis on God and Jesus led all three congregations to identify themselves and their social services implicitly and explicitly with God-centered mission and Jesus-based evangelism. Their long histories of serving their neighbors and their core ministry values of living for and with their neighbors have shaped their identities. This boundary seems to be more influential in shaping their identities because many other PCK congregations within such poor, urban, and industrial environments have not been concerned with engagement with their neighbors. These boundaries mentioned above "shape a congregational culture" within each congregation.[47]

OTHER RELATED LITERATURE

This section addresses other emerging literature regarding the research findings and the emerging theory of this study. The research findings brought to the fore the importance of congregational leadership in the process of listening to the neighbor. Rapidly changing contexts and services appropriate to the neighbor call our attention to the importance of congregational leadership in the view of the research congregations. In this regard, we look at Karl E. Weick and Scott Cormode's notions of leadership as sensemaking and Peter Senge's notions of leadership as nurturing a learning organization.

Weick and Cormode: Sensemaking Leadership

Karl E. Weick emphasizes the importance of leadership as an activity of sensemaking.[48] Weick contends that an organization needs sensemaking leadership when organizational members' understanding of the world becomes unintelligible in the face of a rapidly changing environment.

---

47. Ibid., 145.
48. Weick, *Sensemaking in Organizations*, 9–10.

Sensemaking starts from the following questions of what the story is (identity) and what is going on (event or action) so as to look for meaning within a changing context within and outside an organization. Sensemaking is about interplay of interpretation and action.

However, sensemaking aims to make something *sensible*. Weick notes that sensemaking is not concerned with an interpretation, but the ways people create what they interpret.[49] Weick holds that, "[An] organization is a set of people who share many beliefs, values, and assumptions that encourage them to make mutually-reinforcing interpretations of their own acts and the acts of others."[50] With this in mind, Weick argues that sensemaking *enacts* sensible environments. Weick treats people as "a part of their own environment" and enactment as "action in the world."[51]

Weick highlights that sensemaking is a social process "because what a person does internally is contingent on others."[52] Collective sense-making can be understood as the process whereby groups interactively create social reality, which *becomes* the organizational reality. Weick calls special attention to "talk, discourse, and conversation" as a primary means of social contact in this sense.[53] Action and talk in sensemaking are treated as cycles rather than as a linear sequence. Talk occurs both early and late, as does action. Furthermore, sensemaking is an ongoing process. We constantly try to *bracket* certain moments in the flow of life in order to make sense of them. However, this is temporary and not perfect because life is a continuous flow and sensemaking only looks at some moments of this flow. Sensemaking finally is concerned with *plausibility* rather than *accuracy* because sensemaking is based on reasonable explanations of what *might* be happening rather than scientific discoveries. That is to say, it continually focuses on looking for plausible stories within an organization. Communication through *talk*, *discourse*, and *conversation* is a central component of sensemaking and organizing in this process. The decision-making process is an on-going process of sensemaking within an organization.

---

49. Ibid., 13.
50. Ibid., 73.
51. Ibid., 31–36.
52. Ibid., 40.
53. Ibid., 41.

Scott Cormode, likewise, contends that congregational leadership means to help its members "make spiritual sense."[54] Every time we encounter a new situation, we have to figure out how to make sense of it. Church leadership does not aim to provide an interpretation of the new situation, but an interpretive framework from God's perspective.[55] People look for plausible stories through sharing storytelling as a vehicle for sensemaking in the face of new situations. Responding to new situations, as Cormode says, people within a congregation seek to interpret these situations by "weaving stories from culture's repertoire of meanings" and look for stories that make the most sense of these.[56] Cormode emphasizes that leaders cannot and must not transform or control ongoing stories within a congregation according to the leader-centered-top-down mode. Rather, leaders first need to *listen* to these stories, because they are unavoidably a part of these stories deeply tied to the identity of the congregation.

Cormode notes that sense-making leaders provide biblical and theological vocabularies and categories "to imagine a different way to interpret the world and to construct new course of action."[57] All lead pastors of the study, in this regard, have provided their congregational members with biblical and theological vocabularies. The lead pastors of Heavenly Creek and Holy Hill interpret what the church is and what the church does from the perspective of holistic mission, as we will address in the following chapter. Evangelism and social service, in brief, cannot be separated. The lead pastor of New Community has developed a vocabulary of creating a *web of life* and *village within a city* based on *minjung* theology.

Drawing from Senge, Cormode holds that leaders can help the people of God change the *mental models* that they use to make sense of the world.[58] For instance, by sending letters, the Apostle Paul tried to keep giving many congregations various biblical and theological vocabularies and categories in order for them to deal with their new situations. Sensemaking leadership within a congregation seeks to help all members to make their own spiritual meaning in terms of their congregational identity and mission. Congregational leadership as sensemaking is an

54. Cormode, *Making Spiritual Sense*, xii.
55. Ibid., xi.
56. Ibid., 28–30.
57. Ibid., 66.
58. Ibid.

ongoing, social process, from Cormode's perspective. Peter Northouse similarly defines leadership not as a fixed set of individual roles or attributes, but as a process of relational influence.[59] All processes of sensemaking are temporary and improvisional, and as such, there is no such thing as fixed sensemaking, as Weick noted above.

Pastors as leaders of the research congregations seem to play a role as sense-makers in the process of listening to their neighbors in light of Weick's notion of leadership as an activity of sensemaking. Pastors have tried to make sense of their changing environments and what they heard from their neighbors. They have sought to make meaning to help their members interpret and cope with their situations. The research findings shed light on the fact that pastors seem to have taught and encouraged their members to be involved in serving their neighbors and continually listen to them, while pastors of other congregations in the same areas do not seem to do so. Leaders help congregations' members share their knowledge and views of church, neighbor, mission, and context through internal communications. These congregations have become organizations of making sense of their contexts and their ministries.

Their listening to their neighbors is a continuous social process, as Weick emphasizes sensemaking as a continuous social process in an organization. This is because their environments, including their neighbors, are continuously changing and their interpretations of what they hear from their neighbors are limited and different. The listening process is a cyclical process of action and communication in the sense of Weick's sensemaking. Attitude, skill/method, and outcomes in the research findings can be understood in terms of action, while internal communications can be regarded in terms of communication. The listening process, in light of Weick, can also be treated as a process of seeking *plausibility* of their listening rather than *accuracy*. It is an on-going process open toward future listening and makes decision-making process an on-going process of sensemaking, and vice versa. Therefore, congregational leadership can be understood as sense-making leadership which helps the congregation to make sense of its place within a continually changing context.

Senge: Leadership for a Learning Organization

Senge is primarily concerned with organization and leadership in the face of rapidly-changing contexts. In *The Fifth Discipline*, Senge argues

---

59. Northhouse, *Leadership*, 3.

that all organizations should be learning organizations.[60] Senge maintains that all people should tap into their inner resources and potential in hopes that they can build their own community based on principles of liberty, humanity, and a collective will to learn. He theorizes that learning organizations are as follows:

> ... where people continually expand their capacity to create the results they truly desire, where new and expansive patterns of thinking are nurtured, where collective aspiration is set free, and where people are continually learning how to learn together.[61]

The basic rationale for such organizations is that in situations of rapid change only those that are flexible, adaptive, and productive will excel.

Senge proposes the five primary disciplines of learning: systems thinking, personal mastery, mental models, shared vision, and team learning. *Systems thinking*—the conceptual cornerstone of Senge's argument—is the discipline that integrates the other four disciplines, fusing them into a coherent body of theory and practice.[62] Senge emphasizes that systems thinking aims to comprehend/address the whole rather than the parts, and examine the interrelationship between the parts. Since systems thinking is generally oriented toward the long-term view, "delays and feedback loops are so important."[63] Learning organizations build *feedback loops* designed to maximize the effectiveness of their learning processes. *Personal mastery* is the discipline of continually clarifying and deepening our personal vision, focusing our energies, developing patience, and seeing reality objectively.[64] It is involved in spiritual growth and, at the same time, goes beyond spiritual opening.[65] *Mental models*, for Senge, are "deeply ingrained assumptions, generalizations, or even pictures and images that influence how we understand the world and how we take action."[66] Senge contends that a genuine vision leads to people wanting to excel and learn within learning organizations. Leadership must aim at *building shared visions*. Leaders must translate personal vision into shared vision, fostering a sense of the long-term. Finally, *team learning* is

60. Senge, *The Fifth Discipline*.
61. Ibid., 3.
62. Ibid., 12.
63. Ibid., 92.
64. Ibid., 7.
65. Ibid., 141.
66. Ibid., 8.

"the process of aligning and developing the capacities of a team to create the results its members truly desire."[67]

Senge proposes a new leadership based on these five disciplines in which leaders are designers, stewards, and teachers.[68] Senge emphasizes that the organization's policies, strategies, and systems are key areas of design. Senge argues that leadership is primarily concerned with designing governing ideas, such as the purpose, vision, and values. Leaders are also stewards of shared vision and, as such, their task is to manage the vision for the benefit of others. Leaders have to learn to *listen* to other people's visions and to modify their own where necessary.[69] Regarding leaders as teachers, Senge also holds that their primary responsibility is to define reality and, as such, to help "people achieve more accurate, more insightful and more empowering views of reality."[70]

Senge's ideas of learning organizations and leadership seem to be applicable to understandings of church and leadership seen within the research findings. The church is essentially a *learning organization*, insofar as discipleship is at the heart of the church. Research congregations take seriously a life of witnessing the gospel seen in the life and ministry of Jesus. Their emphasis on listening to their neighbors shows that they can be regarded as learning organizations in terms of their relationship with their neighbors. In particular, their attitudes of listening, such as maintaining humility, remaining open, and maintaining empathic attention, indicate that they are ready to learn from their neighbors. It, thus, seems natural for them that, as a result of their listening, they gain learning from their neighbors or their listening process.

The research congregations seem to have a perspective similar to Senge's perspective of *systems thinking* from which they deal with their members not as separate from the world, but connected to the world. This perspective, as a discipline of seeing the organization as a whole, intends to get a big picture of the *whole* congregation in relation to its environment. Systems thinking is ever changing and growing in terms of the congregation's inner and outer relationships. The research congregations, in this sense, seem to have looked for ways to effectively reach others through their listening to their neighbors and introduced new

---

67. Ibid., 236.
68. Ibid., 340.
69. Ibid., 351.
70. Ibid., 353.

ideas on a new context while influencing systems throughout the entire congregation. They regard their output, such as local ministries, mission outreach, and feedback loops, as a key part of systems thinking. They take for granted that they aim at listening to voices outside them.

The process of the research congregations' listening to their neighbors seems to be a feedback loop from Senge's perspective. It already contains feedback as a method for listening to their neighbors, in a narrow sense. Feedback loops can be understood more broadly. For example, the appointment of deacons and the initiation of Gentile mission in Acts were results of feedback loops in the early church. We, in a similar vein, can understand Roxburgh and Romanuk's argument that missional leaders need to listen to "the stories of the people in their neighborhood."[71] Feedback loops empower organizations to be better learning organizations by opening and humbling themselves. The research congregations' listening processes, as ongoing feedback processes, likewise seem to help them to be more flexible and more adaptive in response to environmental changes. Their listening culture in relation to their neighbors is based on openness to the world in which God has placed them to serve.

Congregations primarily require effective leadership to transform them into learning organizations, from Senge's perspective of learning organization. Learning organizations embrace change and constantly create reference points to precipitate an ever-evolving structure that has a vision of the future built-in. Effective leadership is not based on a traditional hierarchy, but rather, is a mix of different people from all levels of the system who lead in different ways. Congregational leaders can become more effective by mastering the disciplines of transformational leadership—creative tension, mental models, team learning and systems thinking, in Senge's view. The research congregations seem to seek effective leadership, although they seemingly have traditional pastor-centered leadership, which was not addressed in relation to the broader aspects of leadership, but aspects of listening to their neighbors. Internal communications of the research congregations seem to partly include a mix of different people from all levels of the congregations. Their leadership seems to foster trusting personal and organizational relationships in an open-ended manner. This is possible because leaders themselves have taken part in listening to their neighbors. They encourage their members to participate in listening to their neighbors by showing good exemplary

---

71. Roxburgh and Romanuk, *The Missional Leader*, 182.

lives and nurturing internal communications for better listening to their neighbors. They have also provided mental models to do so with a long-term vision. They have aimed to not impose their own visions, but build shared visions through internal communications.

The leader functions as designer, steward, and teacher, from Senge's perspective of leadership. Pastors of the research congregations to some degree seem to have functioned as designers, stewards, and teachers in the process of listening to their neighbors. They have designed purposes, values, and visions of their own congregations; however, they, as the stewards of the shared vision, served for the benefit of others by listening to other people's visions. They have been responsible for defining reality and, as such, enabling all congregation members to define reality more accurately. From the perspective of Senge's leadership, congregational leadership must link to sharing power and authority by opening up space for others to act and basing the decision-making process in all members. This seems apparent as far as pastors of the research congregations have participated in internal communication processes.

CONCLUSION

This chapter has been concerned with theoretical reflections on the research findings in relation to sensitizing concepts and other relevant literature. To begin with, we explored the hermeneutics of the other by undertaking a dialogue between Gadamer and Levinas. Both Gadamer and Levinas take seriously listening to the other. Gadamer regards the other as an equal conversational partner. Listening, in this regard, is regarded as mutual and symmetrical. Levinas understands the other in terms of asymmetrical relationship with the self. The self exists to be responsible for the other. Levinas contends that the other is always a speaker in relation to us. We saw that the research findings seemed to partly include both understandings of the other in relation to the listening process. On the one hand, Gadamer's hermeneutics of the other seemed to be working in the process of the research congregations' listening to their neighbors, in the sense that they regarded their neighbors as their conversational partners in order to communicate with them. On the other hand, Levinas's hermeneutics of the other seemed to be operative to the extent that the research congregations continued to first listen to their neighbors prior to speaking and pay attention to their weaknesses and needs.

We, moreover, addressed the relationship between the research congregations and their environments in terms of OST. We saw that the process of the research congregations' listening to their neighbors seemed to play a key role in adapting and recontextualizing in the face of challenges due to changing contexts. It aimed at seeking a better fit between them and their environment. We also explored Weick, Cormode, and Senge in terms of organizational leadership. Pastors of the research congregations seemed to function as sense-makers, designers, stewards, and teachers in the process of listening to their neighbors. The research congregations appeared to be learning congregations in that listening could be regarded as learning from their neighbors.

6

Biblical and Theological Reflections on the Research Findings

THIS CHAPTER REFLECTS ON and discusses the research findings and the emerging grounded theory of listening to the neighbor in biblical and theological terms by placing these into dialogue with the biblical and theological concepts presented in chapter 3. It also focuses on other literature regarding the research findings and the emerging theory of this study. This chapter takes up the following topics accordingly: biblical perspective, theological perspective, and other related literature.

BIBLICAL PERSPECTIVE

This section is concerned with the research findings and the emerging theory of listening to the neighbor in biblical terms. It focuses on the biblical notions of the neighbor and listening to the neighbor, the kingdom of God, and the church as a Spirit-led community.

The Neighbor and Listening to the Neighbor

We have seen few references to biblical understandings of listening to the neighbor in the research findings. Research participants, however, did implicitly show their biblical understandings of listening to the neighbor through their biblical understandings of neighbor, as well as church and mission. Biblical understandings of the neighbor were at the heart of Heavenly Creek, Holy Hill, and New Community's relationships with their neighbors. Their biblical understandings of their neighbors seemed to shape how they related and listened to their neighbors. These notions overall were based on the NT, and, in particular, in Jesus' life and ministry in the four gospels. Research participants' interpretations of how Jesus had relationships with his neighbors were closely related to both these congregations' understandings of their neighbors and ways of being engaged with their neighbors.

Research participants primarily understood their neighbors as the poor, the marginalized, the widowed, etc. They thought that Jesus took seriously reaching out and caring for the sick, the poor, the marginalized, and the like. This is the reason they had to be concerned with serving and caring for people in need around them. This notion seemed to be closely linked with Matthew 25:31–46 and Luke 10:25–37, although participants did not explicitly mention the exact biblical texts regarding this. There were both commonalities and differences of interpreting these texts among the three congregations. Heavenly Creek and Holy Hill had similar understandings compared to New Community in this regard.

All three congregations seemingly agreed that the above biblical texts showed what their neighbors were like. Their neighbors were the hungry, the sick, the stranger, the naked, the thirsty, the victimized, etc., as described in Matthew 25:31–46 and in Luke 10:25–37. What they first had to do was feed the hungry, welcome strangers, look after the sick, clothe the naked, give the thirsty something to drink, and take care of the victimized. It was also clear that they had their own perspectives concerning who the least of those in need were.

There are rich references in the gospels to Jesus' conversations with people, regardless of who they were, by listening and speaking. Jesus was willing to listen to their stories. He also told his stories to them. Jesus was wise to engage in conversations that took place in terms of his conversation partners, topics, and contexts. Nevertheless, Jesus paid special attention to those who did not generally receive attention in his time—the marginalized and the alienated. For instance, Jesus had conversations with a woman of Samaria, a lame man at the pool of Bethesda, a Canaanite woman, and so on. Jesus allowed children, who were regarded as the despised in his time, to come to him and he blessed them. He earnestly listened to and allowed people in need to state their needs for help. Jesus not only cared about their words, but also their sociopolitical situations. By listening, Jesus made the despised and the marginalized feel valuable and respectful. Jesus was regarded as a friend of sinners. Jesus had not only a listening ear, but also a listening eye and heart in the Levinasian sense of listening.

All three research congregations took it for granted that they listened to their neighbors. For instance, Participant J mentioned that what God wanted J's congregation to do was continue to listen to its neighbors via its programs for its neighbors and this listening would be decisive in determining what to do or where to go. Most participants also seemed to not distinguish their service for their neighbors from evangelism. For example, Participant O said that "bread is the gospel to the poor." They regarded serving their neighbors as not abstract, but concrete and practical. They believed that evangelism included immediately and concretely responding to their neighbors' basic needs, as did the Samaritan traveler in Luke 10:25–37. They felt responsibility toward their neighbors.

We need to dig deeper into Jesus' parable of the Good Samaritan. This shows our dual identity in relationship with the neighbor. Jesus taught that the Samaritan man and the victimized person were neighbors to each other. However, they were not regarded as neighbors from the perspective of the expert in law who talked with Jesus. This is because ordinary Jews did not consider Gentiles to be their neighbors. They also treated Samaritans as their enemies. They were forbidden from touching one who was half dead in order to keep the laws of purification.[1] This was regarded as one way of loving God. Jesus challenged such notions of neighbor. His understanding of neighbor included anyone in need—even enemies. Jesus' emphasis on the Samaritan man as a good neighbor requires us to be a good neighbor to anyone in need.

We now turn to differences regarding the notions of neighbor among the three congregations. Heavenly Creek and Holy Hill dealt with the neighbor in relation with the Great Commandment (Matt 22:36–40). Most participants from these two congregations interpreted loving God as loving their neighbor, and vice versa. They tended to deal with the two aspects of this commandment in a *both/and* manner, rather than in an *either/or* manner. They believed that loving their neighbors was not an abstract concept, but the concrete activity of serving them. They, thus, held that loving their neighbors meant serving them, and *vice versa*.

However, Heavenly Creek and Holy Hill clearly acknowledged that their neighbors had to come to Jesus for the sake of salvation, although they did not want to force their neighbors to do so. They sharply pointed out that many congregations did so in Korea, as they distinguished themselves from others in terms of *church* as a subcategory of *knowledge/*

---

1. See Fitzmyer, *Luke X-XIV*, 882–90.

view. Such congregations directly related their social services for their neighbors to their evangelism and treated their neighbors as objects for their church growth. This critical evaluation of other congregations led Heavenly Creek and Holy Hill to distance themselves from how other congregations related to their neighbors. What mattered to these two congregations was that it was very important to serve people in need, but that this was not enough for salvation to take place. Research participants from these two congregations held that their neighbors needed Jesus for their spiritual needs, although such needs could not be completely separated from their physical needs. This notion seemed to place an emphasis on their neighbors' coming to the church. They believed that everything was God's work in the process and what they did was participate in God's work.

In contrast, New Community seemed to put its focus on Jesus' fellowship with the poor, the marginalized, and the unprivileged rather than their salvation. This seems to be biblically based on the fact that Jesus was "a friend of tax collectors and sinners" (Matt 11:19; Lk 7:34). This notion is influenced by *minjung* theology, as seen later in more detail. New Community took seriously the sociopolitical context of the *minjung* in its neighborhood whose lives were filled with the struggle for survival. New Community was more concerned with political suffering alongside socio-economical suffering compared to Heavenly Creek and Holy Hill. New Community underscored that Jesus not only treated caring for people in need as crucial in terms of salvation, but also identified himself with one of them in Matthew 25. New Community discovered Jesus among the people in need. What Jesus primarily focused on in his ministry was taking care of these people and transforming local villages into new communities rather than promoting the church as a separate religious community. For this reason, it somehow seemed natural that New Community tried to take care of the whole community beyond the church. New Community believed that it might be impossible to meet its poor neighbors' essential needs without transforming the whole community.

The Kingdom of God

The three research congregations took seriously the kingdom of God in relation to understanding of church and mission. The research findings showed that these congregations were commonly concerned with the kingdom of God. All the congregations' websites addressed the kingdom of God in relation to their social services and programs. All three congregations acknowledged themselves and their ministries as instruments of the reign of God in the world in order to witness the gospel. They were sure of themselves as a sign and/or foretaste of the kingdom of God in the world. They believed that their exemplary lives could be regarded as their hermeneutic of the gospel in relation to the kingdom of God. This is because they thought that their neighbors could not help but know and experience what the gospel meant as they addressed their congregations' lives and ministries.

The research congregations' understandings of the kingdom of God tended to be explicitly related to the notions of *building* or *expanding* the kingdom of God, in contrast to biblical notions of *receiving, entering, seeking,* and *inheriting* it.[2] Their emphasis on practical activities and exemplary lives in terms of understanding of the gospel seemed to lead them into such notions, although they rejected treating the gospel only as individual, spiritual, or otherworldly. The research congregations took for granted that they should *build* or *expand* the kingdom of God. They acknowledged that the kingdom signified the rule of God and God was the subject of all their activities in terms of the reformed tradition. At the same time, they borrowed the early missionaries' language of building or expanding only for describing their obedience to God's sovereignty. In this regard, their expressions of "building" or "expanding" God's kingdom have somehow nuanced meanings compared to ordinary understandings in Korea. On the one hand, most congregations tend to believe that building and expanding the kingdom of God is their primary mission to be achieved through church growth. They regard themselves as subjects of mission. On the other hand, the research congregations believe that God is the subject of building or expanding God's kingdom. What they really focused on was their participation in God's work of *building* or *expanding* God's kingdom. There are some differences among the three research congregations in this regard. Heavenly Creek and Holy Hill generally seemed to highlight the dimension of the coming of God's kingdom with a focus on personal salvation, whereas New Community tended to be primarily concerned with the kingdom of God as an earthly kingdom in terms of Jesus' community of hope, justice, and peace on earth.

2. See Van Gelder, *The Essence*, 87.

We need to revisit the Great Commandment of loving God and loving one's neighbor in regard to the kingdom of God. The Great Commandment is inseparably related to the coming reign of God in Mark 12: 28–34. Jesus told the scribe that he was not far from the kingdom of God (Mk 12:34). Jesus related the Great Commandment to inheriting eternal life in the Lukan version (Lk 10:25–28). This saying implicates that we are not *building* or *expanding*, but *entering* or *inheriting* God's kingdom, because God is the builder, sustainer, and ruler of his kingdom. In light of Matthew 25, feeding the hungry, giving drink to the thirsty, welcoming the stranger, and clothing the naked are all essential to *entering* and *inheriting* the reign of God. These activities are a *foretaste* or *sign* of the kingdom of God. All three congregations seemed to have played such roles in their neighborhoods as long as God was the subject of their interactions with their neighbors.

Church as a Spirit-led Community

All three congregations had the tendency to understand themselves as the church of Jesus Christ rather than being Spirit created and led. This seems to have been influenced by Calvinism, as discussed below. Most participants, except pastors, paid little attention to the Spirit in relation to their understandings of church and leadership. There were relatively common understandings of the Spirit. First, many participants generally seemed to relate the Spirit to personal spheres of spirituality and interest. The Spirit, in this regard, moved individuals' hearts and encouraged individuals to participate in their congregations' social services for their neighbors. Second, many participants also understood the Spirit as the Spirit who performed miracles in terms of their personal and organizational relationships with their neighbors.

Third, many participants tended to describe the Spirit as the Spirit of God, which seemed to imply the Spirit as subordinate to God the Father. All participants clearly acknowledged God as the subject of their congregations' relationships with their neighbors, including listening processes, while they did not all seem to relate the Spirit to such relationships.[3] Fourth, God and Jesus were very often mentioned regardless of their relations with researcher's questions, while the Spirit was not addressed until I asked about it, as noted in the research findings. Fifth,

---

3. Nine out of fifteen participants and one out of six groups connected the role of the Spirit to their congregations' relationships with their neighbors.

pastors have relatively rich expressions regarding the Spirit in relation to the Trinity in dealing with their congregational relationships with their neighborhood, although they focused more attention on God the Father and the Son.

In contrast, the research congregations seemed to identify themselves as churches of Jesus Christ and, as such, their social ministries followed Jesus' relationship with his neighbors. They placed Jesus Christ at the heart of their ecclesiological identities. Heavenly Creek and Holy Hill tended to understand Jesus as the full manifestation of God's love and the redeemer of human sins, while New Community seemingly understood Jesus as the one who showed the communal life of God's kingdom and brought a new community of peace. However, they all believed that Jesus came to serve the weak and the sinners and live together with them. They naturally developed their ways of living both *for* and *with* their neighbors from their beginnings. They believed that their neighbors came to know the gospel not through *the Bible*, but through *their daily life* as *witnesses*. From this point of view, all congregations regarded the local congregation as "the only hermeneutic of the gospel is the life of the congregation which believes it," as Newbigin states.[4] All three congregations thus commonly viewed the gospel not as *abstract*, but *concrete*.

THEOLOGICAL PERSPECTIVE

This section addresses the research findings and the emerging theory of listening to the neighbor in relation to Calvin's ecclesiology and missional ecclesiology.

Calvin's Ecclesiology

Research congregations overall seemed to follow the PCK's ecclesiology, which was based on Calvin's ecclesiology. The PCK's version of Calvin's ecclesiology was seasoned by the Westminster Confession of Faith and the early missionaries' understandings of the church, as seen in chapter 2. It tended to emphasize God the Father rather than the Son and the Spirit in terms of the Trinity, while acknowledging the equal and mutual relationship among the three persons. It also seemed to highlight the roles of Jesus and the pastor in ecclesiological terms. Such tendencies appeared within the research findings.

---

4. Newbigin, *The Gospel*, 234.

Calvin's emphasis on God the Father's sovereignty led the research congregations to understand God as the subject of their interactions with their neighbors in terms of mission. Most research participants acknowledged God the Father as the subject of history and the lord of the universe. They believed that God the Father is the God who sent Jesus and the Spirit and has used their congregations as means for God's purpose. They took for granted that God the Father caused Jesus to proclaim the gospel and the Spirit to distribute spiritual gifts. Jesus and the Spirit have served God the Father's will, so the research congregations have tried to also serve it by engaging in God's work for their neighbors. In this regard, some participants explicitly referred to their activities for their neighbors as activities for God's glory. The research congregations' understandings of engagement with God's work are linked with their understandings of the gospel, as discussed later. The suffering of Jesus on the cross is at the heart of their understandings of the gospel. This implicitly influenced their attitude of remaining humility. Relatively speaking, Heavenly Creek and Holy Hill tended to understand this in soteriological terms, while New Community interpreted the suffering of Jesus as his participation in human socio-political suffering. However, all of them addressed the cross of Jesus within God the Father's sovereignty.

All research participants tended to understand the three persons of the Trinity as being hierarchal rather than equal. Their references to God the Father included the Son and the Spirit's activities, but not *vice versa*. A similar pattern to this relationship applied to the relationship between the Son and the Spirit. Such understandings of the Trinity seem to be influenced by the PCK's understandings of the Trinity. The PCK appears to manifest Calvin's God-the-Father-centered Trinity in a more hierarchal manner. On the one hand, Calvin developed teachings on the Father and the Son in theoretical terms, while he did not fully develop his pneumatology. However, Calvin addressed all themes of his *Institutes* in a Trinitarian fashion continuing to relate the Father and/or the Son to the Spirit. On the other hand, the PCK's *Constitution* tends to pay more attention to God according to the hierarchal order of God the Father, the Son, and the Spirit. It mentions "God" 542 times, "Jesus" and/or "Christ" 316 times, and the Spirit 110 times. The research findings showed similar results regarding references to the three persons: God was referred to 173 times, Jesus/Christ was referred 84 times, and the Spirit was referred 50 times.

Most participants did not use the Spirit in explaining or expressing their congregations' interactions with their neighbors until I asked a question regarding the "Spirit," as discussed in chapter 4. In contrast, they naturally used "God" and "Jesus/Christ" regardless of questions. The Westminster Confession of Faith, as the main part of the PCK's *Constitution* in terms of theology, rarely mentions the Spirit until Chapter Thirty-Four of thirty-five chapters, whereas it repeatedly deals with God the Father and Christ over several chapters. The PCK's notions of the relationship of the three persons in the Trinity seem to be more hierarchal rather than equal and mutual. It is to be noted that the *Constitution* rarely mentions the social relationship of the Trinity. Even in addressing Communion, it does not touch on the Trinity in terms of the Trinitarian social relationship.

I argue that the sovereignty of God the Father has been strengthened through Korea's patriarchal culture and the early missionaries' Father-centered understandings of the Trinity. In this respect, the use of *Hananim* for Christian God has been most decisive. Koreans had an essentially monotheistic concept of a Creator-God: *Hananim*. Koreans regarded *Hananim* as the celestial God of the Heavenly Kingdom. The spirits stood on one supreme ruler named *Hananim*. The monotheistic concept of *Hananim* created a primary contact point with Koreans. Missionaries came to regard *Hananim* as suited to their own conception of God.[5] John Ross acknowledged its virtuous function for evangelism in Korea as follows: "The name *Hananim* is so distinctive and so universally used, that there will be no fear, in future translations and preachings, of unseemly squabbles which occurred long ago among Chinese missionaries on this subject."[6]

Hananim, however, hardly includes the *social Trinity* because it referred to only *one God* or the *supreme God* over other lesser gods, although it was a wonderful deity for helping Koreans to believe in the Christian God. The use of *Hananim* is good for emphasizing God's sovereignty, the oneness of the Trinity, and hierarchal relationships among the three persons in the Trinity. This understanding of *Hananim* as a supreme deity in patriarchal terms, along with the Calvinistic emphasis on God's sovereignty and Christ's Headship (or Kingship) of the church,

---

5. Palmer, *Korea and Christianity*, 17–19.
6. Ibid., 17.

has also tended to lead Christians in the PCK to place pastors at the top of the church governance.

The notions of the church within the research findings showed that research participants understood the church in terms of Jesus Christ related to God the Father. Most research participants treated their congregations as communities in relation to Christ, while paying little attention to the Spirit in this regard. This is similar to the PCK's general understanding of the church, which is based on Christology related to God the Father, with relatively little consideration of the Spirit. In contrast, Calvin developed a Christ-centered ecclesiology focusing on the Spirit's help and guidance, as seen in chapter 2. Calvin held that the Spirit led members of the church to form and dwell in a community as the one body of Christ serve Christ as its head, and serve one another. Most research participants, in this regard, seemed to lack an understanding of their communities in relation to the Spirit.

The PCK has a tendency to limit the work of the Spirit to the spheres of personal life and faith in practical terms. This is due decisively to the Great Revival of 1907 and its legacy throughout the history of the PCK.[7] The Great Revival has seemed to reduce the Spirit to a deity who is only concerned with personal, spiritual affairs. Calvin, however, understood the Spirit as the Spirit of being involved in the universe, beyond individuals' faith and the church. Calvin underscores the Spirit's work as preserving, restoring, and guiding creation in the world.[8] Relatively speaking, pastors who were familiar with Calvin's notion of the Spirit tended to easily relate their congregations' activities for their neighbors to the Spirit, while other participants appeared to seek their own personal reasons for why they got involved in these activities in light of the Spirit.

The research congregations' understandings of the church as a church of Christ and a church for witnessing the gospel seem to be closely related to the PCK's ecclesiology in the *Constitution*, where the church exists to witness to Jesus and the gospel. It regards Jesus Christ as the primary agent in leading the church. The church is the result of the activity of Jesus Christ, existing for witnessing to the gospel of Christ. The *Constitution* emphasizes the marks of the true church (such as the pure proclamation of the gospel, the pure administration of the sacraments), and the exercise of church discipline. This is grounded in Calvin's emphasis on

---

7. See the section "The Church as a Spiritual-Renewal-Centered Church" in chapter 2.

8. *Institutes*, I.14.1–22.

Christ as the Word. The church cannot be the church without the role of the pastor, because the church can be a true church only when the Word is preached and the sacraments are administered. This notion has seemed to lead ordinary Christians in Korea to take for granted pastor-centered leadership by treating the role of the pastor as absolute regarding preaching and sacraments. Calvin, however, regarded the pastor as necessary for true marks of the church to the extent that Christ uses the pastor as an instrument, like wine and bread for sacraments, to witness the Word. Calvin also underscored that the Word could not be preached and heard without the Spirit's working in the process.

We, therefore, can understand that Calvin's emphasis on Christ as the Word appears to have an influence on the research participants' notions of a church as a church of Jesus and a church for witnessing the gospel. The research congregations took seriously Christ as the Word in terms of their relationships with their neighbors and, as such, came to seek a community to relate to their neighbors by following the life of Jesus. It seems to some extent natural that the lead pastors played a primary role in research congregations' listening processes and internal communications, reflecting the role of the pastor in Calvin's ecclesiology. If the research congregations had known better Calvin's concept of *union with Christ* in relation to the Spirit, they might have developed their social spirituality through their relationships with their neighbors, as seen from Billings' or Chung's argument in chapter 2.[9] If the lead pastors take seriously teaching of one body of Christ in relation to the Spirit, the research congregations will become more communal and mutual in understanding their congregations and interactions with their neighbors.

Missional Ecclesiology

We take a brief look at the fact that the research findings have some similarities and differences with missional ecclesiology, focusing on God's Trinitarian mission, the church's local context, and church as a Spirit-led community. We later address the understandings of the neighbor/other and listening to the neighbor within the missional church conversation literature.

---

9. Calvin treated *union with Christ* as one of his primary theological themes. He argued that Christians' union with Christ could be achieved only through help of the Spirit, focusing on loving both God and the neighbor in their daily lives. Union with Christ can be regarded as a lively spirituality clothed in concrete, practical forms. See Billings, *Union with Christ*; Chung, *Christian Spirituality*.

First, the research congregations acknowledged that God was the subject of their services for their neighbors, as missional ecclesiology emphasizes. They took it for granted that God, rather than the church, was the subject of mission and church growth did not necessarily mean the success of mission. They believed that they essentially existed to serve God's purpose in the world, in general, and in their neighborhoods, in particular. They, in this sense, identified themselves as *instruments* or *signs* used by God, as Hunsburger understands the church as a *sign, servant, foretaste,* and *messenger* of the kingdom of God.[10] The research congregations were also primarily concerned with witnessing to the gospel in light of God's mission. These understandings of the gospel seemed to depend on how each participant interpreted the life and ministry of Jesus. Participants related the gospel accordingly to love, salvation, the kingdom of God, etc. Most participants understood the gospel as addressing not only spiritual/bodily needs but also personal/communal aspects, although each tended to have different priorities in the process. They also believed that their neighbors first came to know about the gospel through the daily lives of church members in both personal and congregational terms. However, they did not all place the kingdom of God at the center of the gospel to the extent that missional ecclesiology emphasizes God's kingdom.

The research findings showed that the research congregations tended to regard God's mission as a God-the-Father-centered mission, which Jesus and the Spirit served with little attention given to social relationship in the Trinity. Many participants tended to relate the Spirit to the personal spheres of the heart and mind, although they, unlike typical Christians in Korea, did not think that they could control or possess the Spirit through their efforts. Missional ecclesiology, in contrast, has developed the concept of God's mission in terms of mutual social relationships of the Trinity. Missional ecclesiology tends to take seriously understandings of the Trinity because it assumes that understandings of the Trinity tend to shape ecclesiology, leadership, and mission. From the perspective of missional ecclesiology, the research congregations need to take seriously the Trinity by focusing primarily on the dimension of the reciprocal, mutual relationship of the three persons. They have to pay more attention to the Holy Spirit in understanding mission in relation to their neighbors.

---

10. Guder, *Missional Church*, 101–2.

Second, the research congregations took seriously their local contexts, as does missional ecclesiology. The research findings evidence that *context* as a subcategory of knowledge/view had a strong influence on shaping the research congregations' identities and mission. The research congregations definitely understood themselves as a part of their context and larger communities. Most of their members came from their neighborhoods. The research congregations, furthermore, actively responded to their environment and its socio-cultural change in terms of God's mission. The research congregations have been located in urban industrial areas since their beginnings. They did not treat their neighbors as objects for church growth. Instead, they paid special attention to who their neighbors were and what they needed. Their neighbors were the poor, the uneducated, the marginalized, etc. They believed that God wanted them to serve their neighbors. They have become accustomed to first attending to their neighbors' situations and needs in order to serve. All research participants tend to regard their own congregations as churches for/with their neighbors without hesitation. Their listening attitudes (which included remaining open and maintaining humility) and listening skill/method (such as providing open spaces) are largely due to their understandings of their context. Their understandings of context, likewise, seem to influence other primary categories such as outcomes and leadership. Therefore, the emerging grounded theory of listening to the neighbor can be regarded as a result of the fact that the research congregations took seriously their local contexts to serve God's mission. The processes of the research congregations' listening to their neighbors, in this sense, can be regarded as missional processes.

Third, the research findings showed that the research congregations seemed to lack an understanding of themselves in relation to the Spirit, as discussed above. The PCK, including the research congregations, has paid little attention to the role of the Spirit in the sphere of the community and the world, beyond the sphere of personal faith and life. Even research participants (excluding pastors) of New Community, who were strongly influenced by *minjung theology*, did not seem to relate their understandings of the church or interactions with their neighbors to the Spirit, while minjung theology assumes that the Spirit works in the world beyond the church.

In contrast, missional ecclesiology sheds light on the church as a Spirit-led community. Missional ecclesiology highlights the church as a social community, focusing on *perichoresis*—the interrelatedness between three persons of the Trinity. This notion is closely linked with the church as a Spirit-led community of *koinonia*. The Spirit leads all members to serve the church for mutual and communal benefit and, as such, its neighbors. The missional church needs to address its structure and leadership in relation to the Spirit to participate in God's mission in the world. Missional ecclesiology, in this light, seeks to nurture reciprocal, communal, and mutual dimensions of congregational life and mission. Therefore, missional ecclesiology—the church as a Spirit-led community—may help the research congregations become more reciprocal, communal, and mutual in terms of communal life and leadership internally and in their interactions with their neighbors. This is because the research findings showed that they already understood themselves as a community and there were reciprocal, mutual aspects in the process of their internal/external communications in the process of listening to their neighbors.

Missional theology, furthermore, holds that the church's understanding of the Trinity tends to shape leadership, ecclesiology, and its relationship with the neighborhood. In this regard, new understandings of the relationship of the three persons in the Trinity help the research congregations make their leadership more communal rather than hierarchal and help them become more actively involved in their neighborhoods. For example, Moltmann maintains that Trinitarian fellowship as open fellowship guides human relationships.[11] Moltmann contends, in this light, that the church is a free society of equals and an open fellowship of friends and the relationship between the church and the world is open, equal, and reciprocal. This open fellowship of the church includes the solidarity with the oppressed and the poor in the world, open for God, "open for men [sic] and open for the future of both God and men."[12] This might help the research congregations get more actively involved in their neighborhoods. John Zizioulas, in *Communion and Otherness*, attempts to understand the church as communion-in-mission to overcome the individualistic culture of the West, leaning on the Cappadocian Fathers' notions of the Trinity. Zizioulas highlights that the "true personhood is only what we observe in the trinity."[13] He interprets the concept of "person" as including otherness in an inseparable relation with

---

11. Moltmann, *The Trinity*, 54.
12. Moltmann, *The Church*, 2.
13. Zizioulas, *Communion*, 177.

communion.[14] Zizioulas notes that "*to be* and *to be in relation* becomes identical."[15] Zizioulas's notion of personhood in relation to the Trinity also might be helpful for the research congregations to be more actively engaged in their neighborhoods.

Most accounts of the Trinity, however, are ontological in the Levinasian sense. Levinas points out that ontology tends to destroy "the radical alterity of the other."[16] This leads missional theology to necessitate a new approach to the Trinity. We can consider Schroeder and Bevans's notion of the Trinity as dialogue, as discussed in chapter 1.[17] Luther and Calvin have a similar tendency regarding this.[18] Chung, in the same vein, does address the Trinity in relation to God's act of speech rather than God's being.[19] Chung understands God as God-in-dialogue because the triune God manifested Godself as both "God-in-dialogue" and "the Subject of speech" in creation, incarnation, and Pentecost and created human beings as "God's dialogue partners."[20] Such a Trinitarian notion of God-in-dialogue seems to take for granted that the church should get involved in conversation with its neighborhood in a missional sense. Therefore, missional theology might help the research congregations better listen to their neighborhoods as long as it develops its Trinitarian understanding of God-in-dialogue.

OTHER RELATED LITERATURE

This section addresses other emerging literature regarding the research findings and the emerging theory of this study. We, thus, focus on the three primary topics: holistic mission, minjung theology, and dialogue with many missional voices regarding listening to the neighborhood.

---

14. Ibid., 229. "Stasis (being 'as it stands,' as it is 'in itself') is realized in personhood both as ek-stasis (communion, relatedness) and as hypo-stasis (particularity, uniqueness)."

15. Zizioulas, *Being as Communion*, 88. Emphasis in original.

16. Levinas, *Totality and Infinity*, 35–36.

17. Bevans and Schroeder, *Prophetic Dialogue*, 41.

18. Luther, *St. John Chapters*, 5–14; See Bayer, *Martin Luther's Theology*, 340–41; Calvin, *According to John*.

19. Chung, *Hermeneutical Theology*, 353–55. Chung holds that God's word is in action.

20. Ibid., 354–55.

Holistic Mission

The lead pastors of Heavenly Creek and Holy Hill have a tendency to understand mission as holistic mission. Both pastors regarded the church's essence and all activities in light of holistic mission. In particular, the lead pastor of Holy Hill mentioned explicitly in the interview with me that he was considerably dependent on John Stott's notion of holistic mission. We explore more carefully the concept of "holistic mission" with a focus on Stott in what follows.

As a founding leader in the Lausanne Movement, Stott points out that hostility toward Christian mission has been growing world-wide. It is essentially related to the previous aggressive and unidirectional style of evangelism and mission. Stott provides the following three reasons for such a hostile phenomenon: intolerance, arrogance, and violence.[21] These three reasons seem to be directly applicable to the Korean current context. These resonate with research participants' critical evaluations regarding the general Christian mission in and outside Korea.

Stott, accordingly, brings to the fore the concept of *holistic mission*, which seeks to embrace both evangelism and social action. Stott's concept of being "holistic" is based on "the philosophical notion that 'the whole is greater than the sum of its parts.'"[22] Stott tries to understand mission in light of how to relate evangelism to sociopolitical engagement. He regards these two as two extremes—usually, the evangelical/liberal divide—in understanding mission. Stott holds that social action cannot be separated from evangelism.[23] Stott takes into account the partnership between evangelism and social action because "both are expressions of unfeigned love."[24] Stott, in this vein, insists on the inseparability of the Great Commandment ("love your neighbor") and the Great Commission ("go and make disciples").[25]

Nevertheless, Stott places slightly more priority on evangelism rather than sociopolitical action, and, as such, the church *for* its neighbors rather than *with* them. Stott holds that personal salvation in terms of not only soul but also body is at the center of evangelism. Stott's tendency regarding the relationship between evangelism and social action

21. Stott, *The Contemporary Christian*, 321.
22. Ibid., 337.
23. Stott, *Christian Mission*, 23.
24. Ibid., 27.
25. Ibid., 46.

seemed suitable for Heavenly Creek and Holy Hill. This is because these two congregations, with their ultimate concern for evangelism, have been involved in social services for their neighborhoods.

Stott brings to the fore God's missionary nature. Mission is rooted in "the nature of God himself."[26] God's mission is grounded in God's self-giving love, in which God the Father, the Son, and the Spirit are "eternally united to each other."[27] The Scriptures show that God as "a missionary God (Father, Son and Spirit), who creates a missionary people, and is working towards a missionary consummation."[28] Stott emphasizes that Jesus has sent the church "*into the world* to be servant church" as the Father sent him.[29] Stott regards the church's service as *love* for its neighbors. Stott highlights, "Love has no need to justify itself. It merely expresses itself in service wherever it sees need."[30] Stott's notion of the Trinity is God-the-Father-centered Trinity, with pays little attention to the social relationship of the three persons in the Trinity.

Stott has elaborately articulated the dimensions of *dialogue* and *listening* in terms of mission. Stott understands dialogue as "a token of genuine Christian love."[31] Bearing witness to Christ is at the heart of dialogue.[32] God's revelation has often had dialogical aspects. Stott understands that "God not only speaks but listens" by asking questions and waiting for answers.[33] God's attempt at having conversations with sinful human beings is graceful. Jesus too listened to people and asked questions. The Bible shows that Jesus very often entered into serious conversations. Stott claims that a true dialogue has the following four marks: authenticity, humility, integrity, and sensitivity.[34] Ultimately, a true dialogue attempts at "mutual 'listening,' listening in order to understand."[35]

---

26. Ibid., 21.
27. Stott, *The Contemporary Christian*, 148.
28. Ibid., 325.
29. Stott, *Christian Mission*, 24. Emphasis added. Stott continues to stress the dimension of being sent *into the world*.
30. Ibid., 48.
31. Ibid., 81.
32. Ibid., 82.
33. Ibid., 61.
34. Ibid., 71–74.
35. Ibid., 73.

Stott develops the concept of *double listening*—listening to both "the Word and the world."[36] What Christians first need in terms of discipleship is the *listening ear*. Stott provides three dimensions for this. First, Christians have to listen to God. According to Stott, "the living God has spoken and continues to speak."[37] Second, Christians have to listen to one another. A Christian community develops and matures its inner relationships through the communication of speaking and listening to one another. Third, Christians have to listen to the world. Stott views the contemporary world as full of anger, frustration, pain, etc. Accordingly, the better way of mission is "to listen before we speak."[38]

Stott's notions of listening to the other or the world have obvious affinities with the emerging theory of listening to the neighbor within the research findings. Stott presumes *knowledge/view* regarding the Word, the world, mission or evangelism for listening to the world. Stott makes explicit the ultimate *purpose* of listening to the world as follows: "We listen to the world in order to discern which of Christ's riches are needed most and how to present them in their best light."[39] Stott is also concerned with humility, attentiveness, willingness, and readiness in terms of listening *attitudes*, as the emerging theory of this study regards maintaining humility, remaining open, and maintaining empathic attention as listening attitudes. However, Stott also points out the need for a critical attitude in listening to the world, though it is not addressed in the emerging grounded theory. Stott does not articulate concrete *skills* or *methods* for listening to the world. Finally, Stott presents the following *outcomes* of listening: learning from the other/the process, developed relationship, and mutual understanding, which resonate with listening outcomes in the emerging theory, such as learning from the neighbor/process, mutual/reciprocal communication and relationships. However, Stott pays little attention to the role of leadership in the process of listening to the world.

Stott's emphasis on *double listening* through both faithful focus on God's word and effective engagement with the world is likely to be helpful for PCK congregations which have been used to a monological approach to mission. Stott tends to understand evangelism and social action in light

---

36. Stott, *The Contemporary Christian*, 27.
37. Ibid., 103.
38. Ibid., 110.
39. Ibid., 110–111.

of Jesus' love. Such an emphasis on love for neighbors without separating from evangelism was explicitly apparent mostly within Heavenly Creek and Holy Hill. Interview participants from these two congregations tended to understand their social services and evangelism as two aspects of love for their neighbors. Their ultimate concern was the salvation of their neighbors. Heavenly Creek and Holy Hill seemed to regard themselves somewhat as a church *for* rather than *with* its neighbors. To be sure, their understanding of salvation is personal. On the one hand, this dimension is similar to most congregations in the PCK. On the other hand, these congregations seemed to emphasize the salvation of both soul and body, unlike the general PCK congregations' emphasis on the salvation of individual soul. Stott stresses dialogue with neighbors in the context of Christian witness. Likewise, Heavenly Creek and Holy Hill tried to have personal and organizational dialogues with their neighbors.

However, Stott tends to reduce mission to the two primary categories of evangelism and social engagement. Mission is bigger than these, because mission arises out of the nature of God. These two categories cannot cover the whole of mission. Stott has not fully developed his theology of God's mission in Trinitarian terms. Seemingly, Stott's notion of God's mission is dependent on the Trinity of the Western Church (God-the-Father-centered Trinity) rather than the Eastern Church (the relatively-social Trinity).[40] Stott's attention is not on the Holy Spirit being equal to the Father and the Son. Heavenly Creek and Holy Hill similarly paid more attention to God the Father and the Son than to the Spirit.

Minjung Theology

Relatively speaking, New Community seemed to consider itself as a church *with* its neighbors rather than a church *for* them, compared to Heavenly Creek and Holy Hill. Participants within New Community seemed to take seriously treating their neighbors as equals. They seemed to take for granted caring for their local community in light of God's mission. This is because God is a God who is concerned with the world of which New Community is a part. New Community participants rarely used the term *love*. One reason is that they seemed to avoid regarding their relationship with their neighbors as a *benefactor-beneficiary*

---

40. From my perspective, the Trinity of the Eastern Church tends to emphasize the relational social aspects of the Trinity. However, it does not seem to deny that God the Father plays a role as the initiator of the relationship.

relationship.[41] This tendency is to a great degree related to the influence of minjung theology. New Community has developed its understandings of church and mission and relevant activities in light of minjung theology. We need to take a careful look at minjung theology, specifically, its notion of *minjung*, church and mission, and listening in what follows, while it is beyond the scope of this section to discuss minjung theology in great detail.

New Community has understood the poor and marginalized as its neighbors since its beginning. New Community still places priority on the poor and the marginalized, despite its context changing due to an influx of middle-class residents. We cannot understand this without considering the strong influence of minjung theology. Its lead pastor seems to take for granted that New Community is a *minjung* congregation. However, he acknowledges that the concept of a "*minjung* congregation" cannot fully capture its current identity. Thus, he wants New Community to be called "a congregation of the web of life."

Minjung theology is a theological product issuing from the background of the Korean socio-political situation of the 1970s and 80s. Minjung theologians tried getting involved directly in socio-political struggles of the oppressed—the *minjung*—by looking at people's suffering due to oppression by dictatorship and dehumanization as a result of rapid industrialization. The theological understanding of *missio Dei*, which had been introduced by the World Council of the Churches, encouraged them to be actively engaged in people's struggles for justice and human rights in Korea. Minjung theology contributed greatly to the democratization of Korea, challenging the negative consequences brought by industrialization and promoting participation in socio-political struggles of people.

Some scholars divide minjung theology into three generations according to the primary emphasis and the age of theologians.[42] The first generation—minjung theology of the 1970s and 80s—is a theology which paid more attention to the minjung in theological and biblical terms. The second generation of minjung theology tended to utilize Marxist politico-economic theories in order to work together with practitioners of secular minjung movements in the 1980s. The third generation has accepted diverse post-structural and post-modern theories to address

41. See Bosch, *Transforming Mission*, 290, 456.

42. See Choi, "A Generational Identification of Minjung Theology and Diverse Minjung Theologies." The title is my translation.

issues due to the downfall and/or increased capitalism of many socialist countries and the world-wide phenomenon of globalization. However, from my viewpoint, this division is a microscopic understanding of minjung theology. The first generation of minjung theology is still referred to as minjung theology both within and outside Korea.

In fact, there is no clear agreement among minjung theologians regarding the precise definition of the word *minjung*. *Minjung* can be translated into English as "the mass of people." However, this is not adequate for minjung theologians' essential purpose because in terms of Korean culture and history, the *minjung* are regarded as people who have experienced oppression and alienation not only politically, socially, and economically, but also *religiously*. Minjung theologians use the *habiru* (the Hebrew) of Egypt, the *amharets* (the people of the land) of Israel, and the *ochlos* (the crowd) of Galilee as biblical references of *minjung* because these peoples were oppressed politically, exploited economically, alienated socio-religiously, and kept in ignorance. Minjung theologians pay special attention to the relation between the *minjung*'s call for help in the face of oppression and injustice and God's reply in the Bible. They also argue that stories of the *minjung*'s experiences of God form the content of revelation. The *minjung*, thus, are both recipients and participants of God's revelation. The *minjung* are a part of God's revelation itself, rather than just its medium.

Byung-mu Ahn, as one of the founding fathers of minjung theology, provides the biblical foundation for minjung theology with a study on the characteristics of the *ochlos*, literally the "crowd," in the Gospel of Mark. Ahn reinterprets the story of Jesus' life in terms of a "reciprocal relation between Jesus and the *ochlos*" by interpreting the *ochlos* as the people excluded from Jewish society.[43] Jesus promised them the future of God through proclamation of the advent of God's kingdom and identification with the suffering *ochlos* on the cross. Ahn, in this light, translated the *ochlos* into Korean as *minjung*. Taking a further step, Ahn conceptualizes a christological notion of Jesus' socio-biography with the *ochlos-minjung* in light of his theology of the word-event coupled with the *minjung*-event. Therefore, Ahn holds that the gospel urges Christian communities to serve the *minjung* in the world in order to liberate them from the dominating culture of oppression and injustice.

---

43. Chung, Kärkkäinen, and Kim, *Asian Contextual Theology*, 6. Most theologians and church leaders have criticized that, along with Ahn's perspective, minjung theologians' tendency towards reading the Scriptures is *reductionist* and *non-objective*.

Nam-Dong Suh, as one of the pivotal minjung theologians, highlighted this perspective in his article "Missio Dei and Two Stories in Coalescence," in which the theology of God's mission plays an important role in shaping minjung theology as a creative response to God's mission working in the life context of the *minjung*.[44] Suh seeks to make confluent the biblical *minjung* tradition and the Korean *minjung* tradition in light of *han* because both traditions have been led by the Holy Spirit. Suh relates minjung theology to *han* most concretely. According to Suh, there are both negative and positive aspects to *han*:

> On the one hand, it is a dominant feeling of defeat, resignation and nothingness. On the other, it is a feeling with a tenacity of will for life which comes to weaker beings. The first aspect can sometimes be sublimated to great artistic expressions and the second aspect could erupt as the energy for a revolution or rebellion.[45]

The Korean experience of *han* has been expressed as renunciation in Korean literature and culture. However, *han* as the tenacity for life of oppressed spirits also has a tendency for social revolution. For Suh, the Spirit empowers the *minjung* to demolish or overcome the oppressed barriers of their ruling class through the perspective of the accumulated *han* of the *minjung*. Thus, Suh holds that Christians and their congregations' primary task must start from listening to the sighs of the *minjung* as "the voice of Christ knocking on our doors."[46]

Minjung theologians also emphasize that storytelling is a more effective tool in talking about God and dealing with the *han* of the Korean *minjung*. Storytelling in Korean culture has played a role in stimulating one's emotions, activating memories, and visualizing imagination in communities as well as individuals.[47] Minjung theologians hold that, since *minjung* is a living, dynamic, and complex reality which cannot be conceptualized objectively, the reality of the *minjung* can be found in their stories in their everyday lives. There is no distinction between reality and reflection or between the theory and practice in storytelling. Through telling and listening to stories of their individual and communal

---

44. Ibid., 51–68.

45. Commission of Theological Concerns of the Christian Conference of Asia, *Minjung Theology*, 58.

46. Ibid., 68.

47. Ibid., 4.

suffering, the *minjung* find their own identities and try to create a space for their lives and hopes. By so doing, the *minjung* do not become the props of the history of the ruling elites, but the subjects of their own history. Therefore, what Christian communities first have to do is listen to the *minjung*'s stories in order to share their own stories of the crucified Christ.

Minjung theology seemed to strongly influence New Community's interactions with their neighbors, in general, and listening processes, in particular. Minjung theology led New Community to relate its *knowledge/view* regarding the church, the neighbor, context, and mission to the *minjung* in light of God's mission. Minjung theology also seemed to shape New Community's motive/purpose for listening to its neighbors (better serving, making its local community better, and carrying out mission). Listening to the neighbor seemed to be not optional, but necessary for New Community. This is because the *minjung*, as God's primary concern, are at the center of minjung theology. It seemed natural for New Community to consider *humility*, *openness*, and *empathic attention* in the process of listening to its neighbors in terms of attitude and *providing open spaces* in terms of skill/method. New Community's notions of listening appeared to include not only listening to stories of its neighbors but also paying attention to their voiceless suffering. New Community tended to emphasize its neighbors as equal partners, given that minjung theology regards the *minjung* as the subject of history. New Community's caring for their neighbors, thus, can be understood as its solidarity with them rather than its benefaction for them. New Community, in the same sense, took it for granted that listening to its neighbors resulted in learning from its neighbors, mutual/reciprocal communication and relationships, and/or new missional events. Minjung theology helped New Community form a democratic leadership nurturing internal communications throughout the listening process.

However, the lead pastor of New Community shared his critical assessment regarding minjung theology from the perspective of his long-term experience of leading a *minjung* congregation. First, he held that minjung theology paid little attention to the fact that the primary dream of the *minjung* was to leave their present reality of poverty and marginalization. Second, the minjung theology's strong emphasis on the historical and political dimension of the *minjung*-event led to lack a balanced emphasis on everyday lives of the *minjung* in their local communities. In other words, minjung theologians did not deal with the locality of the *minjung*'s daily lives in their local communities to the extent that they were primarily concerned with the *minjung* within the larger society of Korea. Third, he pointed out that minjung theology seemed to focus on the subjectivity of the *minjung* without consideration of God's sovereignty. According to him, when we acknowledge the subjectivity of the *minjung* in light of God's sovereignty, we also deal with sinfulness, weaknesses, and limitations of the *minjung*. From his experience, he sometimes saw that the *minjung* despised or oppressed one another within their communities. Fourth, he asserted that minjung theologians tended to not expand the breadth of minjung theology because of their strict boundary of minjung theology. For example, minjung theologians were slow to start relationships with civil society organizations or other organizations in dealing with issues regarding the *minjung*. Fifth, and foremost, he maintained that *minjung* theology lacked ecclesiology. He wanted minjung theology to develop an ecclesiology as a community of faith and confession. Accordingly, it had weaknesses regarding worship service and evangelism.

We need to address in detail the final point of ecclesiology above. On the whole, minjung theologians did not articulate their ecclesiology until the late 1980s. Most of them tend to understand the church as a new community established on the grounds of an egalitarian socio-political system rather than in biblical terms of its organization. What they had to address most urgently was people's suffering due to the dictatorship and the rapid industrialization since the 1970s. It seems natural for minjung theologians to maintain that the *minjung*, not the church, are God's primary concern. Minjung theologians often argue that the *minjung* are the true members of the church. They sometimes ask the church to fight for the *minjung* against structural evil, while they sometimes speak about the church's solidarity with the *minjung*.

We can ask the following questions: What is the identity of the church? Is the church a community *for*, *with*, or *by* the *minjung*? Such ambiguous ecclesiological notions of relationships between the church and the *minjung* tend to lead church members to ambiguous notions of evangelism. For example, do the *minjung* need to come to church despite God's preference towards them? Such tendencies seemed apparent within New Community. On the one hand, New Community has developed its ecclesiology of church both *for* and *with* the *minjung*. As a result, New Community tried to take care of its whole local community. On the other hand, such notions seem to prevent the members of New

Community from developing how to invite and welcome the *minjung* into New Community. Their negative understandings of church-growth-centered evangelism also seemed to be operative in the process. Minjung theology's notion of the relationship between Jesus and the *minjung* plays a central role in New Community's interactions with its neighbors, while its emphasis on the Spirit's working in the encounter between the church and the *minjung* in the world was rarely seen in New Community's listening processes. The following question can be raised accordingly: why participants, except pastors, did not relate their interactions with their neighbors to the Spirit, given the emphasis on the Spirit within minjung theology?

Listening to the Neighborhood: Dialogue with Various Missional Voices

Most literature regarding the missional church conversation has paid little attention to the topic of listening to the neighbor, although Van Gelder and Zscheile argue that missional theology acknowledges "the integral role of the neighbor [and] the other" in terms of congregational life and mission.[48] As one of contributors to the GOCN's *Missional Church*, Roxburgh explicitly acknowledges that "we ended up spending most of time on church questions [rather than world or neighborhood] questions."[49] The God-church relationship is more dominant than the God/world or church/world relationships in the missional church conversation, although missional theologians emphasize that the church has to participate in the relationship between God and the world. I argue that missional theologians put their primary concern on the crises of the North American church rather than people in need in the world.[50] This is because the missional church conversation was started in order to cope with serious issues in churches rather than people in North America. The data analysis seems to resonate with Roxburgh's primary arguments in *Missional: Joining the Neighborhood*. However, we first need to briefly look at how missional literature has dealt with the topics regarding the concepts of "neighbor," "other," and/or "listening" in terms of the church's relation with its neighborhood, prior to dialogue with Roxburgh.

---

48. Van Gelder and Zscheile, *The Missional Church in Perspective*, 154.
49. Roxburgh, *Missional*, 53.
50. Guder, *Missional Church*, 2.

Listening to the Neighbor in the Missional Conversation

We can regard Patrick R. Keifert's *Welcoming the Stranger* as the first book for dealing with the stranger as the other in missional terms, although not mentioning explicitly the concept of *missional* or *the missional church*.[51] *Welcoming the Stranger* is mainly concerned with hospitality toward the stranger, while paying little attention to listening. Keifert mainly argues that "liturgical worship and effective evangelism can complement and enhance one another."[52] Public worship can be a bridge between the public and private worlds.[53] Keifert defines the stranger in the three following senses: (1) clear outsiders—those who are not members of the congregation, (2) inside outsiders—those who are "between the intimate group, or family leaders of the congregation, and the outsiders," and (3) all outsiders—all members are also outsiders in terms of "the irreducible difference."[54] In this third sense, Keifert understands the congregations as "a company of strangers."[55]

Keifert points out that "the ideology of intimacy" as a present-day guiding paradigm for public worship must be replaced by hospitality to the stranger—welcoming the stranger—to do so.[56] This is because the ideology of intimacy causes the church to exclude others in public worship. Keifert relates hospitality to "opening one's private world to the stranger" rather than "making the stranger feel at home."[57] Keifert, in this sense, continues to emphasize that the congregation needs to reserve a *space* for the stranger in public worship, in terms of atmosphere and liturgy, as well as a physical place. There are two reasons for this:

---

51. Keifert, *Welcoming the Stranger*.
52. Ibid., 5.
53. Ibid., 10–11.
54. Ibid., 8–9.
55. Ibid., 88–92.
56. Ibid., 7–26. Keifert points out that American congregations tend to apply the ideology of intimacy in private life for their public lives. It contains the three tenets as follows: "First, it posits that an enduring, profound human relationship of closeness and warmth is the most—or even the only—valuable experience that life affords. Second, the ideology supposes that we can achieve such an intimate, meaningful relationship only through our own personal effort and will. Third, it assumes that the purpose of human life is the fullest development of one's individual personality, which can take place only within such intimate relationships" (ibid., 24).
57. Ibid., 8.

> First, God is the host of public worship, whose presence is often revealed in and through the stranger.
>
> Second, the God who is present in worship is essentially a gracious God who gives to the stranger.[58]

Keifert, in this light, displays how this hospitality to the stranger works in a reciprocal manner. Drawing upon numerous biblical images and his own pastoral experiences, Keifert contends that the relationship between the congregation as a host and the stranger as a guest can be subverted, as with the relationship between the disciples and the stranger along the road to Emmaus from the Gospel of Luke.[59]

Keifert's argument on welcoming the stranger has some similarities with the research findings. First, it is related to acknowledging the otherness of the stranger, as the research findings show that remaining open as a listening attitude means recognizing and acknowledging the otherness of the other. Second, Keifert takes seriously the need for a space for the stranger, as research congregations tried to provide their neighbors with an open space. Third, Keifert also considers "the sense of openness" in the process of welcoming the stranger, as the research findings treat openness as important in relation to one's listening attitude toward one's neighbor. Fourth, Keifert understands God as a God who has revealed Godself in and through the stranger. The research findings, in a similar sense, indicated that God has led research congregations to new missional events or directions through listening to the neighbor.

However, Keifert's notion of *stranger* does not seem to include all neighbors of the congregation, given his purpose in studying public worship. His notion of stranger tends to include only those who are interested in public worship, whether they belong to the congregation or not. In contrast, the concept of neighbor within the research findings includes those who are not interested in all affairs of the congregation, to say nothing of worship. The role or space of the stranger in public worship is uncertain compared to Keifert's emphasis on it. Finally, barriers between the stranger and the congregation seem to be easily overcome and transformed into reciprocal relationship through hospitality toward

---

58. Ibid., 58.

59. Ibid., 155–57. The disciples hosted the dinner for the stranger and, then, the stranger as a host transformed it into the Eucharist for them.

the stranger, although Keifert underscores that "the encounter with the stranger as the other is *profoundly threatening*."[60]

I argue that Keifert's tendency to do this is due to his inattention to Levinas's emphasis on the asymmetrical relationship between one and the other. His book is greatly dependent on Levinas's understanding of the other, as Keifert uses implicitly and explicitly Levinasian terms or concepts, such as *hospitality to the other, the stranger, the other, the face-to-face encounter with the other, welcoming the stranger*, and so on. Keifert seems to address reciprocity between the host and the guest by drawing upon Levinas's notion of the other. However, Levinas emphasizes that the other is totally transcendent from the self and, as such, there is an *asymmetrical* relationship between the other and the self. Levinas argues that all the self has to do is welcome and listen to the other, as discussed in chapter 5. Keifert needs to explain how the congregation and the stranger can move toward a reciprocal relationship, while depending on Levinas.

Inagrace T. Dietterich, in *Missional Church*, sheds light on the hospitality of missional communities toward the stranger, although not dealing with the dimension of listening to him/her.[61] Dietterich refers to strangers as those who are "other than we are."[62] Dietterich argues that the stranger has played a central role as "spiritual guide" in the Bible and "[by] honoring others precisely in their otherness, we embrace the new, the mysterious, and the unexpected."[63] She also points out that "Jesus came as a stranger" and Jesus' life is "the manifestation of God's hospitality."[64] Jesus extended God's hospitality beyond socio-cultural barriers of his day. Dietterich spells this out as follows: "Such hospitality indicates the crossing of boundaries (ethnic origin, economic condition, political orientation, gender status, social experience, educational background) by being open to and welcoming of the other."[65] She includes openness and receptivity in her concept of Christian hospitality. This enables missional communities to provide safe, free, and fearless spaces for strangers. Dietterich seems to inseparably relate welcoming the stranger to such concrete practices.

60. Ibid., 89. Emphasis added.
61. Dietterich, "Missional Community," 142–82.
62. Ibid., 179.
63. Ibid., 177–78.
64. Ibid., 178–79.
65. Ibid., 177.

We see some similarities and differences between Dietterich's hospitality and the research findings. On the one hand, Dietterich implicitly relates the stranger to the neighbor as long as the neighbor is regarded as unknown. She highlights openness and receptivity toward the other, as do the research findings. She also takes seriously providing strangers with free and fearless spaces, similar to research congregations' providing open spaces for their neighbors. On the other hand, Dietterich tends to stress the primary role of the Holy Spirit in relation to Christian hospitality, while research participants seemed to focus on the role of God the Father rather than the Spirit in terms of their congregations' relationships with their neighbors. Dietterich also pays little attention to listening to the neighbor, although she emphasizes the central role of the stranger as a spiritual guide in biblical terms. She focuses on how missional communities relate to strangers, but not vice versa. She does not seem to be concerned with missional congregations' long-term, two-way relationships with their neighbors because strangers are those who are strange to these congregations.

Dale A. Ziemer, in *Treasure in Clay Jars*, similarly draws upon the concept of "welcoming the other" in terms of hospitality through case studies of diverse missional churches.[66] Ziemer argues that the church's communal life is a foretaste of the reign of God. Ziemer highlights that "the redemptive relationships in community" show what a "gospel-formed community" is like.[67] Ziemer, in this sense, contends that Christian hospitality embraces three primary practices: listening to one another, active helpfulness, and bearing with one another.[68] These practices work together and lead us to "confront difference and engage the other-ness of those who are other than ourselves."[69] These practices result in welcoming the other within and outside community and seeking reconciliation with one another. The missional churches Ziemer researched wanted strangers or visitors to feel *welcomed* rather than *recruited* in the process.

We need to take a close look at Ziemer's emphasis on listening to one another for this study. Ziemer regards listening to one another in a community as a fundamental characteristic of redemptive relationships. Ziemer holds that such listening is naturally related to learning from,

---

66. Ziemer, "Pattern 4," 84–99.
67. Ibid., 84–85.
68. Ibid., 86–92.
69. Ibid., 92.

helping, and bearing with one another. For Ziemer, "listening to one another also corresponds with the practice of listening to God."[70] Both listening to one another and God essentially aim to "discern God's direction and call for the future."[71] These listening practices have enabled missional communities to get involved in listening to their neighbors. Ziemer underscores that "listening involves not only offering one's ear but one's living space, a bed, meals, and an address."[72] Listening to the neighbor includes "taking risks to welcome the 'other' and offer *space* for fostering redemptive relationships in community."[73]

Ziemer's concept of listening is similar to understandings of listening within the research findings. Ziemer's listening includes learning from the other, as the research findings do. The study showed that maintaining humility as a listening attitude and learning from the neighbor or listening process seemed to include the dimension of learning from the other. Ziemer's understanding of relationship between listening to and helping one another also implies that listening is related to paying attention to the other's needs, as listening is related to paying attention to the neighbor's needs within the research findings. The connection of listening with welcoming the other shows that listening to the other seems to mean acknowledging the otherness of the other and ultimately seeks to reconcile with the other. In a similar sense, the research findings indicated that remaining open as a listening attitude meant recognizing and acknowledging the otherness of the other. Mutual/reciprocal communications and relationships as listening outcomes can be understood in terms of Ziemer's notion of reconciliation with the other. Ziemer tends to take seriously fostering space in listening to the neighbor, as research congregations tried to provide their neighbors with open spaces.

However, there are some differences between Ziemer's notion of listening and listening in relation to the research findings. Ziemer places the emphasis on congregations' internal listening, while the research findings focus on congregations' outer listening. This essentially results from the fact that Ziemer's primary research interest is in looking at his research congregations' internal relationships in missional terms, while I am primarily concerned with my research congregations' relationship

---

70. Ibid., 87.
71. Ibid., 88.
72. Ibid., 93–94.
73. Ibid., 94. Italics added.

with to their neighbors. Ziemer's research congregations address listening to the neighbor as a result of listening to one another within their missional communities, but not vice versa. From Ziemer's perspective, it seems uncertain that research congregations of this study have come to listen to their neighbors due to overflowing of rich, internal relationships through listening one another, although research congregations' internal communications can be regarded as internal listening processes. However, Ziemer pays little attention to reciprocal and mutual relationships with the neighbor through listening to the neighbor, while addressing such relationships with one another as a result of listening to one another within community. Ziemer partly underscores his research congregations' contribution to their neighbors with little consideration of the benefits from listening to their neighbors. In contrast, the research findings show that research congregations have learned from their neighbors through listening to them and they can be somehow regarded as co-partners with research congregations in creating new missional events.

Dialogue with Roxburgh

The arguments and practical steps Roxburgh discusses in *Missional* greatly resonate with the research findings in terms of listening to the neighbor. We take a careful look at his primary arguments and concepts in the book, and then dig deeper into Roxburgh's understandings of neighbor and listening in relation to the neighbor. Roxburgh points out that the missional church conversation seems to have been a *monologue* focusing on church questions, while Newbigin's work, which has decisively contributed to its development of the missional church conversation, is based on a "*trialogue* (a three-way conversation) between gospel, church, and culture."[74] This is because "[the] language house of churches in North America continues to make the church the center of its social imaginary even as it uses new words, such as *missional* and *emergent*."[75] Therefore, Roxburgh's primary agenda of the book is to construct "a radically different language house and social imaginary" for the missional church conversation.[76]

Roxburgh employs the concepts of *social imaginary* and *language house* to do this, as seen above. Roxburgh embraces Charles Taylor's

---

74. Roxburgh, *Missional*, 51, 90. Italics in original.
75. Ibid., 62. Italics in original.
76. Ibid., 66.

notion of *social imaginary* as "the ways in which we are shaped by these basic kinds of stories that lie in the background of our lives like the props in a stage play."[77] Roxburgh, depending on Mark Lau Branson, espouses the concept of *language house* as "the house in which we live provides us with the symbols and basic elements that give identity, meaning, and the resources for our life."[78] These two are the ways of seeing the world. Roxburgh utilizes the concept of *language house* as his primary concept throughout the book in dealing with his agenda. This is because Roxburgh understands language as "indispensable to being human," as Gadamer did in the previous chapter. *Service for local society* (Heavenly Creek), *local mission* (New Community), and *social wellbeing service* (Holy Hill) can be understood from Roxburgh's perspective of language house.

Roxburgh provides the narrative of Luke-Acts as a way forward toward shifting the language house of North American churches. Roxburgh observes that Luke-Acts was written for Christians in a time of upheaval, similar to the present-day North American context. Luke-Acts, focusing on the faith that God was the subject of God's mission in the world, encouraged them to participate in God's mission in the world. The story of the sending of the seventy followers in Luke 10 is at the heart of Roxburgh's reading of Luke-Acts. He sheds light on radical discipleship, leaving baggage behind, the ordinariness of the seventy, and so on in the story.

Roxburgh, based on his interpretation of Luke 10:1–12, suggests ten rules that help enact change on a local level as follows:

(1) Go local.

(2) Leave your baggage at home.

(3) Don't move from house to house.

(4) Eat what is set before you.

(5) Become poets of the ordinary.

(6) Move the static into the unpredictable.

(7) Listen people into speech.

(8) Experiment around the edges.

(9) Cultivate experiments, not BEHAGS (Big Hairy Audacious Goals).

---

77. Ibid., 59.
78. Ibid., 61.

(10) Repeat rules one through nine over and over again.[79]

Roxburgh continues to suggest nine practical steps for moving back into the neighborhoods as follows:

(1) Prepare the local church.

(2) Develop new eyes for your neighborhood.

(3) Teach Radical neighborliness.

(4) Map the neighborhood.

(5) Listen to neighborhood stories.

(6) Discern what God is up to in the neighborhood.

(7) Get involved.

(8) Report—what are we learning?

(9) Commit—what do we do next?[80]

---

79. Ibid., 167–78. The first rule is concerned with both "the ordinary lives of the people of a local congregation through which the Spirit is shaping a new future" and "the local contexts as the venues for discerning and engaging that culture" (ibid., 167–68). The second rule indicates that the local church, like a stranger, needs to relate to its neighbors without any strategies and intent for making members, receiving hospitality from them. Roxburgh suggests that Christians must approach their neighbors as strangers, rather than hosts, who need hospitality. This is a kind of reversal of identity. The third rule means that the local church makes its neighborhood its primary location with a vow of stability. The fourth rule deals with being ready to enter into the world of the other from her/his point of view. The fifth rule, primarily focusing on the role of the congregational leadership, is that we not only listen to our neighbors' stories and connect them with God's story, but we also get changed and our stories are reshaped in the process. Roxburgh holds through the sixth rule that the Spirit leads the church beyond its static and, as such, it needs to "create spaces for the unpredictable" (ibid., 175). The seventh rule, based on the Spirit's working in the community, is concerned with "the skill of creating the spaces where people can give voice to their anxieties, hopes, and fears, as well as the music that lies beneath" (ibid., 175). Roxburgh takes for granted that this skill helps the church listen to its neighbors. New simple, experiments around the edges thorough the listening process can help the church discover alternatives or create a new space for thinking about how to live as God's people in a changing world. The ninth rule, as a subset of the eighth rule, leads the church to both "resist BEHAGs" in spiritual terms and focus on "moving back into the neighborhoods." Finally, the tenth rule emphasizes that changes can come through continually repeating these rules.

80. Ibid., 181–90.

Roxburgh, in doing so, presumes that the Spirit is working in the neighborhood and the church, as the people of God, has to join in the Spirit's working there.

We need to look at whether Roxburgh's primary text—Luke 10: 1–12—is applicable to the local congregation's relationship with their neighborhood prior to comparing Roxburgh's theory of listening to the neighbor with the emergent theory of listening to the neighbor in this study. Roxburgh gives us little explanation regarding Luke 10:10–12 in addressing the text. There are important reasons for paying attention to Luke 10:10–12 in order to understand the whole text. *Shaking off the dust* (Lk 10:11) means "a sign of God's rejection" against those who did not welcome missionaries and the gospel of God's kingdom.[81] It may apply to our neighbors who do not welcome us and the gospel in terms of the local church's relations with their neighbors. Verses 10–12, along with "the harvest" (v. 2), highlight the urgency of mission work.[82] Roxburgh seems to relate the urgency of this whole text to Christians' ordinary, daily encounter with their neighbors. Such urgency shows that primary mission work in the text focuses on *proclamation* rather than *dialogue* in terms of evangelism. Bevans and Schroeder hold that mission requires both dimensions of proclamation and dialogue, and that dialogue emphasizes the dimension of respecting and being open toward the other, while proclamation is related to the prophetic aspect of the gospel.[83] The text of Luke 10:1–12 does not seem to give us enough room for *deeply* listening to the neighbor to the extent that it is primarily concerned with proclaiming the kingdom of God as an urgent task, although it includes involvement with listening in terms of the dwelling with the neighbor. Thus, Roxburgh needs to bring his interpretation of Luke 10:10–12 into discussion so as to justify his aforementioned understanding of Luke 10:1–12.

We turn to looking at Roxburgh's theory of listening to the neighbor from the emerging theory within the research findings. We can regard the ways in which Roxburgh treats the concept of listening to the neighbor throughout the book as a theory, although Roxburgh does not articulate it. The concept of *listening to the neighbor* plays a central role in Roxburgh's missional project of moving back into the neighborhood.

81. Fitzmyer, *Luke X-XIV*, 841–49; Nolland, *Luke*, 840–45; Bock, *Luke*, 986–1000.

82. Nolland, *Luke*, 844.

83. Bevans, *Prophetic Dialogue*, 19–55. Bevans and Schroeder hold that both are inseparable and go together.

Roxburgh wants to move our attention from the church to the neighborhood through listening to the neighborhood. This is a project of turning the *church-centric language house* into the *neighborhood-centric* language house, given that the Spirit is ahead of us in the process. Roxburgh's emphasis on the Spirit as "the boundary-breaking spirit" in the process of listening to the neighbor seems to be decisively different from the emerging theory, although there are many similarities between the two, as will be discussed.[84]

Roxburgh holds that listening is a crucial part of the process of "back-and-forth dialogue" requiring "listening to the other."[85] Most research participants, too, regarded listening as an important part of their communications with their neighbors. *Knowledge* and *views* regarding *church, neighbor, mission,* and *context*—a primary category of the emerging theory—seem to be operative in Roxburgh's theory of listening to the neighbor. Roxburgh also shows that *motive/purpose* lead us to listen to our neighbors, as does the emergent theory. Roxburgh tends to regard listening to the neighbor as both participating in and discovering God's mission in the neighborhood. Roxburgh wants Christians to link their neighbors to God's stories through listening to their stories. This listening process also aims at discerning "what God is up to" in our neighborhoods.[86]

Roxburgh continues to address with listening attitudes. The emerging theory of this study provided *maintaining humility, remaining open,* and *maintaining empathic attention* as a subcategory of *attitude*. Roxburgh similarly emphasizes willingness, readiness, and openness as to listening attitudes. Roxburgh, in this respect, understands listening in relation to attending, comprehending, knowing, learning, receiving, encountering, and so on. Roxburgh's notion of attending to and learning from the other can be regarded as maintaining humility. This helps us avoid treating our neighbors as objects for our plans.[87] Seeking to comprehend, know, and receive what the other says seems to be linked with the attitude of remaining open toward the other. Roxburgh also relates listening to the stories of the neighbors to paying attention to stories behind such stories by trying to understand the other's position. Many

---

84. Roxburgh, *Missional*, 103.
85. Ibid., 42, 145.
86. Ibid., 149.
87. Ibid., 126.

research participants, in a similar sense, did not focus on listening to only their neighbors' verbal expressions, but also their feelings. These three dimensions regarding listening attitude are inseparably related to one another within Roxburgh's theory of listening to the neighbor.

Roxburgh considers *creating spaces* for listening in terms of *skill*, similar to the emerging theory's providing *open spaces*. Roxburgh generally uses *space* and *place* interchangeably, as many research participants did.[88] Roxburgh depicts the Spirit as not only breaking barriers or boundaries, but also opening up new spaces.[89] Roxburgh contends that "listening into speech involves *the skill of creating the spaces* where people can give voice to their anxieties, hopes, and fears, as well as the music that lies beneath."[90] Where Christians are to do so is not in the church, but in the neighborhood as a public space.

In so doing, Roxburgh brings the metaphor of *sitting at the table* of the neighbor to the fore.[91] Roxburgh regards neighbors' tables as the most appropriate space for listening to them because they can share their stories most comfortably. Christians come to sit at their neighbors' tables to listen to their neighbors, expecting hospitality from them op-

---

88. John Inge argues that we need to distinguish *place* from *space*. According to him, the former is used in concrete, physical, and visible terms, whereas the latter is used for abstract and invisible meanings. Inge points out that modernism brought the demise of place and the prevailing of space, while the Bible takes seriously place and depicts God in relation to concrete places. Inge ultimately aims at highlighting the understanding of the church as a *place* by tracing biblical notions of place. See Inge, *A Christian Theology of Place*, 1–32; Chung also maintains that the theology of God's *topos* (God's place) focusing on God's presence in concrete places can help Christian theology get involved in socio-economic justice issues in the public sphere because the God of place is *concretely* rather than *abstractly* with people in the world. See Chung, *Cave and Butterfly*, 21–47.

89. Roxburgh, *Missional*, 103–14.

90. Ibid., 176. Emphasis added.

91. Ibid., 144. "The table is a symbol of where God is taking all of creation. More than a symbol, it is a sacrament that can engage us directly in the life of God. That is, perhaps, one of the reasons the world of modernity has created the belief that fast food, quick meals, and busy lives are the symbols of success—they release us from the sacraments and rhythms that restore and root us in our humanity and personhood. But for humans to flourish, we need to be embedded in such a life. The table is a symbol of the eschaton (God's healed creation in Christ), which has already started among us. These early followers of Jesus were not entering the households as blank slates; they came with the news of God's shalom, their own announcement that God's promised future had come among them. These disciples brought their narrative of God's coming in Jesus to the table."

posite to the general understanding of Christian hospitality toward their neighbors. Roxburgh argues for the neighbor as the provider of the space compared to the research congregations as the providers of spaces within the emerging theory.

However, some questions can be raised regarding Roxburgh's symbolic use of *the table of the neighbor*. First, Lukan uses of *table* are not likely to support Roxburgh's assumption that the table can be a representative image for expressing a space of ordinary neighbors. The term *table* in the Bible is generally used for rituals and banquets and, as such, the table is depicted as the table of God, a king, or a rich man, or the table for a Sabbath or wedding banquet.[92] All usages of table (except Lk 24:30) in Luke seem to follow such patterns because *table* is referred to in the scenes of banquet or dinner provided by the rich or king (Lk 5:29, 7:36, 49; 11:37, 14:10, 16:21, 17:7, 22:30) and the last supper—a Passover dinner—as a ritual banquet (Lk 22:7–39). The dinner table of the risen Jesus and his two disciples of Emmaus (Lk 24:30) can be understood in relation to the last supper in Eucharistic terms. Sitting at table symbolizes honor and intimacy given by the host. The fact that the poor and the sinner sat with Jesus at table means to be a special blessing given to them. Thus, table implies *extraordinariness* of the rich or those in authority rather than *ordinariness* of the populace.

Second, it does not seem too hard for Christians to sit at the table of the neighbor to the extent that Roxburgh makes it explicit that there no longer exists the culture of welcoming the stranger in North America which was taken for granted by seventy disciples in Luke 10.[93] He emphasizes that Christians' receiving hospitality from the neighbor is risky business in North America because Christians are ready to accept harsh rejection. Given the culture of fearing the stranger in both North America and Korea, Christians' neighbors rather than Christians seem to take more risks in the process of welcoming the other. Roxburgh remains silent in how to deal with the culture of fearing the other in the neighborhood and how to enter into the neighbors' homes under such conditions. Roxburgh, in some sense, seemingly holds that the local church is completely dependent upon the Spirit in the process.

---

92. Bromiley, et al., "Table," 706–7; references regarding table in Luke (Lk 5:29, 7:36, 49; 11:37, 14:10, 16:21, 17:7, 22:30, 24:30) See Fitzmyer, *Luke X–XIV*; Nolland, *Luke*; Bock, *Luke*.

93. Ibid., 123–27, 195.

Third, Roxburgh pays little attention to the fact that there needs to be open spaces where neighbors can easily know who the church is and speak to it before allowing it to enter into their homes and sit at their tables. Many Koreans outside the church have criticized Korean churches' aggressive evangelism which is related to entering into their neighbors' homes and sitting at their tables. All research congregations acknowledged this fact. That is why the research congregations tried to provide their neighbors with open spaces. They also considered that their neighbors did not usually have enough space to live because of their poverty. Open spaces help Christians and their neighbors communicate with one another with freedom and comfort and build trust relationship for furtherer and more intimate communications.

We move to *listening outcomes* within Roxburgh's theory of listening to the neighbor, given that the emerging theory provides three kinds of outcomes: learning from the neighbor/process, mutual/reciprocal communications and relationships, and new missional events. Roxburgh holds that listening to the neighbors means learning from them and building relationships with them, as the emerging theory does. It also leads the local church to realize what God is up to in the neighborhood. This can be called a *missional event*. The local church's listening to the neighbors helps them connect their stories with God's stories. This listening also helps the church as follows:

> As we listen to the story of a neighbor, we too become shaped by that story and start to see that God's story doesn't only connect with the neighbor but it also challenges and, often, questions the ways we have automatically assumed what the gospel is all about.[94]

Roxburgh also takes seriously leadership in the process of listening to the neighbor from the perspective of the emerging theory of this study. He pays special attention to the primary role of leaders which is concerned with helping people look at what is going on in the neighborhood, while the emergent theory seems to emphasize the primary role of the lead pastor, given in the Korean context. Roxburgh compares leaders to poets who listen to stories beneath peoples' external stories and help them connect to bigger stories.[95] Leaders within Roxburgh's theory listen to both their people's stories and their neighbors' stories and

---

94. Ibid., 173.
95. Ibid.

encourage their people to keep listening to their neighbors.[96] Leadership is also engaged in the ongoing discernment process of what God is up to throughout the entire listening process. In some sense, the internal communications within the emerging theory can be regarded as an ongoing discernment process, although not thoroughly enough to focus on what God is up to in the neighborhood to the extent that leadership does within Roxburgh's theory.

In conclusion, Roxburgh's theory of listening to the neighbor holds that listening to the neighbor is an ongoing, cyclical, and a developmental process, as does the emergent theory of this study. The reason why it can be regarded as a developmental process is that it is essentially dependent on the Spirit's leading compared to the emerging theory's lack of focus on the Spirit in the process of listening. Roxburgh's theory of listening is primarily concerned with language-based and story-focused listening in the Gadamerian sense. It seems weak in listening to people from other languages or the voiceless saying of the poor or the marginalized in the Levinasian sense.[97]

CONCLUSION

In relation to the research findings and the emerging theory, we discussed the neighbor and listening to the neighbor, the kingdom of God, and church as a Spirit-led community in biblical terms. We also addressed Calvin's ecclesiology, missional ecclesiology, Stott's holistic mission, minjung theology, and notions of listening to the neighbor within the missional conversation in general and Roxburgh in particular in terms of theology. The research congregations understood the neighbor in light of Jesus' understanding of neighbor. They regarded their neighbors as the poor and the marginalized, based on the following biblical texts Matthew 22:36–40, 25:31–46, and Luke 10:25–37. They understood listening to the neighbor implicitly through reflecting on Jesus' relationships with people in need. They treated themselves and their ministries as instruments of the reign of God in the world in order to witness the gospel. They recognized God as the subject of mission and their interactions with their neighbors, while being concerned with *building* or *expanding* the kingdom of God. They lacked understanding the church as a Spirit-led

---

96. Ibid., 176.

97. For example, Christians who can only speak English cannot listen to the stories of those who are foreigners and cannot speak English.

community and the Spirit's working in the process of listening, focusing primarily on church as a community of Jesus Christ.

We looked at how much the PCK's version of Calvin's ecclesiology worked in the process of the research congregations' listening to their neighbors. Such ecclesiology seemed to have an influence on their notions of God-the-Father-centered mission, Christ-centered church, the pastor-centered leadership, and inattention to the Spirit in the process of listening to their neighbors. Missional ecclesiology showed that the research congregations did not have understandings of the Trinity in social or relational terms or the dimension of a Sprit-led community in terms of ecclesiology, leadership, and mission. We also saw that Stott's concept of holistic mission was operative in Heavenly Creek and Holy Hill as to ecclesiology and mission. Stott's double listening encouraged both congregations to listening to the Bible and their neighborhoods. In contrast, minjung theology influenced New Community's understanding of the church and mission in general and interaction with its neighbor in particular. Minjung theology led New Community to focus on making its larger community better in terms of God's mission.

Finally, we briefly dealt with notions of the neighbor or listening to the neighbor within the missional church conversation in relation to the emerging grounded theory of this study and a number of related literatures. We came to know that the missional church conversation did not develop such notions to the extent that it emphasized the importance of the church's local context. Roxburgh pointed out that this was essentially because the missional church conversation was grounded in a church-centered language house.

Nevertheless, we saw a primary concern for the stranger/neighbor in terms of hospitality within the following theologians: Keifert, Dietterich, Ziemer, and Roxburgh. They commonly emphasized hospitality and importance of the open, free, and/or safe space in relation to the stranger/neighbor. Keifert portrayed hospitality to the stranger in terms of public worship and the possibility of reciprocal relationship between the church and the stranger. However, his notion of the stranger tended to exclude those who were not interested in the church's affairs, including public worship, in the light of the emerging theory. Keifert held that hospitality seemed to enable the church to easily overcome barriers between the church and the stranger and transform these barriers into a reciprocal relationship, while his emphasis on threatening of the stranger did not seem to be appropriately resolved through hospitality to the stranger.

Dietterich shed light on the stranger as spiritual guide and hospitality to the stranger as crossing socio-cultural boundaries. She underscored the role of the Spirit in the process. However, Dietterich paid little attention to reciprocal or mutual relationship between the church and the stranger in the light of the emerging theory. Ziemer maintained that listening to both God and one another in the church naturally led to listening to the stranger/neighbor, whereas he did not address the dimension of reciprocal or mutual relationship between the church and the neighbor.

Roxburgh argued that listening to the neighborhood helped the missional conversation change its language house from being church-centered to the neighborhood-centered. He presumed that the Spirit, as a boundary-breaking Spirit, was already working in the neighborhood. In light of Luke 10:1–12, Roxburgh articulated a theory of listening to the neighbor. This seemed to resonate with the emerging theory of this study. Roxburgh's theory of listening to the neighbor held that listening to the neighbor was an ongoing, cyclical, and developmental moving-forward process, as did the emerging theory of this study. On the one hand, this theory's focus on the Spirit may help the research congregations to pay attention to the Spirit's working in the process of listening to their neighbors. Roxburgh's theory of listening seemed weak in listening to people from other languages or the voiceless saying of the poor/marginalized in the Levinasian sense, because it was primarily concerned with language-based and story-focused listening in the Gadamerian sense. The next chapter touches on achievements and limitations of this study, the summary of the emerging grounded theory of listening to the neighbor, missional implications, and a brief conclusion with possibilities for future research and my personal reflections.

7

Conclusion

THIS CHAPTER BEGINS WITH addressing achievements and limitations of the research. It discusses an overview of the research findings and the emergent theory of listening to the neighbor. This is followed by a summary of the implications of the study. The chapter then concludes with recommendations for future research and culminating statements which include my reflections.

This concluding chapter begins with addressing achievements and limitations of the research. It discusses an overview of the research findings and the emergent theory of listening to the neighbor. This is followed by a summary of the implications of the study. The chapter then concludes with recommendations for future research and culminating statements which include my reflections.

ACHIEVEMENTS AND LIMITATIONS OF THE STUDY

I chose a constructivist grounded theory as a methodology to explore the following research question: For the PCK congregations which have been actively involved in their neighborhoods, what are the understandings and practices of their listening to their neighbors? This question embraced three primary aims which were: (1) to explore the ways and phenomena of congregational listening to the neighborhood in terms of local mission, (2) to describe the congregations' understandings of their listening to their neighbors, and (3) to construct a grounded theory of their listening experiences in relation to their neighborhoods. I achieved these aims by constructing a grounded theory of listening to the neighbor through a constructivist grounded methodology journey. The research findings showed that the research congregations' listening to their neighbors was a missional activity insofar as it was a part of their missional involvement in their neighborhoods and God was the subject of this. It was also an *integrated, intricate, multifaceted,* and *ongoing* process. This process had six primary categories (knowledge/view, motive/purpose, attitude, skill/method, outcomes, and leadership). It had the following three phases: pre-listening (knowledge/view and motive/purpose), present-listening (attitude and skill/method), and post-listening (outcomes), while leadership appeared to be operative throughout the whole listening process (see figure 1). It was also a sequential, cyclical, and developmental process.

Figure 1: The Process of Listening to the Neighbor

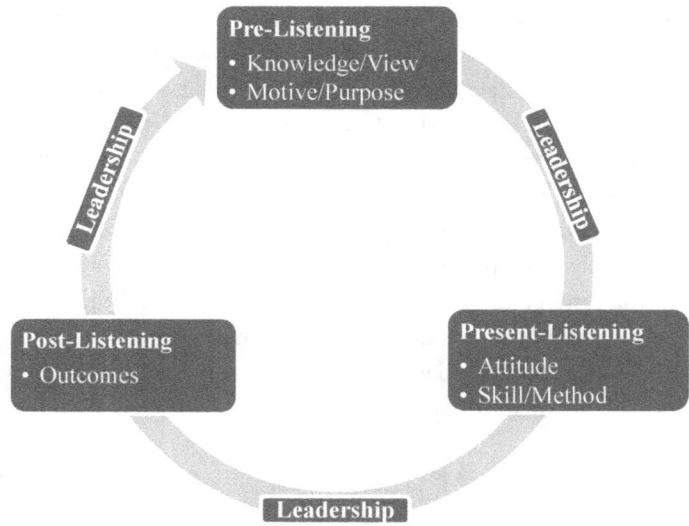

I have become increasingly aware of constructivist research journey as a listening process similar to the emergent theory. Charmaz's constructivist grounded theory embraces both the importance of a solid foundation in data and interpretive, analytic aspects of grounded theory inquiry. Since this study was an inductive approach in terms of the former, I worked to avoid importing preconceived ideas on the data and used systematic procedures and constant comparisons until data no longer triggered new theoretical insights.[1] This was truly a listening process because the research required both "openness" toward and "empathetic understanding of the participants' meanings, actions, and worlds."[2] In other words, I had to first listen to what the data said. This was really a learning process because it helped me realize that it was difficult to first listen to the other, including the text in the Gadamerian sense.

I, at the same time, have enjoyed this constructivist methodological journey in interpretive, analytic terms, because it was very creative. Constructivist grounded theory highlights both co-construction of knowledge by both participants and me and interpretive renderings of a reality rather than objective reports of it. I, in this regard, raised the research question from my interest rather than the research participants' interest in listening to the neighbor, although the research was concerned with the research participants' notions of listening to their neighbor. Sensitizing concepts helped me begin this study and interpret the data. Therefore, the research findings and the emergent theory within this study resulted from my creative interpretation of the research congregations' listening to their neighbors, although these were all grounded in the data.

However, embedded within this study are several important limitations that require consideration when assessing the research. First, this study lies firmly within the interpretive tradition because it was conducted from a constructivist perspective. There, thus, can be different interpretations of the same data which might be dissimilar to my interpretation.

Second, the research was conducted within the qualitative tradition with specific attention focused on the individual perspectives of participants and meanings they gave to their realities and behaviors in relation to listening to their neighbors. Generalization to the other populations is not applicable. The research engaged only with those who were involved in their own congregations' social services for their neighbors over three years in terms of local mission. Even other members within the same research congregations who are not involved in their congregations' interactions with their neighbors may have different understandings of their congregations' listening to their neighbors. Moreover, this study did not touch on the research congregations' listening to their neighborhoods from the perspectives of their neighbors.

---

1. Charmaz, *Constructing Grounded Theory*, 51, 165.
2. Ibid., 184.

Third, the small number of participants in the study can be considered a limitation. I conducted only fifteen personal interviews and six focus groups within three congregations. Maximum variation was not achieved in the sample.

Fourth, understandings of the church, context, mission, and leadership which were addressed as key concepts within this study seem to have limitations in being applied to the research congregations' original understandings regarding them. This is because these understandings within the study were indirect results of this study, while this study focused primarily on the dynamics of their congregations' listening to their neighbors. This study, in this sense, did not primarily focus on internal listening processes within the research congregations.

Fifth, this study paid little attention to understandings and practices related to listening in terms of culture. It did not touch on how Korean culture shaped or influenced the research congregations' listening to their neighbor, given that Margarete Imhof and Laura Janusik hold that different cultures bring different emphases in understanding listening.[3] This is partly because there are few studies regarding the church's listening to the neighborhood given different cultural contexts.

RESEARCH FINDINGS AND THE EMERGENT GROUNDED THEORY

This research focused on participants' understandings of their own congregations' listening to their neighbors, while most listening literature is primarily concerned with individuals' understandings of listening. The former addresses individuals' understandings of organizational listening in terms of the organizational relationship with the neighbors, while the latter pays attention to individuals' understandings of listening on an individual level. Listening within the research findings was understood as not being a simple, linear process, but rather being a multi-faceted, ongoing process. The research findings showed the following six primary categories of the research congregations' listening to their neighbors: (1) knowledge/view, (2) motive/purpose, (3) attitude, (4) skill/method, (5) outcomes, and (6) leadership.

---

3. Imhof and Janusik, "Development and Validation," 79–98.

Knowledge/View

Knowledge/view influenced the research congregations' listening to their neighbors. Knowledge/view contained *church, neighbor, mission*, and *context* as subcategories, which were interrelated. The research congregations' knowledge/view of church, neighbor, mission, and context seemed to be operative when the research congregations listened to their neighbors. In other words, the research congregations began listening to their neighbors with their pre-understandings of church, neighbor, mission, and context. The research participants' understandings of the church and neighbor seemed to influence each other, while they were affected by the other two categories—mission and context—which had an influence on each other. The category of knowledge/view influenced on all other categories within the emergent theory of the church's listening to the neighbor.

The research participants tended to identify their congregations as churches for their neighbors, churches with their neighbors, churches distinguished from other churches in Korea, and churches of Jesus Christ. The last notion of themselves was at the center of their identities, related to their understandings of the gospel. Regarding their congregations as churches of Jesus, the research participants posited that their congregations were churches for/with their neighbors, because Jesus lived for and with his neighbors. They, in the same sense, distinguished their congregations from other congregations in Korea which were self-centered and sought one-way approaches to mission in terms of their relationships with their neighbors.

The research congregations also understood their neighbors as people in need, local residents, and those who needed the gospel. These notions were consonant with the research congregations' notions of the church. Relatively speaking, *people in need* seemed suitable for the notion of the church *for the neighbor*, while *local residents* fit the notion of the church *with neighbor*. *Those who needed the gospel* seemed to link to the notion of the church *of Jesus Christ* in the same sense. Neighbor as a subcategory of knowledge/view was also influenced by the research congregations' views of mission and context.

The research congregations' notions of mission were primarily concerned with *witnessing the gospel* and *God's mission*. Research participants related the gospel to love, salvation, and/or the kingdom of God. Most participants addressed the gospel in terms of both spiritual and bodily needs and both personal/communal aspects, although each tended to have different priorities. They believed that their neighbors first came to know about the gospel through their daily lives, regarding their daily lives as their hermeneutics of the gospel in relation to God's kingdom. The research congregations acknowledged themselves and their ministries as instruments of the reign of God in the world so as to witness the gospel. They held that God's kingdom should be *built* or *expanded* by God and, as such, they should participate in God mission in the world. On the one hand, this notion somehow seemed to be influenced by the Korean church's traditional understanding of building or expanding God's kingdom as the church's primary work. On the other hand, the research congregations emphasized God's agency in the whole process of mission in light of God's mission.

The research congregations took into account that God was the subject of their social services and mission because God was the subject of history and the universe. They congregations tended to regard God's mission as God-the-Father-centered mission, which Jesus and the Spirit served with little attention given to social relationship in the Trinity. Most participants, except pastors, seem to hardly relate the Spirit to the process of listening to their neighbors. They generally understood the Spirit in relation to the personal, spiritual sphere. They paid little attention to the Spirit in the process of listening to their neighbors compared to their emphasis on both Jesus Christ in terms of ecclesiology and the gospel and God the Father in terms of God's mission.

Moreover, the research findings highlighted *context* as one of subcategories of knowledge/view. Context influenced the research congregations' understandings of church, neighbor, and mission. The research congregations understood themselves as churches for/with their neighbors and their neighbors as people in need, because they were located in poor, industrial areas. They were also concerned with their neighbors' poor living conditions in terms of mission. They, thus, got used to paying primarily attention to their neighbors' needs. The recent changes to their contexts, such as an influx of middle-class residents due to local redevelopment projects, led all research congregations to develop relevant programs and/or alternative approaches to these environmental changes. Therefore, the research congregations took for granted listening to their neighbors in order to serve God's mission, taking seriously their local contexts.

Motive/Purpose

Motive/purpose led the research congregations to get involved in listening to their neighbors. Motive/purpose was discovered as a primary category within the emergent theory of listening to the neighbor, containing *better serving the neighbor, making their local communities better,* and *carrying out mission* as subcategories. The category of motive/purpose was concerned with what motivated participants to listen to their neighbors. The concept of *motive* was used for what individual participants valued and what drove them to act and behave in certain ways on a personal level, while the concept of *purpose* appeared to be a goal or aim for which participants existed or acted on a congregational level. However, these two seemed to be inseparable.

The research findings showed that the research congregations tried to listen to their neighbors to better serve them. This appeared as the most dominant notion in relation to the category of motive/purpose. Their knowledge/view regarding church, neighbor, mission, and context led them to first pay attention to their neighbors' needs. The research participants, in this regard, used both paying attention and listening to their neighbors interchangeably. The category of better serving the neighbor seemed to reflect *asymmetrical relationships* between the research congregations and their neighbors because they tried to better serve their neighbors and their neighbors did not listen to them in the first place.

The research congregations also listened to their neighbors so as to make their communities better. They participated in communications with their neighbors on both personal and congregational levels, acknowledging themselves as part of their larger communities. Given their knowledge/view of church, neighbor, mission, and context, they continued to get involved in communications with their local governments and civic organizations in order to make their communities better because their communities were located in poor industrial areas. This notion presumed a symmetrical relationship between the research congregations and their neighbors taking seriously the importance of respecting or acknowledging each other for communication.

Carrying out mission was the ultimate concern of the research congregations in listening to their neighbors. This subcategory seemed to be an indirect, but essential purpose, while the above two subcategories appeared to be linked to direct purposes. The research congregations related mission to witnessing the gospel and serve God's mission in this regard.

Attitude

Attitude emerged as the third category of listening to the neighbor. It included *maintaining humility, remaining open,* and *maintaining empathic attention* as its subcategories, which were interrelated. The research participants acknowledged that they tried to keep humble in listening to their neighbors, because they wanted to serve their neighbors. They understood listening to their neighbors as humility. This attitude showed that the research congregations first considered their neighbors' interests, feelings, and positions rather than their own. They did not treat their neighbors as objects for their satisfaction or making their church members through their services. The attitude of maintaining humility also seemed to include attitudes of respecting and learning from neighbors.

The attitude of remaining open meant that the research congregations were receptive to whatever their neighbors spoke or asked for. This meant that they tried to pay attention to their neighbors with an open mind, despite giving up or imposing their positions or intentions on their neighbors. This attitude also appeared to contain recognizing and acknowledging the otherness of their neighbors and be flexible in the process of listening to their neighbors.

The research congregations regarded maintaining empathic attention or attentive empathy as crucial in the process of listening to their neighbors. They seemed to pay attention to both their neighbors' physical needs and emotional pain with empathy rather than judgment in this process. They considered that most of the marginalized or the poor really wanted to hide both their poverty or current social status and emotional pain. The research participants appeared to try to be empathic listeners while their neighbors spoke about their pain and weaknesses. These three subcategories (maintaining humility, remaining open, maintaining empathic attention) appeared to work together and be sharply distinguished from one another, as seen above. Furthermore, the category of *attitude* was seemingly influenced by the above primary categories of *knowledge/view* and *motive/purpose*, but not vice versa.

Skill/Method

The research congregations took seriously *skill/method*—the fourth category—in listening to their neighbors. Skill/method appeared to contain the following subcategories: *using personal/organizational relationships, providing open spaces*, and *utilizing feedback/using media*. It seemed contingent on the above primary categories (knowledge/view, motive/purpose, and attitude). The research congregations' long-term relationships with their neighborhood via their local services created trusting relationships between both parties. They used their organizational relationships as official conduits of listening to their neighbors, while they used their members' private relationships as unofficial channels in the process of listening.

The research congregations provided open spaces for their neighbors in regard to listening and communication. *Open* meant placing no limitations in both physical and psychological terms. Participants also used the concept of *space* in both physical and psychological terms. Providing open spaces were related to the research congregations' considerations of both their neighbors' poor living conditions and openness toward their neighbors.

The research congregations utilized feedback (including surveys and conferences) or media, such as newspapers, websites, and social networks, to listen to their neighbors. Media was used for both providing information regarding who they were and what they were doing. They used their feedback loops for improving existing programs and services for the neighborhood. These processes were also open toward their neighbors' other opinions, no matter what those opinions were.

Outcomes

The research congregations received *outcomes* through listening to their neighbors. *Outcomes* as the fifth category of theory of listening to the neighbor included *learning from the neighbor/process, mutual/reciprocal communication and relationship*, and *new missional events*. The research findings showed that the research congregations learned from their neighbors in listening to them and/or the listening process itself. They also reached mutual/reciprocal communications and relationships with their neighbors through the listening process. The research findings indicated that communications and relationships appeared to be closely related. The research congregations' listening to their neighbors led them to experience new missional events as unexpected outcomes.

On the one hand, the first two sub-categories seemed to be consistent results of the listening process, while the last sub-category tended to be an inconsistent result of listening to the neighbor. On the other hand, these three subcategories were dependent on one another and the first two categories could be as new missional events as long as the process of listening to the neighbor was missional. The primary category of *outcomes*, as its title implies, was influenced by the previous primary categories (knowledge/view, motive/purpose, attitude, and skill/method), and vice versa.

Leadership

Leadership as the sixth category of the emergent theory played a central role throughout the listening process. It was constituted by the following subcategories: *the primary role of the lead pastor* and *internal communication*. On the one hand, the lead pastors as parts of their congregations were under the influence of the previous categories (knowledge/view, motive/purpose, attitude, skill/method, and outcomes). On the other hand, they had a strong influence on forming those categories through their teachings and leadership. They themselves also played central roles as primary listeners in their congregations' listening to their neighbors. Calvinistic emphasis on the role of the pastor tended to strongly influence this.

Internal communication as a subcategory of leadership also appeared to be working throughout the research congregations' listening to their neighbors. The research congregations used *personal dialogues* and *regular group meetings* as the two main tools for internal communications. Internal communications seemed to be contingent on the category of the primary role of the lead pastor, because the lead pastors were regarded as primary in terms of decision-making within the research congregations. The category of internal communication tended to be more related to the primary categories of attitude, skill/method, and outcomes, whereas the category of the primary role of the lead pastor was more concerned with the primary categories of knowledge/view and motive/purpose.

Summary

Taken together, both the category of leadership as well as all other categories influenced each other. The category of knowledge/view influenced all other categories, while leadership was concerned with constituting knowledge/view and the category of outcomes brought new knowledge/view to it. The category of motive/purpose was influenced by the categories of knowledge/view, outcomes, and leadership, while it had an impact on the categories of attitude, skill/method, outcomes, and leadership. The category of attitude was contingent on the categories of knowledge/view, motive/purpose, outcomes, and leadership, while it had an impact on the categories of skill/method, outcomes, and leadership. The category of skill/method had an effect on the categories of outcomes and leadership, whereas all others, including the category of outcomes and leadership, influenced this category. The category of outcomes was influenced by all other categories, including leadership, while the former was also likely to regenerate the latter.

The research findings, furthermore, indicated that the research congregations' listening to their neighbors was an *intricate, ongoing, multifaceted,* and *integrated* process. This process seemed to be distinguished into the three distinct, albeit inseparable phases (pre-listening, present-listening, and post-listening). *Knowledge/view* and *motive/purpose* appeared to be seemingly regarded as the phase of *pre-listening, attitude* and *skill/method* as the phase of *present-listening,* and *outcomes* as the phase of *post-listening;* leadership was involved throughout all phases of listening. The process of listening seemed to be continually *sequential, cyclical,* and *developmental,* as was Gadamer's dialogue-based hermeneutics in chapter 5.

MISSIONAL IMPLICATIONS

We have seen that the process of the church's listening to its neighbors is an ongoing, multifaceted process. It shows that listening to the neighbor cannot be achieved by launching a program or learning techniques regarding it. Listening to the neighbor needs various transformations of the church's understandings of itself, its neighbor, mission, context, and so on. Considering this, three implications of this thesis are highlighted here: missional understandings of the neighbor, missional understandings of listening, and sensemaking leadership in the listening process.

Missional Understandings of the Neighbor

This study has shown that understanding the other greatly influences how one relates and, as such, listens to the other. Most churches in Korea have had a monological approach to their neighbors because they have been accustomed to treating their neighbors as objects for their growth or mission. In contrast, the research congregations appeared to understand their neighbors as both others to serve and conversational partners. They, thus, took for granted listening to their neighbors.

First, this study highlights the notion of the *neighbor* as *the other to serve*. Most churches in Korea have placed the church-centered mission and narrow-minded understandings of salvation at the heart of their mission, which have weakened their understandings of neighbors as others to serve. How could the research congregations understand their neighbors as others to serve, given this context? Calvin's emphasis on the Bible in general and Jesus Christ in particular seemed to take seriously Jesus' life for serving the other in the world. The early missionaries tended to address social services for the neighborhood as complementary means for evangelism, although they emphasized the importance of the Bible and Christ. Many churches have followed this tendency regarding activities for serving their neighbors. In contrast, the lead pastors of the research congregations helped their members regard their services for their neighbors as not complementary, but essential in terms of mission, as we will see. They provided different mental models in understanding mission and the other.

The research congregations believed that the gospel could not be separated from serving the other, because Jesus came to serve the other— the sinner, the sick, the poor, the marginalized, and the like. For this reason, they tried to listen to their neighbors in order to better serve them. They placed their priority on the poor, the marginalized, the sick, and so on in the process. Calvin regarded love of one's neighbor as integral for Christians' lives.[4] Calvin also emphasized that the church had to play a central role in helping people in need in his time.[5] Levinas regarded serving the other as primary in ethical terms, relating the other to the vulnerable, such as the poor, the stranger, the widowed, the orphan, and so on. For Levinas, this asymmetrical service for the other is not one's

---

4. Billings, *Union with Christ*, 10.

5. This is partly because the Protestant Church had to become a substitute for the Catholic Church, which covered education and welfare services in Switzerland.

beneficial activity, but responsibility, and listening to the other is necessarily required because God speaks to one through the face of the other. Dietrich Bonhoeffer, likewise, asks the church to pay attention to others outside it because "Jesus is there *only* for others."[6] Bonhoeffer relates others to "those who suffer"—"the outcast, the suspects, the maltreated, the powerless, the oppressed, the reviled, [and the like.]"[7] The research congregations took for granted the church for the other, as does Bonhoeffer. Therefore, this notion of the neighbor as the other to serve may help the church first listen to its neighbors.

Second, this study sheds light on the notion of the *neighbor as a conversational partner*. This notion of the neighbor as a conversational partner shows that mission has a dimension of two-way symmetrical communication. It indicates that the church is ready to listen to its neighbors in order to communicate. The church's participation in this dialogical communication with its neighbors means participating in God's mission in its context as long as God is working in its neighborhood. Given that conversational partners participate in a community of subject-matter in the Gadamerian sense, the church and its neighbors can be regarded as both participating explicitly in a community of their common subject-matter and implicitly in a community of God's mission. Gadamer points out that those who provide charitable or welfare services may dominate their relationships with the receivers of their services, unless they keep focused on the subject-matter between both parties.[8] *Listening outcomes*, in the Gadamerian sense, within the research findings (learning from the neighbor/process, reciprocal/mutual communication and relationship, and new missional events) can be understood as social constructions shared by both the research congregations and their neighbors who participated in their social services. Both parties, thus, can be regarded as a community of God's mission from the perspective of the research congregations. This is because the research congregations acknowledged that God was the subject of their interactions with their neighbors.

This notion of the neighbor as a conversational partner indicates that the research congregations appeared to understand themselves as churches with their neighbors. Bosch introduces *mission as the*

---

6. Bonhoeffer, *Letters and Papers*, emphasis added.
7. Ibid., 17.
8. See Gadamer, *Truth and Method*, 353–54.

church-with-others as an emerging ecumenical missionary paradigm.[9] In so doing, Bosch draws from Sundermeier's criticism of Bonhoeffer's notion of the church-for-others as *western helper syndrome*, showing the church-with-others as a substitute.[10] However, Sundermeier pays little attention to Bonhoeffer's notion of others as those who suffer emphasizing "the view from below" rather than the view "from above."[11] The research findings showed that both notions of the church for/with the other worked together in the process of listening to the neighbor in a *both/and* fashion rather than an *either/or* fashion. Nevertheless, the church for others seems to have a slight edge over the church with the neighbor within the emergent theory of listening to the neighbor, given that neighbors are unlikely to have relationships with the church in the first place. Therefore, the church's notion of the neighbor as a conversational partner may help the church have dialogical relationships with its neighbor, based on the notion of the neighbor as the other to serve.

Missional Understandings of Listening

Listening to the neighbor could be regarded as missional because it was an important part in participating in God's mission in their neighborhood. We, in this regard, address both *paying attention* and *learning* as missional understandings of listening. These two notions are closely interrelated without separation.

First, the listening to the other has a dimension of first paying attention to the other in light of the emergent theory. The research congregations first paid attention to their neighbors—their neighbors' needs in particular. They did not care about whether their neighbors listened to them. They took seriously listening to their neighbors as their primary concern of following Jesus. This notion somehow resonates with Levinas' notion of asymmetrical listening to the other, as discussed earlier. The church must always be a listener in relation to its neighbors and exist for them, focusing on caring for them. Listening as paying attention also includes listening to nonverbal aspects of the other—voiceless suffering of the other. The church, thus, must develop *listening eyes* to do this in the Levinasian sense. We can also listen to the voice of God in direct ways of listening to the face of the other—the poor, the widowed, the orphan, the

---

9. Bosch, *Transforming Mission*, 368–89.
10. Ibid., 375.
11. Bonhoeffer, *Letters and Papers*, 17.

stranger, and so on. Paying attention to the other may help the church serve the least in its neighborhood, as the PCK hopes.

Second, listening also has a dimension of learning. The listening process, in this regard, is essentially a learning process, as this study shows. The church must have a *listening heart* to learn from the neighbor or the process of listening. *Humility* and *openness* can be considered in this regard in light of the emergent theory of listening to the neighbor. Humility is related to first considering neighbors' needs and feelings, respecting neighbors' positions. Openness can be understood as readiness or willingness to listen to whoever the other is and trying to accept whatever the other requests. It also includes acknowledging the otherness of the neighbor by opening up spaces in physical and psychological terms and even accepting something against us. This openness always needs to work together with humility in the process of the church's listening to the neighbor. Furthermore, listening to the neighbor may help the PCK create reciprocal/mutual communications and relationships with its neighbors and lead it new missional events as long as listening aims at learning from them.

Sense Making Leadership

Pastors, in particular, the lead pastors, played a role as sense-makers in the process of listening to their neighbors, as Weick regards leadership as an activity of sensemaking. They tried to help their members make sense of their changing situations and mission in the listening process from the perspective of God's mission. They provided their members with theological and biblical vocabularies to do this with a long-term vision although they did not provide interpretive frame works. Their leadership fostered trusting personal and organizational relationships in an open-ended manner. The lead pastors nurtured internal communications for better listening to their neighbors. They did not forcibly impose their own visions, but tried to build shared, long-term visions through internal communications as well as their teachings.

The leadership of their lead pastors greatly influenced the research congregations' listening to their neighbors, given most churches' monological approaches to their neighbors in Korea. This, in another sense, was possible due to pastor-centered leadership in Korea. Ordinary congregations within the PCK require the transformation of their leadership into *sensemaking* leadership in order to listen to their neighbors and create a dialogical approach to mission. There is no fixed sensemaking in terms of leadership, because congregations' internal/external situations continue to change.

Furthermore, Korean churches, including the research congregations, need to nurture a more communal leadership from a long-term, missional perspective. This is because pastor-centered leadership tends to easily emphasize a top-down leadership focusing on an individual leader and the success of congregational leadership seems to depend on who the lead pastor is in Korea. In contrast, the Spirit-led leadership will empower a more communal leadership embracing diverse voices within/outside the church in order to seek the will of the Spirit as well as the common good and unity of the church. If the PCK takes seriously teachings of the Spirit related to ecclesiology and leadership in missional terms, its leadership and interactions with its neighbors may become more communal and mutual.

FUTURE RESEARCH

This study has explored how the three PCK congregations which have been actively involved in their neighborhoods listen to their neighbors. It provides diverse possibilities for future research regarding the church's listening to its neighborhood. First, future research could explore the PCK's ordinary congregations' listening to their neighbors. Second, future research could address direct relationships between the church's listening and its understandings of the church, neighbor, mission, or leadership. Third, the church's listening to its neighbors could be addressed from its neighbors' perspective. Fourth, the relationship between the internal listening process within the church and external listening process in relation to its neighborhood could be researched. Fifth, we could explore how missional input in general and teachings on the Spirit in particular might influence the research congregations' listening to their neighbors.

CONCLUSION

This study concludes by mentioning my culminating statement, including personal reflections. For me, this study has been a journey of learning how difficult it is for one to listen to the other. It reminds me that listening is not a technique, but a multifaceted, learning process. This study also has shown that listening to our neighbor is necessary as long as the church hopes to create a dialogical approach to mission in terms of its interactions with the neighborhood. The church must listen to its neighbors because God is working in its neighborhood. The church must create *listening eyes* and *hearts* to pay attention to the sigh of the least of its neighbors so that it may listen to the voice of Christ knocking on its doors in the process. Therefore, this listening process would appear to play a crucial part in looking for where the Spirit is working in the church's neighborhood.

Appendix A

Personal Interview Questions

Q 1. Please share with me a bit about your background.
  1) How long have you attended this congregation?
  2) In what kinds of activities have you been involved?

Q 2. Who you do understand your neighbors to be?
  1) Describe your definitions and/or understandings of your neighbors.
  2) What do you think of your neighbors' understanding of your congregation?

Q 3. In what kinds of activities or relations with your neighborhood has your congregation been involved?
  1) When were they started? Why?
  2) Describe any experiences of these activities in the past 3–5 years. Can you illustrate them with a story?
  3) What have been the evaluations of your neighbors regarding these activities?

Q 4. What has your congregation done to listen to its neighbors in the process?
  1) How do you define "listening to your neighbor"? Why?
  2) What are the main ways in which this is done? E.g., does your congregation have any conversations with your neighbors at the personal/communal level?

3) Has your congregation ever changed its approach to local mission and/or social activities to the neighborhood because of this listening process? If yes, can you illustrate your experience of it with a story?

4) What might help your congregation more fully pay attention to its neighbors?

Q 5. Tell me what you think God is doing in your neighborhood.
1) Tell me a story about what God is doing through your congregation in the process.
2) Tell me a story about how God speaks to your congregation through your neighbors.
3) Tell me a story about what the Spirit is doing in the process of the conversation between your congregation and it neighborhood.

Q 6. What is your role in the process of your congregation's listening to your neighborhood?
1) What are your primary texts/perspectives/concepts involved in playing your role?
2) What does your leadership take seriously?

Q 7. Is there anything we have not discussed that you would like to add? Thank you!

Appendix B

Focus Group Interview Questions

1) Invite the participants to fill out the demographic data sheet upon arrival.
2) Introduce the Interviewer and the Scribe.
3) Briefly explain the site visit and purpose.
4) Invite the participants to say a bit about their role and tenure in the congregation.

Q 1. Who you do understand your neighbors to be?
   1) Describe your definitions and/or understandings of neighbor.
   2) What do you think of your neighbors' understanding of your congregation?

Q 2. In what kinds of activities or relations with your neighborhood has your congregation been involved?
   1) When were they started? Why?
   2) Describe any experiences of these activities in the past 3–5 years. Can you illustrate them with a story?
   3) What have been the evaluations of your neighbors regarding these activities?

Q 3. What has your congregation done to listen to neighbors in the process?
   1) How do you define "listening to your neighbor"? Why?

2) What are the main ways in which this is done? E.g., does your congregation have any conversations with your neighbors at the personal/communal level?

3) Has your congregation ever changed its approaches to local mission and/or social activities to the neighborhood because of this listening process? If yes, can you illustrate your experience of it with a story?

4) What might help your congregation more fully pay attention to its neighbors?

Q 4. Tell me what you think God is doing in your neighborhood.
1) Tell me a story about what God is doing through your congregation in the process.
2) Tell me a story about how God speaks to your congregation through your neighbors.
3) Tell me a story about what the Spirit is doing in the process of the conversation between your congregation and it neighborhood.

Q 5. What is your role in the process of your congregation's listening to your neighborhood?
1) What are your primary texts/perspectives/concepts involved in playing your role?
2) What does your leadership take seriously?

Q 6. Is there anything we have not discussed that you would like to add? Thank you!

Appendix C

Informed Consent Form (Personal Interview)

YOU ARE INVITED TO be in a research study exploring the dynamics of PCK congregations' listening to their neighbors. Put in more detail, this research aims to explore the following: For the PCK congregations which have been actively involved in their neighborhoods in light of mission, what are the understandings and practices of their listening to their neighbors? For this study, you have been selected as a possible participant because you have been involved in your congregation's engagement with its neighbors for over three years. I ask that you read this form and ask any questions you may have before agreeing to be in the study.

This study is being conducted by me as part of my PhD dissertation project in Congregational Mission and Leadership at Luther Seminary. My advisor is Craig Van Gelder, Professor of Congregational Mission and Leadership at Luther Seminary in St. Paul, MN, USA.

If you agree to be in this study, I would ask you to do the following things. First, I will conduct a personal interview with you regarding the above research project. Second, I will ask you seven main questions and some sub-questions. Third, your interview will be recorded via an mp3 audio file. Fourth, this interview will require 40–45 minutes of your time to complete.

This research does not have any anticipated risks. I will not offer any direct benefits (money, credit, etc.) for your participation in this research. However, it will provide you with indirect benefits as follows: (1) This research will help look at the dynamics of the PCK congregations' listening to their neighbors. (2) This research will also be a helpful source for your congregation to pay more attention to your congregations' listening to its neighbors.

The records of this study will be kept confidential. If I publish any type of report, I will not include any information that will make it possible to identify you. All data will be kept in a locked file in my office; only I and my advisor, Dr. Craig Van Gelder, will have access to the data and video recording. If members of my research committee want to have access to this data, this will be possible only with your consent. I will not identify you by name in the report or in any conversations with other people. While I will make every effort to ensure confidentiality, anonymity cannot be guaranteed. If the research is terminated for any reason, all data and recordings will be destroyed. The raw data mentioned above will be destroyed ten years after the completion of the research work.

Your decision whether or not to participate will not affect your current or future relations with Luther Seminary and/or your congregation. If you decide to participate, you are free to withdraw at any time without affecting those relationships.

I appreciate your participation. The researcher conducting this study is Byungohk Lee. You may ask any questions you have now. If you have questions later, you may contact me at 1570 Eustis ST #102 Lauderdale, MN 55108, blee001@luthersem.edu, or 651-278-1409 (cell). You may also contact my advisor, Dr. Craig Van Gelder, Professor of Congregational Mission and Leadership at Luther Seminary, St. Paul, MN 55108, at 651-641-3218 or cvangeld@luthersem.edu.

You will be given a copy of this form to keep for your records.

STATEMENT OF CONSENT:

I have read the above information or have had it read to me. I have received answers to questions asked. I consent to participate in the study.

Signature_____
Date_____

Signature of Investigator_____
Date_____

Created 04/12/2012

Appendix D
Informed Consent Form (Focus Group)

YOU ARE INVITED TO be in a research study exploring the dynamics of PCK congregations' listening to their neighbors. Put in more detail, this research aims to explore the following: For the PCK congregations which have been actively involved in their neighborhoods in light of mission, what are the understandings and practices of their listening to their neighbors? For this study, you have been selected as a possible participant because you have been involved in your congregation's engagement with its neighbors for over three years. I ask that you read this form and ask any questions you may have before agreeing to be in the study.

This study is being conducted by me as part of my PhD dissertation project in Congregational Mission and Leadership at Luther Seminary. My advisor is Craig Van Gelder, Professor of Congregational Mission and Leadership at Luther Seminary in St. Paul, MN, USA.

If you agree to be in this study, I would ask you to do the following things. First, I will conduct a focus group conversation regarding the above research project. Second, I will ask you seven main questions and some sub-questions. Third, this conversation will be recorded via an mp3 audio file. Fourth, this conversation will require 1 hour and 30–45 minutes of your time to complete.

This research does not have any anticipated risks. I will not offer any direct benefits (money, credit, etc.) for your participation in this research. However, it will provide you with indirect benefits as follows: (1) This research will help look at the dynamics of the PCK congregations' listening to their neighbors. (2) This research will also be a helpful source for your congregation to pay more attention to your congregations' listening to its neighbors.

The records of this study will be kept confidential. If I publish any type of report, I will not include any information that will make it possible to identify you. All data will be kept in a locked file in my office; only I and my advisor, Dr. Craig Van Gelder, will have access to the data and video recording. If members of my research committee want to have access to this data, this will be possible only with your consent. I will not identify you by name in the report or in any conversations with other people. While I will make every effort to ensure confidentiality, anonymity cannot be guaranteed. If the research is terminated for any reason, all data and recordings will be destroyed. The raw data mentioned above will be destroyed ten years after the completion of the research work.

Your decision whether or not to participate will not affect your current or future relations with Luther Seminary and/or your congregation. If you decide to participate, you are free to withdraw at any time without affecting those relationships.

I appreciate your participation. The researcher conducting this study is Byungohk Lee. You may ask any questions you have now. If you have questions later, you may contact me at 1570 Eustis ST #102 Lauderdale, MN 55108, blee001@luthersem.edu, *or* 651-278-1409 (cell). You may also contact my advisor, Dr. Craig Van Gelder, Professor of Congregational Mission and Leadership at Luther Seminary, St. Paul, MN 55108, at 651-641-3218 or cvangeld@luthersem.edu.

You will be given a copy of this form to keep for your records.

STATEMENT OF CONSENT:

I have read the above information or have had it read to me. I have received answers to questions asked. I consent to participate in the study.

Signature_____
Date_____

Signature of Investigator_____
Date_____

Created 04/12/2012

Appendix E

Consent Form (Translator/Auditor)

I, _____, translator or auditor, agree to maintain full confidentiality in regards to all data from Byungohk Lee related to his doctoral study on "Listening to the Neighbor: From A Missional Perspective of the Other." Furthermore, I agree:

1) To hold in strictest confidence the identification of any individual related the data;

2) To not make copies of any data or media;

3) To delete all electronic files containing study-related documents from my computer hard drive and any backup devices.

I am aware that I can be held legally liable for any breach of this confidentiality agreement, and for any harm incurred by individuals if I disclose identifiable information contained in the data to which I will have access.

Translator's or Auditor's name (printed)_____

Translator's or Auditor's signature_____

Date_____

Bibliography

Adams, Daniel J. *Christ and Culture in Asia: Explorations from Korea.* Quezon City, Philippines: New Day, 2002.
———. "Church Growth in Korea: A Paradigm Shift from Ecclesiology to Nationalism." In *Perspectives on Christianity in Korea and Japan: The Gospel and Culture in East Asia*, edited by Mark R. Mullins and Richard Fox Young, 13–28. New York: Edwin Mellen, 1995.
Barth, Karl. *Church Dogmatics.* 2 vols. Translated and edited by G. W. Bromiley and T. F. Torrance. New York: T. & T. Clark, 2004.
Barro, Antonio Carlos. "Election, Predestination and the Mission of God." In *John Calvin and Evangelical Theology: Legacy and Prospect: In Celebration of the Quincentenary of John Calvin*, edited by Sung Wook Chung, 181–98. Louisville: Westminster John Knox, 2009.
Barrett, Lois Y., et al. *Treasure in Clay Jars: Patterns in Missional Faithfulness.* Grand Rapids: Eerdmans, 2004.
Bayer, Oswald. *Martin Luther's Theology: A Contemporary Interpretation.* Translated by Thomas H. Trapp. Grand Rapids: Eerdmans, 2008.
Beaver, R. Pierce. "The Genevan Mission to Brazil." In *The Heritage of John Calvin: Heritage Hall Lectures*, edited by John H. Bratt, 55–73. Grand Rapids: Eerdmans, 1973.
Bevans, Stephen B. "Mission as Prophetic Dialogue." *Missionaries of the Precious Blood Kansas City Province.* No Pages. Online: https://www.relforcon.org/sites/default/files/Transform_Wkshp-MISSION_AS_PROPHETIC_DIALOGUE-final.pdf.pdf.
Bevans, Stephen B., and Roger Schroeder. *Prophetic Dialogue: Reflections on Christian Mission Today.* Maryknoll, NY: Orbis, 2011.
Billings, J. Todd. *Calvin, Participation, and the Gift: The Activity of Believers in Union with Christ.* New York: Oxford University Press, 2007.
———. *Union with Christ: Reframing Theology and Ministry for the Church.* Grand Rapids: Baker Academic, 2011.
Blauw, Johannes. *The Missionary Nature of the Church: A Survey of the Biblical Theology of Mission.* New York: McGraw-Hill, 1962.
Blumer, Herbert. "What is Wrong with Social Theory?" *American Sociological Review* 18 (1954) 3–10.
Bock, Darrell L. *Luke.* Vol. 3 of *Baker Exegetical Commentary on the New Testament.* Grand Rapids: Baker, 1996.

Bonhoeffer, Dietrich. *Letters and Papers from Prison.* Translated and edited by Eberhard Bethge. New York: Macmillan, 1971.

Bosch, David Jacobus. *Transforming Mission: Paradigm Shifts in Theology of Mission.* American Society of Missiology Series 16. Maryknoll, NY: Orbis, 1991.

Bromiley, Geoffrey W., et al. "Table." In *The International Standard Bible Encyclopedia,* edited by Geoggrey W. Bromiley et al., 706-7. Grand Rapids: Eerdmans, 1988.

Brown, Delwin, Sheila Greeve Davaney, and Kathryn Tanner, editors. *Converging on Culture: Theologians in Dialogue with Cultural Analysis and Criticism.* Oxford: Oxford University Press, 2001.

Buswell, Robert E. Jr., and Timothy S. Lee, editors. *Christianity in Korea.* Honolulu: University Of Hawaii Press, 2006.

Butin, Philip W. *Revelation, Redemption, and Response: Calvin's Trinitarian Understanding of the Divine-Human Relationship.* New York: Oxford University Press, 1995.

Camion, Clement. "The Right of Resistance in Jean Calvin and the Monarchomachs." *Ithaque—Revue de Philosophie de l'Université de Montréal* 5 (2009) 1-25. Online: http://www.revueithaque.org/fichiers/Ithaque5/03Camion.pdf.

Calhoun, David B. "John Calvin: Missionary Hero or Missionary Failure?" *Presbyterian Covenant Seminary Review* (1979) 16-33.

Calvin, John. "Commentary on the First Epistle to the Corinthians." Vol. 20 of *Calvin's Commentaries.* Translated by Calvin Translation Society. Edited by John King. Grand Rapids: Baker, 1981.

―――. "Commentaries on the First Epistle to Timothy." Vol. 21 of *Calvin's Commentaries.* Translated by Calvin Translation Society. Edited by John King. Grand Rapids: Baker, 1981.

―――. *Commentary on the Gospel According to John.* 2 vols. Translated by William Pringle. Grand Rapids: Eerdmans, 1949.

―――. "Commentary on a Harmony of the Evangelists." Vol. 17 of *Calvin's Commentaries.* Translated by Calvin Translation Society. Edited by John King. Grand Rapids: Baker, 1981.

―――. "Commentaries on Micah." Vol. 14 of *Calvin's Commentaries.* Translated by Calvin Translation Society. Edited by John King. Grand Rapids: Baker, 1981.

―――. *Institutes of the Christian Religion.* 2 Vols. Translated by Ford Lewis Battles. Edited by John T. McNeill. Louisville: Westminster John Knox, 2006.

―――. "Short Treatise on the Supper of Our Lord." The Highway. http://www.the-highway.com/supper1_Calvin.html (accessed January 23, 2013).

Canlis, Julie. *Calvin's Ladder: A Spiritual Theology of Ascent and Ascension.* Grand Rapids: Eerdmans, 2010.

Charmaz, Kathy. *Constructing Grounded Theory: A Practical Guide through Qualitative Analysis.* Thousand Oaks, CA: Sage, 2006.

Choi, Hyeongmuk. "A Generational Identification of Minjung Theology and Diverse Minjung Theologies." *Theologia.* No Pages. Online: http://theologia.kr/zeroboard/zboard.php?id=koreatheo&page=1&sn1=&divpage=1&category=6&sn=off&ss=on&sc=on&select_arrange=headnum&desc=asc&no=347&PHPSESSID=89f15da943b266d65ab7433aa4d4dda1.

Chung, David. *Syncretism: The Religious Context of Christian Beginnings in Korea,* Edited by Kang-nam Oh. Albany, NY: State University of New York Press, 2001.

Chung, Paul S. *Cave and Butterfly: An Intercultural Theory of Interpretation and Religion in the Public Sphere*. Eugene, OR: Cascade, 2011.
———. *Christian Spirituality and Ethical Life: Calvin's View on the Spirit in Ecumenical Context*. Eugene, OR: Pickwick, 2010.
———. *Hermeneutical Theology and the Imperative of Public Ethics: Confessing Christ in a Post-Colonial World Christianity*. Eugene, OR: Pickwick, 2013.
———. *Public Theology in an Age of World Christianity: God's Mission as Word-Event*. New York: Palgrave Macmillan, 2010.
———. *The Spirit of God Transforming Life: The Reformation and Theology of the Holy Spirit*. New York: Palgrave Macmillan, 2009.
———. *Spirituality and Social Ethics in John Calvin: A Pneumatological Perspective*. Lanham, MD: University Press of America, 2000.
Chung, Paul S., Veli-Matti Kärkkäinen, and Kim Kyung-Jae, editors. *Asian Contextual Theology for the Third Millennium: Theology of Minjung in Fourth-Eye Formation*. Princeton Theological Monograph Series 70. Eugene, OR: Pickwick, 2007.
Clark, Charles A. *Digest of the Presbyterian Church of Korea*. Seoul: Korean Religious Book and Tract Society, 1918.
———. *The Korean Church and the Nevius Methods*. New York: Revell, 1930.
Clark, Donald N. *Christianity in Modern Korea*. Lanham, MD: University Press of America. New York: Asia Society, 1986.
Commission of Theological Concerns of the Christian Conference of Asia, editor. *Minjung Theology: People as the Subjects of History*. Maryknoll, NY: Orbis, 1983.
Confucius. *The Analects of Confucius: A Philosophical Translation*. Translated by Roger T. Ames and Henry Rosemont Jr. New York: Ballantine, 1998.
Cormode, Scott. *Making Spiritual Sense: Christian Leaders as Spiritual Interpreters*. Nashville: Abingdon, 2006.
Creswell, John W. *Research Design: Qualitative, Quantitative, and Mixed Methods Approaches*. 3rd ed. Thousand Oaks, CA: Sage, 2009.
Fitzmyer, Joseph A. *The Gospel According to Luke X–XIV: Introduction, Translation, and Notes*. Vol. 28A of *The Anchor Bible*. New York: Doubleday, 1985.
Flett, John G. *The Witness of God: The Trinity, Missio Dei, Karl Barth, and the Nature of Christian Community*. Grand Rapids: Eerdmans, 2010.
Gadamer, Hans-Georg. *Truth and Method*. 2nd ed. Translated by Joel Weinsheimer and Donald G. Marshall. New York: Continuum, 2004.
Glaser, Barney G. *Theoretical Sensitivity: Advances in the Methodology of Grounded Theory*. Mill Valley, CA: The Sociology Press, 1978.
Glaser, Barney G., and Anselm L. Strauss. *The Discovery of Grounded Theory: Strategies for Qualitative Research*. Chicago, IL: Aldine Transaction, 1967.
Geertz, Clifford. *The Interpretation of Cultures: Selected Essays*. New York: Basic, 1973.
Guder, Darrell L., editor. *Missional Church: A Vision for the Sending of the Church in North America*. Grand Rapids: Eerdmans, 1998.
Hatch, Mary Jo. *Organization Theory: Modern Symbolic and Postmodern Perspectives*, 2nd ed. New York: Oxford University Press, 2006.
Helm, Paul. *Calvin: A Guide for the Perplexed*. New York: T. & T. Clark, 2008.
Hughes, Philip E. "John Calvin: Director of Missions." In *The Heritage of John Calvin: Heritage Hall Lectures*. Edited by John H. Bratt. Grand Rapids: Eerdmans, 1973.
Hunt, Everett Nichols Jr. *Protestant Pioneers in Korea*. Maryknoll, NY: Orbis, 1980.

Imhof, Margarete, and Laura Janusik. "Development and Validation of the Imhof-Janusik Listening Concepts Inventory to Measure Listening Conceptualization Differences between Cultures." *Journal of Intercultural Communication Research* 35:2 (2006) 79–98.

Inge, John. *A Christian Theology of Place: Explorations of Practical, Pastoral, and Empirical Theology.* Burlington, VT: Ashgate, 2003.

Jowers, Dennis W. "In What Sense Does Calvin Affirm 'Extra Ecclesiam Nulla Salus'?" In *John Calvin's Ecclesiology: Ecumenical Perspectives,* edited by Gerard Mannion and Eduardus Van Der Borght, 50–68. New York: T. & T. Clark, 2011.

Keifert, Patrick R. *We Are Here Now: A New Missional Era.* Eagle, ID: Allelon, 2006.

———. *Welcoming the Stranger: A Public Theology of Worship and Evangelism.* Minneapolis: Fortress, 1992.

Keifert, Patrick R., et al. *Testing the Spirits: How Theology Informs the Study of Congregations.* Grand Rapids: Eerdmans, 2009.

Kil, Sun Chu. *Haetaron [Treatise on Laziness].* Seoul: Korean Religious Tract Society, 1904.

Kim, In Soo. *Protestants and the Formation of Modern Korean Nationalism, 1885–1920: A Study of the Contributions of Horace G. Underwood and Sun Chu Kil.* New York: Peter Lang, 1996.

Kim, John T. *Protestant Church Growth in Korea.* Belleville: Essence, 1996.

Koyama, Kosuke. *Water Buffalo Theology.* Revised ed. Maryknoll, NY: Orbis, 1999.

Küng, Hans. *The Church.* Translated by Ray and Rosaleen Ockenden. New York: Sheed and Ward, 1967.

Lake, Frank. *Clinical Theology: A Theological and Psychiatric Basis to Clinical Pastoral Care* Vol. 1. Lexington, KY: Emeth, 2005.

Latini, Theresa F. *The Church and the Crisis of Community: A Practical Theology of Small-Group Ministry.* Grand Rapids: Eerdmans, 2011.

Levinas, Emmanuel. *Basic Philosophical Writings.* Edited by Addrian T. Pepperzak, Simon Crtichley, and Robert Bernasconi. Bloomington, IN: Indiana University Press.

———. *Ethics and Infinity: Conversations with Philippe Nemo.* Translated by Richard Cohen. Pittsburgh: Duquesne University Press, 1985.

———. *Otherwise than Being: Or Beyond Essence.* Translated by Alphonso Lingis. Pittsburgh: Duquesne University Press, 1998.

———. *Totality and Infinity: An Essay on Exteriority.* Translated by Alphonso Lingis. Pittsburgh: Duquesne University Press, 1969.

———. "Trace in the Other." Translated by Alphonso Lingis. In *Deconstruction in Context,* edited by Mark C. Taylor, 345–59. Chicago: University of Chicago Press, 1986.

Luther, Martin. *Sermons on the Gospel of St. John Chapters 1–4.* Vol. 22 of *Luther's Works.* Edited and Translated by Jaroslav Pelikan. St. Louis: Concordia, 1955.

Makra, Mary Lelia, transator. *The Hsiao Ching.* Edited by Paul K. T. Sih. New York: St. John's University Press, 1961.

Mayama, Alain. *Emmanuel Levinas' Conceptual Affinities with Liberation Theology.* New York: Peter Lang, 2010.

McConnel, Tim. "The Old Princeton Apologetics: Common Sense or Reformed?" *The Journal of The Evangelical Theological Society* 46:4 (2003) 647–72.

Moltmann, Jürgen. *The Church in the Power of the Spirit: A Contribution to Messianic Ecclesiology*. Translated by Margaret Kohl. Minneapolis: Fortress, 1993.

———. *God in Creation: A New Theology of Creation and the Spirit of God*. Translated by Margaret Kohl. San Francisco: Harper and Row, 1985.

———. *The Trinity and the Kingdom: The Doctrine of God*. Translated by Margaret Kohl. Minneapolis: Fortress, 1993.

Nagata, Akifumi. "American Missionaries in Korea and U.S.-Japan Relations 1910–1920." *The Japanese Journal of American Studies* 16 (2005) 159–79.

Nevius, John L. *The Planting and Development of Missionary Churches*. Grand Rapids: Baker, 1958.

Newbigin, Lesslie. *The Gospel in a Pluralist Society*. Grand Rapids: Eerdmans, 1989.

New World Encyclopedia. "Christianity in Korea." No Pages. Online: http://www.newworldencyclopedia.org/entry/Christianity_in_Korea.

Nolland, John. *Luke*. Vol. 35B of *Word Biblical Commentary*. Dallas: Word, 1993.

Northhouse, Peter. *Leadership: Theory and Practice*. 5th ed. Thousand Oaks, CA: Sage, 2010.

Paik, George L. *The History of Protestant Missions in Korea 1832–1910*. Pyeng Yang, Korea: Union Christian College Press, 1929.

Pak, Ung Kyu. *Millennialism in the Korean Protestant Church*. New York: Peter Lang, 2005.

Palmer, Spencer J. *Korea and Christianity: The Problem of Identification with Tradition*. Seoul, Korea: Hollym, 1967.

Park, Chung-shin. *Protestantism and Politics in Korea*. Seattle: University of Washington Press, 2003.

Pettegree, Andrew. "The Spread of Calvin's Thought." In *The Cambridge Companion to John Calvin*, edited by Donald K. Mckim, 207–24. Cambridge: Cambridge University Press, 2004.

Purdy, Michael. "Listening, Culture, and Structures of Consciousness: Ways of Studying Listening." *International Journal of Listening* 14 (2000) 47–68.

Ralston, Joshua. "Preaching Makes the Church: Recovering a Missing Ecclesial Mark." In *John Calvin's Ecclesiology: Ecumenical Perspectives*, edited by Gerard Mannion and Eduardus Van Der Borght, 125–42. New York: T. & T. Clark, 2011.

Rhodes, Harry A., and Arch Campbell, eds. *History of the Korea Mission Presbyterian Church U.S.A. 1884–1934*. Seoul: Chosen Mission Presbyterian Church USA, 1934.

Roxburgh, Alan J. *Missional: Joining God in the Neighborhood*. Grand Rapids: Baker, 2011.

———. *Moving Back into the Neighborhood: The Work Book*. West Vancouver, BC: Roxburgh Missional Network, 2010.

Roxburgh, Alan J., and Fred Romanuk. *The Missional Leader: Equipping Your Church to Reach A Changing World*. Leadership Network Series. San Francisco: Jossey-Bass, 2006.

Sanneh, Lamin O. *Translating the Message: The Missionary Impact on Culture*. Rev. ed. Maryknoll, NY: Orbis, 2009.

Schnapp, Diana C. "Listening in Context: Religion and Spirituality." *International Journal of Listening* 22 (2008) 133–40.

Schirrmacher, Thomas, ed. *Calvin and World Mission: Essays*. Nürnberg: VTR, 2009.

Shotter, John. "Listening in a *Way* that Recognizes/Realizes the World of 'the Other.'" *International Journal of Listening* 23 (2009) 21–43.

Senge, Peter M. *The Fifth Discipline: The Art and Practice of the Learning Organization.* New York: Doubleday, 1990.
Smith, Steven G. *The Argument to the Other: Reason beyond Reason in the Thought of Karl Barth and Emmanuel Levinas.* Chico, CA: Scholars, 1983.
Stott, John. *Christian Mission in the Modern World: What the Church Should Be Doing Now!* Downers Grove, IL: InterVarsity, 1975.
———. *The Contemporary Christian: Applying God's Word to Today's World.* Downers Grove, IL: InterVarsity, 1992.
Strauss, Anselm L., and Juliet Corbiton. *Basics of Qualitative Research: Grounded Theory Procedures and Techniques.* Newbury, CA: Sage, 1990.
The Presbyterian Church of Korea. *Constitution.* No Pages. Online: http://www.pck.or.kr/PckInfo/law01.asp?Depth=4&volume#.
Underwood, Horace G. *The Call of Korea: Political-Social-Religious.* New York: Fleming H. Revell, 1908.
———. "Principles of Self-Support in Korea." *The Korea Mission Field* 4:6 (June 1908) 91–94.
Vessey, David. "Gadamer's Account of Friendship as an Alternative to an Account of Intersubjectivity." *Philosophy Today* 49:5 (2005) 61–67.
Van Gelder, Craig. *The Essence of the Church: A Community Created by the Spirit.* Grand Rapids: Baker, 2000.
———. *The Ministry of the Missional Church: A Community Led by the Spirit.* Grand Rapids: Baker, 2007.
———, editor. *The Missional Church and Denominations: Helping Congregations Develop a Missional Identity.* Grand Rapids: Eerdmans, 2008.
———, editor. *The Missional Church in Context: Helping Congregations Develop Contextual Ministry.* Grand Rapids: Eerdmans, 2007.
Van Gelder, Craig, and Dwight J. Zscheile. *The Missional Church in Perspective: Mapping Trends and Shaping Conversation.* Grand Rapids: Baker Academic, 2011.
Walls, Andrew F. *The Missionary Movement in Christian History: Studies in the Transmission of Faith.* Maryknoll, NY: Orbis, 1996.
Warfield, Benjamin. *Calvin and Augustine.* Edited by Samuel G. Craig. Philadelphia: P. & R., 1856.
Weick, Karl E. *Sensemaking in Organizations.* Foundations for Organizational Science. Thousand Oaks, CA: Sage, 1995.
Welker, Michael. "Calvin's Doctrine of the 'Civil Government': Its Orienting Power in Pluralism and Globalization." In *Calvin Today: Reformed Theology and the Future of the Church*, edited by Michael Welker, Michael Weinrich, and Ulrich Möller, 206–14. New York: T. & T. Clark, 2011.
———. *God the Spirit.* Translated by John F. Hoffmeyer. Minneapolis: Fortress, 1994.
Wells, Kenneth M. *New God, New Nation: Protestants and Self-Reconstruction Nationalism in Korea, 1896–1937.* Honolulu: University of Hawaii Press, 1990.
Zizioulas, John D. *Being as Communion: Studies in Personhood and the Church.* Contemporary Greek Theologians. Crestwood, NY: St. Vladimir's Seminary Press, 1985.
———. *Communion and Otherness: Further Studies in Personhood and the Church.* Edited by Paul McPartlan. New York: T. & T. Clark, 2006.
Zscheile, Dwight J. *People of the Way: Renewing Episcopal Identity.* New York: Morehouse, 2012.

Index

alterity, 51, 120–21, 125, 154

Barth, Karl, 30–31, 59–60
Bevans, Stephen, 3, 9, 154, 173
Billings, J. Todd, 33–35, 37, 58, 150, 190
body of Christ, 23, 36, 38–43, 57, 149–50
Bosch, David, 2–3, 10, 25, 29–30, 159, 193–94

Calvin, John, 7, 28–46, 57–59, 70–71, 146–50, 154, 178–79, 190, 192
  ecclesiology, 6, 15, 23, 37–46, 57–58, 70, 146–50, 178
  understanding of mission, 16, 29–37
Charmaz, Kathy, 11–14, 48–49, 61, 65–66, 68, 70, 82–83, 182–83
church growth, 4–5, 7–8, 16–17, 20, 22–23, 28, 41, 46, 56, 73–74, 80, 87, 95, 101, 130, 143–44, 151–52, 164
Chung, Paul, 7, 29, 31–35, 37, 43–44, 50–51, 121, 154, 160, 175
coding, 61, 65–67, 70, 82–83
communication, 2, 13, 69, 75, 81, 84, 94–97, 102, 104–11, 118–19, 130, 132, 134, 137–38, 150, 153, 157, 162, 169–70, 174, 177–78, 187, 189–90, 193, 195
communion, 9, 20, 36, 38, 42–43, 46, 58–59, 118, 148, 153–54,

conceptual category, 12, 49–51, 61, 65–66, 68, 71, 82–86, 88–89, 92–93, 95–96, 99–100, 102, 104–13, 118, 120, 124–27, 129–30, 133, 142, 152, 158, 174, 182–91
constructivist grounded theory, 11–14, 48–49, 67–68, 70, 181–83
context (contextuality), ix-x, 2–3, 7–8, 11, 21–23, 45–46, 52–53, 57–64, 71–73, 82, 84–86, 91–92, 95, 102, 104, 111, 115, 127–28, 130–32, 134, 137, 139, 141, 143, 150, 152, 155, 158–62, 172, 174, 179, 184–87, 191–93
Cormode, Scott, 131, 133–34, 139

dialogue, 2–9, 11, 13–15, 39, 41, 50, 78, 94–95, 106, 109, 113–15, 138, 140, 154, 156, 158, 164, 170, 173–74, 190–91, 193–94, 196
Dietterich, Inagrace, 10, 167–68, 179–80
double listening, 157–58, 179

election, 29–32, 34–35, 58
evangelization, 5, 16–19, 24–26, 46, 56, 75

face (metaphor of), 51–52, 120–25, 127–28, 167, 193–94
fundamentalism, 18–19, 40, 56
fusion of horizons, 50–51, 115–16

Index

Gadamer, x, 50, 114–19, 123–24, 126, 138, 171, 178, 180, 183, 191, 193
God's kingdom, 5–6, 8, 15, 17, 22, 27–29, 36, 38, 46, 54–56, 60, 70, 73, 88–90, 95–96, 140, 143–46, 148, 151, 160, 173, 178, 185–86
God's mission (*missio Dei*), ix-xi, 3–7, 9–11, 13, 17, 21–22, 30–31, 46, 58–59, 74, 89–96, 151–53, 156–59, 161–62, 171, 174, 185–88, 193–95
gospel, ix-x, 4, 13, 18–22, 29–31, 37–38, 40, 56, 60–61, 79–81, 88–90, 95–96, 141–42, 144, 146–47, 149–51, 160, 173, 177–78, 185–88, 192
Great Revival, 26–27, 147
grounded theory, x, 7, 11–14, 48–49, 61, 66, 68, 70, 110, 130, 152, 181–83

hermeneutics of the other, 9, 14, 50–52, 70, 114–26, 138
holistic mission, 15, 74, 81, 133, 154–58, 178–79
hospitality, 10, 165–68, 172, 175–76, 179–80,

illeity, 121–22

Keifert, Patrick, 7, 10–11, 165–67, 179
Kil, Sun Chu, 18, 24, 26–27, 40

language (nature of), 13, 20–21, 50–51, 114–15, 120, 123–24, 171, 174, 178, 180
language house, 170–71, 174, 179–80
leadership, 26, 28, 41, 53, 60, 71, 74, 78, 80, 84, 108–13, 116, 127–28, 131–39, 145, 150–53, 157, 162, 172, 177–79, 182, 184, 190–91, 195–96
learning organization, 131, 134–37
Levinas, Emmanuel, x, 7, 51–52, 114, 119–26, 138, 141, 154, 167, 178, 180, 192, 194
listening, 2–3, 7–8, 10–11, 13–15, 41, 48, 54–55, 68–70, 82–85, 89, 91–119, 121, 123–28, 130–32, 134, 136–42, 145–46, 150, 152–54, 156–57, 159, 161–62, 164–70, 172–75, 177–97
ear, 8, 141, 157
eye, 124–25, 141, 194, 197
local mission, 5–7, 48, 62, 64, 77–78, 86, 114, 129, 171, 181, 183

minjung, 8–9, 75–76, 143, 159–79
minjung theology, x, 7–9, 15, 75, 78, 133, 143, 152, 154, 158–79
missional
ecclesiology, 3–5, 9–10, 31, 43, 45–46, 58–60, 70, 81, 146, 150–54, 178–79
event, 84, 104–5, 107–9, 111–12, 118–19, 162, 166, 177, 189, 190, 193, 195
theology, x, 3–5, 7, 9–10, 12, 14–15, 17, 20–21, 31–32, 34, 41, 46, 60, 81, 154, 164–80
mission-in-dialogue, 3, 6–11
Moltmann, Jürgen, 10, 59, 153
monologue, 2, 5–6, 118, 157, 170, 192, 195

neighbor, x, 2–4, 7–11, 14–15, 18, 37, 43, 47–48, 54–55, 70–73, 76, 78–89, 91–120, 122–31, 134, 136–53, 155–59, 162, 164–66, 168–70, 172–97
Neo-Confucianism, 19, 40–41
Nevius Method, 22–23, 25

open systems theory, 14–15, 50, 52–54, 70, 126–31, 139
other, ix-x, 9–10, 13, 41, 50–52, 55, 97–100, 114–26, 136–38, 157, 166–69, 173–74, 192–96
otherness, 9, 41, 51–52, 98, 116, 120, 123–26, 153–54, 166–67, 169, 188, 195

perichoresis, 9, 58–60, 152
PCK
ecclesiology, 16, 23–29, 40–41, 46, 56, 58, 71, 127, 146, 149, 179

PCK, cont.
   understanding of mission, 5-6, 8, 16-23, 32, 40, 46, 56, 71
   process (of listening), 83, 85, 91, 96, 99-102, 104-10, 112-13, 116-17, 119, 126, 128, 130-31, 134-39, 145, 150, 153, 157, 162, 164, 169-70, 172, 174, 177-80, 182-84, 186, 188-91, 194-95

reciprocity, ix-x, 84, 106-8, 118-19, 121, 151, 153, 157, 160, 162, 166-67, 169-70, 179-80, 189
Roxburgh, Alan, 10-11, 137, 164, 170-180

Sanneh, Lamin, 13, 21
Schroeder, Roger, 3, 9, 154, 173
Senge, Peter, 53, 131, 133-39,
sensitizing concepts, x, 14-15, 49-50, 64, 70, 113-14, 138, 183
space, 34, 68, 73, 79, 84, 91, 94, 98, 100, 102-4, 111, 117, 127, 138, 152, 162, 165-69, 172, 175-77, 179, 189, 195
Spirit, 3-5, 7, 10, 13, 17, 19-24, 26, 31-46, 56-58, 60-61, 87, 90-91, 105, 122, 145-53, 156, 158, 161, 164, 168, 172-76, 178-80, 186, 196-97

Spirit-led community, 3, 15, 52, 54, 57-58, 60, 70, 140, 145, 150, 152-53, 178
spirituality, 10, 19, 26-27, 35-37, 40, 43, 46, 145, 147, 150-51
Stott, John, 155-58, 178-79
stranger, 10, 51, 120-21, 124, 126, 141, 145, 165-68, 172, 176, 179-80, 192, 195

table (metaphor of), 175-77
Trinity, 3, 7, 9-10, 12-13, 30-31, 33, 41, 46, 58-60, 90, 146-48, 151, 153-54, 158, 179, 186

Underwood, Horace, 18, 22-25, 55-56
union with Christ, 35-37, 42-43, 46, 58, 150

Van Gelder, Craig, 4, 7, 9-10, 22, 40, 45, 52, 54, 56, 59, 128-30, 144, 164
vernacular translation, 19-22

Weick, Karl, 131-34, 139, 195
witness, ix-x, 13, 59-61, 89, 93, 95-96, 106, 136, 144, 146, 149-51, 156, 158, 178, 185-86, 188

Ziemer, Dale, 168-70, 179-80
Zizioulas, John, 9, 59, 153-54
Zscheile, Dwight, 10-11, 164

www.ingramcontent.com/pod-product-compliance
Lightning Source LLC
Chambersburg PA
CBHW062023220426
43662CB00010B/1452